The Parrot's Perch

To Phyllis,
Never ever ever
give up

Karen Keilt

The Parrot's Perch

Karen Keilt

To order additional copies of this book, contact:
Xlibris Corporation
1-888-795-4274
www.Xlibris.com
Orders@Xlibris.com
100725

This book is dedicated to Jack, Rick and Edie; my home team. And to Mom, my angel.

Jack, thank you for showing me that it's OK to dream, thank you for your tireless editing and for your support and always, for your love.

Rick, I'm glad you know that dreams do come true. Thanks for your IT expertise and for patiently taking all my panic calls with a smile.

Edieeeee, I'm eternally grateful for your constant love and support.

"T", thanks for always listening, Bonnie thanks for accepting, and Carolyn thank you for showing me the way to be steadfast and for teaching me that:

Forgiveness is letting go of the hope that the past could ever be different.

Knowing this and with all of you I've learned to soar!

AN OPEN LETTER TO THE PRESIDENT OF BRAZIL

Dear President Dilma Rousseff,

The story you are about to read is a true story. I have changed names, locations and some elements of the story for my protection. I am certain you will relate to this story, because you were arrested, abused and tortured by the Brazilian criminal justice system. You were arrested for your role in the kidnapping of United States Ambassador Charles Burke Elbrik, who was later released unharmed. The kidnapping was your valiant but misguided attempt to bring attention to the violation of Human Rights and torture that are common-place in Brazil.

On April 30, 2010 Tom Cahill of Amnesty International made the following statement: "In a country that sees thousands of extra-judicial killings every year at the hands of security officials and where many more are tortured in police stations and prisons, this ruling clearly signals that in Brazil nobody is held responsible when the state kills and tortures its own citizens." Mr. Cahill made this statement when the Brazilian Supreme Court voted to uphold a 1979 law protecting torturers from prosecution.

Today, I appeal to you as the recently elected President of the People of the Republic of Brasil and implore you to repeal and reverse that law, giving thousands of people the justice they deserve for the heinous crimes that were perpetrated against them.

Use all the power of your office and the media to protect your people by stopping the brutality and violations of human rights that go on every single day once and for all.

President Rousseff, I implore you to put an end to the systemic corruption that runs like poisoned blood through the veins of our great nation's cultural consciousness.

Sincerely,
Karen Keilt

PART ONE

FRESH BLOOD

B RUSHING BACK HER gleaming long red hair, Erin O'Grady gives herself a Colgate smile in the mirror over the sink in Canaday Hall. She knows she was lucky to get into the newest dorm on campus as a freshman. In fact she tells everyone back home in Gloucester, that she's in the same room that Academy Award winning actress Mia Sorvino, used during her freshman year at Harvard. Of course, Erin smiled, that was probably just a rumor every freshman tells their friends. But it made her feel like she was on the verge of stardom herself!

As if she could feel any closer to fame at 18, with a full ride science scholarship at Harvard. Sometimes, though, that designation made her feel like a geek. Science Scholar. Sheesh. Who'd a guessed?

At 5'6" with piercing blue eyes and piles of waist length, wavy red hair, a porcelain complexion, intermittently dotted with just the right amount of freckles, and a trim, but curvy figure, Erin's anything but geeky, and tonight when she makes an entrance at the "Lizard" with her friends to see her hometown boys "The FS Rockers" play their favorite venue in Cambridge, she intends for all of them to know she's not just a small town girl with big dreams. Yep. She wants them to know she's a drop dead, knock-out sexy, wicked-smart, Harvard undergrad. She inspects her carefully applied "natural-look" makeup, decides she looks perfect, and smiles approvingly again. She shimmies into her "de riguer" destroyed "Seven" jeans, and her crimson v-neck sweater accentuates her tiny silver crucifix, just a hint of rosy cleavage, and completes the very carefully put together, yet, oh so casual campus "look". Skipping back into her room, she switches her real ID for her fake one, slides her feet into her favorite cowgirl boots, then heads down to the "Yahd" to meet her friends Melissa, Jamey, and Mags. It's gonna to be a fun night and she's ready to wow the hometown boys, and all the new faces in Cambridge, too. Take that, Glostah!

As the girls walk towards Harvard Square giggling conspiratorially, they look like all the other privileged "twenty something's" in the rarefied evening air.

Mags and Jamey are the oldest, all of 21, and they huddle close, as they inspect the fake ID's that'll gain Melissa and Erin entrance to the popular club. Erin's ID alias is Erin Brady, close enough to her own name so she can remember it if she gets carded after a few beers. And even if she ever did get carded, she can still proclaim to be Tom Brady's cousin, which automatically guarantees her celebrity status, rendering her, untouchable. In addition to that, the only other alteration to the I.D. is the year of her birth, changing it from 1987 to 1984, making her eligible for a few famous Bleeding Crimson Shooters, no

...ked. The Gloucester address is real, so there's not much to trip her ...or a freshman, it was a rite of passage to get this ID from a respected ...ssmen. Nervously, Erin anticipates another rite of passage tonight, ...itiation into the drug culture at Harvard. Surprisingly, the number of students involved in this pass-time is much greater than she expected. She's not really sure she wants to try it, but Mags and Jamey insist it's the thing to do, and so, deferring to their wisdom, she's agreed. Erin wonders if maybe this is all too stupid, but quickly decides that it's only for one night, and she has nothing to worry about. Mags had already picked up the small pills and tonight Erin's going to try one. She's determined to be relaxed, and to feel like one of the "regulars" when the old neighborhood crowd see her at the "Lizard".

The girls each dry-swallow one of the pills, cleverly imprinted with a stylized "H" and then dig into their purses for their ID's, and the obligatory five buck cover charge as they reach the red door at 9:30 PM.

The distracted doorman gives the girls' ID's a cursory glance, much more interested in making eye contact with the eye candy, than in doing his job. He stamps their hands with the requisite signature faded red lizard, granting them the freedom to drink at the bar all night.

Inside the volume is full blast, the party well under way. The large space smells a bit like any Massachusetts swamp at low tide. A swamp of stale beer and sweat, strangely mingled with hints of Obsession, baby powder and minty shampoo. Students chug-a-lug red Jello shots and beers at the bar with reckless abandon. Guys hit on girls, girls ask guys to dance, groups laugh together and yell over the heads of their friends to the busy bartenders trying so hard to keep up with their customers and ensure the generous tips they need to pay their rent, utilities or tuition.

The band is setting up, talking and laughing amongst themselves and getting pumped up by the excitement they are feeling from the crowd.

"The FS Rockers" have been around the Boston music scene for a few years, and as usual they have a small entourage of girlfriends and groupies on display who fit right in with the local Cambridge crowd.

The lead singer's sexy, gritty rocker voice quickly makes temperatures rise and from Erin's perspective, even the walls seem to sweat.

Swaying from side to side she watches the guitarist ignite the crowd, and the bassist thrums his instrument until it seems to purr like a wild animal. She feels a bit like a wild animal herself, staring at the hunky bass player, Rick, who's the one she's really come to see. She's had a crush on him since she was a freshman in high school, but he never gave her any indication that he even knows she's alive.

The band is treating the revelers to a proper rocking, East Coast style, inciting them to pound and stamp the dance floor. The four coeds laugh and dance together at the edge of the dance floor, just beneath the raised stage. Several guys give Erin intense meaningful looks, but Erin is only interested in seeing if any of the band members recognize her. Standing just a few feet away from Rick, she waves and yells, calling out his name.

But he's into his gig, mesmerized by the crowd and doesn't notice her. The music plays on, getting louder and louder. Erin seems dazed as the crowd sways enveloping her in its breathing, writhing cocoon.

As the last notes of one song meld seamlessly into the pumping beat of the next one, Erin puts her hand to her head and shuts her eyes.

"Are you OK?", Mags mouths next to her. It's too loud for Erin to hear her. Squinting through her tightly scrunched eyelids, Erin shakes her head "no" and turns away from the stage.

"I have to get out of here. I feel dizzy, like I might puke."

"Don't worry about it", Mags reassures her, "It's just the pill kicking in. You'll be in heaven in a minute. Take a deep breath."

Erin shakes her head again, like a fighter clearing blood from his eyes, and in the glare of the strobe lights, her eyes are glazed and unfocused, her pupils tiny and bright. Mags grab her by the shoulder pulling her away from the dance floor. The crowd knowingly smiles and nods, as the two girls push their way toward the exit. It's obvious to them Erin's a "rookie", having a hard time keeping up. Many of them have been there before. Jamey and Melissa notice their friends leaving the dance floor and fight through the crowd to catch up.

As they reach the door, Erin stumbles and would've fallen head-first, if the cute doorman hadn't seen her coming, and put out a strong arm to hold her up, ushering her into the cool indifferent night.

Just outside now, a small group huddles around Erin, who sinks to the ground, grimacing. Incoherent and mumbling, beads of sweat glistening on her brow she suddenly vomits, spewing her dinner, and beer all over the feet and legs of her friends.

"Ugh. Gross. It's not even 10:30. This isn't gonna be such a fun night." But it's plain to see, something's seriously wrong. The vomit is bright red, and unless she's had nothing but cherry Jello for dinner, it looks like it's laced with blood. The now frightened bouncer quickly pulls out his cell phone and punches in 911.

"We need an ambulance here at the "Lizard", right now. There's a girl here who's been poisoned or something. She's puking blood." He closed his phone and turned to Mags, Jamey and Melissa who are shocked by their friend's rapidly deteriorating condition.

Fearing the worst, the agitated bouncer shouts, "What did she take? This isn't happening because she had a few beers."

Mags opens her mouth to respond, when Erin suddenly slumps face first onto the sidewalk and begins thrashing and moaning, spittle, vomit and red foam covering her chin and neck.

Mags, beside herself with anxiety, clutches the doorman's arms, begging for some help.

"Oh my God. Do something. She's choking. Somebody help her."

In the background the keening wail of the approaching ambulance pierces the night and as they stare helplessly at their beautiful friend, Erin takes a deep ragged breath then is still. Falling to her knees beside her friend, Jamey looks up at the crowd and implores everyone to help them.

"Jesus. Oh God. Jesus. Do something. She's dying. She's dying."

The ambulance screeches to a halt, the paramedics jump out, radios crackling and sputtering, and as they rush to kneel next to Erin, the senior EMT calls out.

"What's her name?" Mags replies in a shaky, somber whisper.

"Erin."

The EMT takes control, pushing Jamey aside. "Come on Erin, open your eyes. You're going to be OK. We've got you now."

He quickly cuts through her sweater and bra, peeling them apart, pulling her crucifix away from her throat, opening her mouth and clearing her airway, placing a breathing bag over her nose and mouth, and begins the life saving techniques of compression, and resuscitation on the pale and disheveled college freshman. Every few seconds they check the pulse in her neck and on her wrist, while her friends, the doorman, and a growing crowd of onlookers watch in abject silence. The lead EMT begins pounding harder on her chest.

"Erin. Erin. Stay with us now. Stay with us, honey. Come on, now."

A police car arrives and two detectives step out to stand next to Mags and the others, anxiously watching the EMT's do their job. In a moment the EMT's stand up looking grim, shaking their heads with deep regret.

"She's gone. We lost her. She OD'd."

Inside, the music keeps right on playing, and the crowd keeps screaming the refrain to the Laura Brannigan hit song, "Gloria. G L O R I A. Gloooria. I want to shout all night."

PARANOIA

FREDDY LAURIA HATED his father. It was that simple. Hated him. With a vengeance.

The hate was so all consuming it had completely blinded him to the opportunities his mother had sacrificed so much for on his behalf; never asking for anything in return.

If pressed, his eyes would glaze over and Freddy would say the hate started a long time ago, when he was six years old. He'd been enjoying an idyllic afternoon, dressed in his favorite cowboy outfit, complete with boots, white hat, and cap pistols on his hips, racing around the yard on his trusted steed, the brand new shiny red tricycle he'd received as a birthday present a month earlier. Freddy had just left his tricycle in front of the garage, rushing into the kitchen to gulp down a tall glass of freshly made lemonade. But the minute turned into a few, and those minutes turned into a few hours, and soon Freddy forgot all about his loyal mount waiting patiently for him outside. He'd gotten hooked watching a Zorro rerun. Today, whenever Freddy closed his eyes and remembered, he could still smell the vaguely sulfuric smoke of all those caps he'd shot at imaginary cowboys dressed in villainous black hats.

A few hours later that day his father stormed into the house screaming Freddy's name, a mangled red handlebar hanging from his raised fist.

Walther Lauria had crumpled the new tricycle with his car when he'd arrived home from work following a stressful day at work, and he was pissed.

Not for the first time in his young life, Freddy endured a beating with his father's belt, and a tongue lashing he would not soon forget either, and was sent to his room without supper, left on his own, trying to understand why he just couldn't seem to ever please his father.

That was why when years later when Freddy's Mom sent him six thousand miles away from home in Brazil to the finest boarding school money could buy in Connecticut, Freddy thought he was being punished because he was a disappointment to his father. He never realized his Mom was trying to give him a chance to escape. So he made a point to disappoint his father every chance he got. Drinking, fighting, screwing up however he could, the thinking wasn't rational, but it gave Freddy satisfaction. Freddy got into as much trouble as possible, fermenting cider on his window cill, staying out past curfew, and getting into fights, but somehow he managed to get decent grades. And his hate for his father grew.

After graduation from prep-school, Freddy was accepted at Harvard and knew he would do whatever it took to even the imaginary score.

Freddy had a simple plan. Walther had opened a bank account in Freddy's name, with enough money in it to pay for everything at the ivy league school; enough money for tuition, room and board, and all his expenses for four years. It was a sizable account. Surely this was some kind of test, and so Freddy decided he would double Walther's money, and put himself through college.

He had a simple plan to accomplish that. He'd gamble the money. He couldn't lose. He'd studied Black Jack and Poker, they were his best games, and they were the games of choice on campus. He'd been playing for months, making small bets, winning all the time, and learning all the "tells" of the other regular players. Not one of them was a match for Freddy. He was a master. He knew luck didn't have anything to do with it. It was all skill. And numbers.

He had skill, and he knew numbers. He had the ability to memorize all the cards, so he practiced and counted, then on a pre-determined night, when all his parameters were in place, he bet it all. And he lost it. All of it.

Freddy put the recurring thought of that tricycle out of his head, and looked at the stacks of hundred dollar bills again.

He hadn't won that night four years ago, so he'd done what he had to, to make up for the huge loss. Freddy had started selling drugs. He was making small change at first. Just enough to get by. But then he expanded, and pretty soon he was making more money than his father ever had. And soon, he'd be going back home to Brazil, and he'd show his father who was really "the boss".

He'd live the life he always wanted. It'd be his show. Time for payback. He didn't need his father for anything anymore. He lovingly breathed in the scent of the money, shut the safe door and keyed in his code, locking it safely away for another few weeks.

Still, Freddy Lauria walked downstairs as if the weight of the world was on his shoulders. The evening air was sultry and warm, and students were out in force taking advantage of the perfect springtime evening. Freddy was headed to his best friend's house. Wayne was hosting another of his infamous parties, and Freddy was supplying the party favors, but even that couldn't shake his gloomy mood.

He shuffled through busy Cambridge streets, past "Out of Town News", the landmark news kiosk, in Harvard Square. Something's bothering him, a feeling he just can't seem to shake, and can't put his finger on, so he walks with his head down, occasionally casting furtive looks over his shoulder. A

KAREN KEILT

few students wave and nod at the Harvard legend, but Freddy, lost in his thoughts, doesn't even notice.

Freddy doesn't really fit in with his peers. He never has. He's something of a freak, a throwback to some other era, to 1960, maybe. Like a slightly civilized Charlie Manson. His look is all wrong for Harvard, but he doesn't care. He's got the money, so fuck 'em. He can do whatever he wants to. No one seems to care. He's just Freddy.

At 5'11" with a scruffy beard and long dirty-blonde hair, wearing baggy old cords, more to hide his expanding belly, than to make a fashion statement, Freddy keeps his faux army jacket buttoned tightly around his neck. He looks more like a bum than like a Harvard student.

As he raises his hand to push the buzzer on the apartment door, he listens for a moment to the sounds coming from inside. The party is in full swing, but there's an air of expectation, and Freddy knows it's him they're waiting for. He touches the buzzer, and for a just a second, the apartment is still before the door swings open, and Wayne welcomes his friend inside.

"Freddy! Come on in, man. We've been waiting for you."

Wayne Buckford Roberts III, 'Bucky' to his friends, is the antithesis of Freddy.

At 6'1", handsome, athletic, and sharply dressed, he seems to be greeting a much less fortunate soul. Freddy's beady gray eyes glance quickly around the room. Wayne claps him on the back ushering him warmly into the party. It's clear these two are the best of friends, as Freddy looks up into Wayne's handsome face and really smiles for the first time all day.

They met at the hockey rink, and became fast friends when Freddy, skating like a dervish, head up and shoulder down, plowed full speed into a defense-man who was skating hard, aiming for Wayne, who was about to shoot the puck into the open net.

Wayne hadn't seen his attacker, a gargantuan senior, zeroing in on him like a guided missile from the opposite bench. Everyone said that if Freddy hadn't intercepted the hit, Wayne would probably still be sifting through cobwebs. It was one of those moments that became lore in the annals of Crimson Hockey. Every time the story was retold the defense-man was even bigger and meaner, Wayne's blood on the ice was redder, and Freddy's knee was bent at an utterly improbable angle. Still, Wayne's uninterrupted shot had won the game, and Freddy had ended up with a twisted bulbous nose and a shattered knee that ended his questionable hockey career when the burly defense-man took his anger at losing the game out on him. Wayne knew he owed Freddy, and had looked out for him ever since. "Come on

Freddy. Let's get this party started. Did you bring the stuff? Everyone's waiting."

Freddy reaches into the large pockets of his overstuffed jacket, and pulls out several large zip lock bags. One is filled with colored pills, another with marijuana, and the third with cocaine. As he hands them to Wayne, everyone in the room whoops and hollers. "Whoo hoo Freddy's here! You da man! You know he knows how to make a party a PARTAY!" Freddy watches as these smart-ass kids line up, wallets and cash in hand, ready to make deals with him.

After a few minutes of negotiations, as couples pair off to snort, smoke or swallow pills, Freddy and Wayne sit down on the shabby-chic overstuffed leather couch, and Wayne turns to Freddy while he chops up lines of cocaine on a small mirror on his Pottery Barn table coffee table.

"Wow. Can you believe it man? We're finally going to graduate. Just a few more weeks and we'll be outa here! I can't wait man. A shiny new office in the burbs . . . some hot little housewives letting me check out their pearly whites, and anything else I can get my hands on."

He rolls up one of the hundred dollar bills someone just handed him, and snorts a couple of lines of cocaine. "This is some good shit, Freddy. Probably some of the best we've had. You always get the best shit. Come on man, party up!" Freddy reaches over and pulls the mirror closer, and snorts a line into each nostril. "Yeah, yeah. I need a good bump." "No shit. You've been a wreck for days. You need to chill out and enjoy these last few weeks. Pretty soon all this will be over."

He spreads open his arms to encompass the room. The wide screen TV is on, music is pumping from the "B & O" CD player, and several cute young women are standing together watching Wayne and Freddy, laughing and giggling. It's a pretty nice apartment. Well decorated. Wayne either has great taste or an interior designer for a girlfriend. Seemingly perplexed Wayne questions his friend.

"What's with you, man? Why are you so bummed?" "I don't know", Freddy replies glumly. I haven't slept in days. I feel like someone's watching me. I can't sleep. I think they're after me." Trying to distract his friend, Wayne calmly speaks up again.

"No one's after you, man! You're paranoid. Get over it, man. Relax. Chill. We're almost there. You've been the go-to man on campus for four years. You're a legend, dude! You're about to graduate from Harvard, and you've already got more of your own money than anyone I know.

You don't look like it, but you do. And you're going to Brazil man! What's to worry about?"

"Shit. I don't know. I just feel like someone's watching me. Something's not right." Wayne hums the easily recognized theme from "The Twilight Zone". "Too do do do, too do do do." He snorts another line and nods at the group of girls watching them from across the room, then agrees with Freddy, and tilts his head towards the group of girls.

"You're right. Someone's watching you all right. It's Cindy over there. She's always watching you. She wants you to fuck her, and she probably wants some of this shit. Go on man, enjoy the party."

Freddy leans over to snort a couple more lines. Getting up, he walks over to the window and pushing a corner of the drapes aside, furtively looks at the street below. Wayne joins the group of girls as Cindy separates herself from the small group and walks over to Freddy, who's pacing between the window and the couch. He's nervous and unsociable.

Leaning seductively against him and rubbing his arm, Cindy whispers, "Come on Freddy. Let me show you something in the bedroom. I bet I can take your mind off whatever's got you so uptight."

Freddy backs away, hands up in the air. "Not tonight Cindy. I've got some work to catch up on at home. I'll catch you another time."

He wanders restlessly around the apartment for a few more minutes, then deciding to leave, waves goodbye to his buddy, and walks out the door.

Wayne shouts after him, but the door has already closed.

"I'll see you in the morning man. We'll straighten out the cash."

Cambridge is quiet now, as Freddy makes his way back to his apartment, with only a few other late night stragglers on the sidewalks. He walks quickly and nervously back past the closed news stand, and past the other closed shops and restaurants. Before walking up to his front steps, he stops again, looking up and down the empty street.

His eyes halt at the sight of the Comcast cable panel truck parked across the street and down a few buildings from his. He seems to recall having seen it there earlier.

But he shakes it off; he's tired and like Wayne said, paranoid. Wayne's right, he's letting stuff get to him, so he just mumbles to himself, and turns back to his building. It seems there's always some kind of panel truck on the street.

Inside the truck, two men monitor Freddy as he moves into the building. The younger of the two quickly summarizes the close encounter.

"That was too close. He almost spotted us. Switch on the audio. I don't want to miss anything. Especially, if he makes any calls. We probably could've busted him right there on the street. I bet he's carrying and he's high as a kite. He looks like he's about to fall over that railing."

In an obvious attempt to keep his partner calm, the older man responds.

"Look, we've got our orders. Don't jump the gun and screw this up. We'll blow all the time we've put into this, and I don't want to be left scratching my balls."

Thinking about spending more time on surveillance discourages the rookie cop from doing anything foolish, so he concedes and switches his attention to the scene playing out on the small black and white camera mounted on a console inside the van.

"You're right. We'll sit tight 'till the boss gets here. OK. I've got him inside now. It looks like he's taking some kind of pills. He's probably too wired to sleep. First they get wired, then they want to get down. Stupid Fuckers."

Inside the building is quiet, and after popping two Ambien, Freddy goes to the kitchen after double checking that all the locks on the windows and door are properly secured. Passing through the filthy kitchen he swallows a couple more pills. Stripping out of his clothes he slides into bed, where he tosses and turns, punching the pillow and trying to settle down. The sheets are wrinkled and stink, and he thinks wistfully about the maids back home in Brazil, and pushes the ratty blanket to a heap at the foot of the bed. Freddy tosses and turns some more, and moans out loud, but in a few minutes the pills kick in, and he falls into a deep, drug-induced sleep.

The room is sparsely furnished, with a beat up four-drawer dresser, a metal folding chair, and an old, padlocked, steamer trunk. The trunk sits on the floor beneath a loudly thumping, rusted window air conditioner. The only thing the old machine does is obscure any outside noises, effectively masking any sounds from the apartments and street below.

A black sheet hangs from a few bent nails unevenly hammered into the wall over the window. The room is stuffy, and a slight haze hangs in the air. On the beat up night stand a brass key ring sits next to a bulky leather wallet, a half burned candle, and a small light fixture with a bent navy blue shade. The dresser is dusty, and water stained, and an empty beer bottle leans precariously against the filmy mirror.

On the other side of the bed is another small table, covered by an open paperback, a large bottle of water, a large bottle of generic aspirin, a few prescription pill bottles and an alarm clock. It's digital display reads 5:00AM.

Freddy's clothes lie in a crumpled heap on the floor by the foot of the bed.

On the sidewalk outside the building, a group of DEA officers, and undercover cops huddle by the panel van Freddy had nervously examined a few hours earlier. Two uniformed SWAT team officers stand alertly with guns drawn, on either side of the entrance to the building. Two more are poised at the base of the steps.

Four more officers are kneeling in-between several unmarked cars pulled up to the curb. The men are full of nervous energy and ready to move.

DEA Agent In Charge, Reggie "Red" Tucker wants to add another collar to his arrest record. He hasn't been feeling great about his status on the force lately, and he knows he better get this bust right. He speaks quietly into the microphone clipped to his collar.

"All right. Everyone is clear on the task at hand. We've gone over safety procedures, and we know our objective.

"We're going in on my go. Everyone check in."

The officers' replies echo in his earpiece one at a time, as they each respond.

"Unit 93, ready."

"Ready Niner-Seven, Captain."

"Nine-one. I'm go, sir."

"Ready, Niner-Four."

"Unit Nine-Five, ready."

"Niner-Six on your mark, sir." "Niner-Niner go." Dropping his arm, as nervous energy seems to crackle through the mikes, AIC Tucker whispers. "OK boys, this is it! Move. We're going in, now! Everyone on your toes!"

In a blur, the officers stationed at the front entrance swiftly break through the door, rushing up the stairs to Apartment Number 2B. Receiving no response to their loud knock, they quickly bust down the door, entering the apartment weapons extended. Multiple padlocks dangle from the splintered door jamb, slivers of wood shower the floor. With boots pounding in staccato precision, the team advances into the musty, dark apartment.

The men fan around the living room and kitchen, and one officer silently checks for anyone hiding in the bathroom. Radios silenced, they each nod affirmation that everyone is in position, and no one is in the front rooms of the apartment.

AIC Red Tucker, and Agent Jack Kelly make their way, weapons extended cautiously, into the bedroom. As they enter the room, Freddy wakes up, a look of terror on his face. Red Tucker smiles and points his weapon at him.

"Good Morning Sunshine! Time to rise and shine. Out of bed mother-fucker!"

Captain Kelly pulls back the sheets and yanks Freddy out of bed, to his feet.

Stammering, looking dazed, Freddy groggily shakes his head responding in a sleep-slurred voice.

"What? Wait. What's going on? Who are you guys? What are you doing here? Who you guys?"

When he's not on duty Red Tucker's a movie buff, he laughs in recognition of the lines erupting from Freddy's mouth, though he's sure Freddy has no clue he's quoting *Butch Cassidy and The Sundance Kid*.

"Wow! That's one of my favorite movies! "Who are those guys?" Tucker shakes his head, and smiling conspiratorially, nods at the two officers and at his partner, Jack Kelly. Loving the spotlight he continues to play Freddy. "Butch and Sundance aren't going to ride in and save the day, and Katherine Ross ain't bringing you breakfast in bed, pal." Still shaking his head, cowering, covering his genitals with his hands, Freddy inches toward the window, confusion evident in his expression.

"I didn't order any."

Seizing the opportunity to get back on track, Tucker responds.

"Right, now you're getting it Freddy. And I'm not the tooth fairy either. Look at you. What happened Freddy? Did you forget to put your Hulk PJ's on before you went to bed?"

He shoves Freddy to the other side of the room, and snickers, as he adds in an amused tone.

"You have an ass like a girl, Freddy. Anyone ever tell you that?"

The officers all share a laugh at Freddy's expense, smirking, while AIC Tucker shakes out a sheet of crumpled paper and pretends to read it.

"This is a search warrant Freddy. We're going to take this place apart. We have credible information that you're the Big Man On Campus when it comes to drugs. Is that so, Freddy? Answer me!"

Stammering Freddy professes his innocence, getting defensive. "I don't know what you're talking about. I'm a senior at Harvard.

I'm going to graduate in a couple of weeks. This is all just a horrible mistake. I don't know what you're talking about. You can't just barge in here. I want a lawyer. Who are you guys?"

Interrupting, Kelly responds curtly.

"Asked and answered. Now move it, shitbag. Cooperate now, and things will go easier for you when we get downtown."

Freddy reaches down, picking up his clothes, hastily pulling on his pants and a grungy undershirt, nervously misaligning the buttons of his a long sleeve shirt. Trying desperately to sway the situation, now that he's completely awake, he attempts to be a bit more genial, Freddy smiles and suddenly becomes conciliatory.

"Hey. Please. Let me, uh, get my bearings. I think you guys have the wrong guy. You leave and we'll pretend this never happened. I promise I won't press any charges. This is just a huge mistake. Leave it at that."

Tucker responds sarcastically.

"Oh. Oh, sure Freddy. We should just leave?"

He scratches his head and looks pensive for a moment, as if considering Freddy's idea.

He points towards the closed closet door with the butt of his gun, and waving it at the SWAT officer, asks innocently.

"On our way out we'll just take a quick peek around. You don't mind, right, Freddy? After all, nothing to hide here. This is just a mistake, right?"

Smashing the door handle with the butt of his assault rifle, the SWAT officer opens the door, and rips the clothing from the hangars, tossing everything to the ground. Shaking his head at his Boss, apologetic.

"Nothing in here, Boss." Red Tucker leans in and looks over at the pile of clothes on the floor of the closet, then turns to Freddy. "Well, Freddy, it looks like you may be right. Maybe we should just leave. Try next door, maybe? My bad." Lowering his voice conspiratorially, Tucker slides up next to Freddy and whispers in his ear.

"But since we're already here, I'll just let the guys look around. I don't want them to think I wimped out. Know what I mean? No Harvard graduate would be involved with drug dealing, am I right? What were we thinking? This is probably a paper-work screw up." He shoves Freddy against the door jamb and laughs at the already befuddled student even more.

Turning, he nods at the SWAT officer standing in the doorway with a sledgehammer. The officer pushes past Freddy, takes a wide swing at the closet, smashing through the back wall and the door frame.

Like a toad trying to escape the gaping jaws of a predator, Freddy jumps away as the officer flings shattered wood, clothing and shoes out onto the bedroom floor. Sounding dismayed the SWAT officer informs the men in the room.

"Oops, guess I got carried away. Nothing in here, Boss. Maybe we are in the wrong place."

The officers all laugh, Freddy tries to maintain his cool, as the SWAT officer looks to the AIC for direction. Freddy tries to regain his composure by sounding unconcerned. "Uh . . . Oh . . . Right, right. No harm, no foul. You can still leave and I won't make a complaint. I won't say a thing."

The SWAT Officer moves over to the dresser slinging out drawers, letting them crash to the floor, pulling out the contents, dumping everything in a heap on the floor, while Red Tucker and Jack Kelly watch in amusement. Laughing the officer holds out a pair of boxer briefs.

"Look Boss, he's a boxer's guy. No Super Heroes, though. I would have bet Super Heroes. He must be a smart guy. Smart guys all wear boxers right?"

Slumped against the wall, Red interjects. "Nah, that's just for the ones who think they need more space for their junk. Looks like Freddy here can go back to teeny briefs."

Hoping desperately to take charge of the situation in his apartment, Freddy tries to intervene.

"Please, Officer, please. Let me . . ."

But Kelly's having none of it, and interrupts him immediately. "What? Blow me? Plenty of time for that where you're going. Besides I don't think you want to do that in front of all these guys, do ya? Sit down, and shut the fuck up."

He reaches back and slams a vicious punch at Freddy's solar plexus, and Freddy slumps, groaning, to the floor. Watching everything unfold and noticing a few concerned looks from some of the men, Tucker orders them to proceed.

"OK boys. Let's find the buried treasure. You know it's in here. Time's a wastin'."

The kitchen sink and counter are piled high with dirty dishes, pots and pans, empty pizza boxes and takeout containers. A pass-through eating counter is host to at least ten empty, smashed beer cans, and a couple of overflowing ashtrays.

The living room window is draped with a sheet to block out the light, a large tower of stereo equipment stands precariously in the corner of the room next to a large crate stacked with CD's and DVD's. The couch has seen better days; it's torn and stained. A coffee table offers up porn magazines, a white-streaked mirror and razor blade, another ashtray overflowing with ashes, and a half-smoked joint. Seemingly discarded, a small bag of marijuana is almost hidden by empty beer cans.

The officers tear up everything in the room. They rifle through books, pour out half-filled bottles onto the floor, kicking through the contents of emptied drawers and cabinets.

In the cramped bedroom, they pull the mattress away from the bed frame, tearing off the stained sheets and blankets, slashing open the mattress and sending stuffing and feathers flying.

They smash open the padlock on the steamer trunk, and AIC Tucker slowly lifts the lid. His eyes double in size when he sees several huge glass cookie jars filled with a variety of pills. He reaches in lifting out a jar. "Well, well, well. What do we have, here? Looks like a pharmacy lab. What did you say you were studying?" He lifts another jar, looking meaningfully at Freddy.

"Jesus. What do these little "H's" on these pills stand for? Heaven? Looks like you're busted asshole."

He nods at his men; they keep on working.

"Keep looking, boys there's got to be more. And the money's here too."

Intently the men methodically remodel the apartment.

Emptying kitchen drawers onto the floor, pulling canned goods out of cabinets, they casually drop dishes and glassware. Freddy covers his eyes with his forearm as Agent Kelly drags him to the living room. One of the officers opens the freezer and pulls out several brick sized parcels wrapped in frost covered aluminum foil.

As he peels back a flap of the icy, silver paper, revealing a frozen brick of marijuana, the officer turns to Freddy.

"What's this? Special vegetarian meatloaf Mommy sent you from home? Tag it and bag it boys, we're on a roll."

The officers continue rifling through the rest of the apartment finally coming to stand in the center of the living room. Red Tucker faces Freddy, who has slid to his haunches, sitting trancelike on the floor in the living room. Leaning down he, speaks quietly to Freddy.

"OK, asshole. Last chance. Where is it?"

"What? What do you want? You've ruined everything. You got it all. I'm finished. Let's get this over with."

He holds out his wrists, and looks up at Tucker who shakes his head, sighing. Looking over at his men, he reaches down and grabs Freddy by the neck, and slings him into the wall opposite the couch, screaming.

"Where's the money, mother-fucker? I don't fucking have all day. Where is it?"

Shaking his head in disgust, at Freddy's continued refusal to cooperate, Tucker turns once more to the officer with the sledgehammer, nodding at him. The officer swings at the wood paneling and starts prying it off the wall. Freddy screams.

"I told you. You got it all. I don't have any money. I don't know what you're talking about. You got everything."

Looking around at the wreckage it appears as if an F-4 tornado touched down inside, destroying everything in it's path. The only thing untouched is the plasma TV hanging from the ceiling. Almost as one, the officers turn and stare at the shiny huge screen hanging from a bracket in the ceiling. It's the only thing left intact. Agent Kelly walks over, stares up at it, and takes the sledgehammer from the SWAT officer.

"Please, please don't bust my TV! That thing's 3D-HD. It cost me over ten grand. It's the only thing left in here. There's nothing else. I told you. There's nothing else!" Kelly slowly turns to face Freddy. "Do I look stupid to you? I know I don't have a Harvard degree ass-wipe, but I didn't get off the fishing boat like some fucking "goombah" yesterday." Approaching Freddy, he menacingly raises the sledgehammer, but at the last moment turns and swings the sledgehammer into the brilliant, shining, new TV.

Pulverized components and sparkling shards of glass fly across the room. The impact leaves the retractable bracket dangling precariously from the wood panelled wall. Behind the new wood paneling metal glimmers in the wall. AIC Tucker looks relieved.

"Bingo. And Jackpot. It looks like someone may have a secret stash after all, boys."

Moving swiftly, the men peel back the wood panelling revealing a hidden compartment in the hollow wall housing a floor to ceiling safe. Suddenly grabbing Freddy again, Red Tucker slams his fist into his face. Bone crunches and blood flies. Some of the officers look away as Freddy screams in shock and pain, while covering his bloodied and broken nose with his hands. His face inches from Freddy's, Tucker whispers ominously.

"OK, now mother-fucker, open it, or you're going to have more than just a broken nose." Barely coherent through bubbling blood, shattered bone, and torn lip, Freddy mumbles.

"You can't do this. This is police brutality. I want a lawyer."

Shrugging his shoulders innocently at his men, Tucker says. "Police brutality, my ass. He was like that when he got here tonight wasn't he? Didn't surveillance say he tripped going back into his apartment tonight?"

Ignoring the rest of the officers, Tucker reaches over grabbing Freddy's arm, twisting it behind his back, as the officers look away. "I'll fucking snap it in two in 30 seconds if you don't get over there and open that fucking safe. Now. 30 . . . 29 . . . 28 . . . 27." Screaming in pain, Freddy cries out. "OK, OK. I'll do it, I'll do it. Let me go, please!"

Freddy reaches through the jagged opening in the wall, presses the keypad, waits then presses a few more keys, and tumblers click into place as the mechanism opens. Freddy steps back, cradling his arm, and watches as Red Tucker swings the door open, staring at the contents in awe and smiling. Gloating over the spoils, he nods at his men, indicating they should remove the contents of the safe.

In a few minutes stacks of cash, and shoebox size packages of cocaine are piled on the floor in the middle of the room along with the rest of the drug evidence. Red Tucker pulls handcuffs off his belt, approaching Freddy.

"Looks like you're headed to the slammer for a long time. Want to tell me how much is in there? A million? Two? 50 keys? Not bad for an ivy league business school punk."

Freddy glances quickly around the room watching officers mark and photograph the evidence before removing it from the apartment. Urgently, he whispers to the AIC.

"Sir. Can we make a deal here? There's enough in that safe for all of us. You can keep a nice chunk, split a few bucks with your team, and report that you got the wrong place. It happens all the time."

Jack Kelly had been listening to the exchange, his eyes light up and he interjects.

"It sounds like a TV show. "Let's Make A Deal With Freddy."

Red Tucker creases his brow in thought for a moment, and egging him on, slides closer to Freddy putting his arms around his shoulders.

"Whoa. Wait. Let's think about this. You're offering me early retirement? I can get away from the fucking cold winters? I won't ever have to deal with jerks like you again? That sounds great to me. I sure can use the cash."

Freddy's eyes gleam with possibility, he gets ready to negotiate the best deal of his young life, as he responds in an excited and newly nasal voice. "Right. Right. We can all get out of here. No one has to know about this. There's enough in there for all of us. What do you say?"

Nodding in ascent at Red Tucker, Jack Kelly agrees. "Man wouldn't I just love that? My dream has always been to get away to someplace warm. Now I can "just do it."

Quickly, Kelly spins Freddy around and violently shoves him face first into the wall, punching him, then kicking his feet apart viciously. Pulling the handcuffs tighter on his wrists, he leans in and whispers in his ear, reading him his Miranda Rights.

"I say this, asshole. You have the right to shut your big-college-boy mouth the fuck up. You have the right to any fucking attorney your filthy rich family can afford. If you cannot find one good enough for your piece of shit ass, the Public Defender's office will assign the very best one they have to defend it for you. Do you understand these rights as I've just read them to you? I live to get scum like you off the street."

Freddy tries to plead for a bargain again, but Jack Kelly kicks in the backs of his knees, Freddy slumps crying, to the ground, as Kelly tells the officers to wrap it up.

"Get this piece of shit out of my sight."

THE DEAL

RED TUCKER AND Jack Kelly leave the apartment as one of the SWAT officers touches the microphone on his collar, calling for a squad car and officers to escort the prisoner downtown.

A few hours later Freddy stares blindly at a scarred and stained metal table where he sits in the bare interrogation room at Cambridge Police Headquarters. He looks up anxiously as the two DEA agents enter the room, and announces without preamble.

"I want a lawyer." Looking directly at Freddy, Red Tucker replies. "You can get a lawyer anytime you want one, but what I want to say to you first can help you get through this." Red sits opposite Freddy. Jack walks to the other side of the room crossing his arms, and stands, hulk-like over Freddy, while his partner continues. "If you choose to have a lawyer present during questioning, we won't be able to offer you this deal, and things will take their own course. Do you want to listen to us first?"

Shaking his head side-to-side like a caged chimpanzee, Freddy responds. "I don't know. What are you offering me?" While Jack watches silently, Freddy and Red argue back and forth. It's a verbal dance he's heard before.

"Are you waiving your right to an attorney?"

"Yes. But I can change my mind anytime I want to, right?"

"Right. OK. Here are the facts. This morning officers from the Cambridge PD, SWAT and the DEA entered your apartment with a search warrant. We've had you under SAT surveillance for months."

Freddy looks anxiously from one agent to the other as Red rattles off the events that went down a few hours ago. It seems like a lifetime ago, and Freddy is still stunned. Now Jack Kelly speaks.

"We have you cold, on video and wire taps. It seems you've been the main supplier at Harvard for a long time. You became a person of interest then, and when a young woman OD'd during a concert at the "Lizard" last night, your fate was sealed.

"Does the name Erin O'Grady ring any bells for you? She's dead, because of the shit she bought from you. Some little designer pills with little "H's" imprinted on 'em. When her friends were interviewed at the scene, they gave us your name. We've been waiting to talk to you. Waiting just paid off."

More distressed than he was a few minutes earlier, Freddy answers quickly.

"So your charging me with murder? You can't pin that on me! You can't prove she bought anything from me. I don't know what you're talking about. I've never heard of any Erin O'Grady. You can't pin that on me!"

"You dumb fuck. We can and we will!"

Jack Kelly, who grew up in Gloucester, knew the girls' family. The tragedy was now the topic of conversation all over the North Shore. The fishing community there was looking for blood, and now it seemed they knew where to find it. Kelly loses it, shouting at Freddy.

"You scumbag. She was a beautiful, sweet girl with her whole life ahead of her. I oughta make you pay right here, right now."

Red Tucker quickly intervenes and regains control of the situation and settling his partner down, speaking softly to Freddy.

"We want your ass, but we want someone bigger than you, you're just a cog in the wheel. We want your supplier. And you're going to give him to us on a silver platter. Or else you're going to rot in prison for a very long time. Your choice."

Shaken, Freddy realizes where this is heading and doesn't want to go there. "Are you crazy? There's no way I can do that. I'd be dead before I could get home. They're not stupid."

Leaning in to close the deal, Tucker replies. "They may not be stupid, but they're greedy. And you can get them to a meet using that greed."

Freddy shakes his head in dismay.

"Fuck. No way. There's no way I'd come out alive."

Red Tucker leans in closer to Freddy, crowding him even further, and leans in, pressing his lips to Freddy's ear.

"Here's what you're looking at, pal. Multiple counts of distribution of a Class A substance, trafficking across state lines, mail fraud, involuntary manslaughter, tax evasion, oh and yeah, add attempted bribery of a federal officer. All in all I'd say you're looking at Oh, ... 120 Years. What do you say to that mother-fucker? Want to bet on that?"

Freddy covers his head with his hands, trying to block everything out and cries out.

"You don't understand. Those guys are killers. They'll tear me apart if I give them up."

Walking back towards the other side of the room, Tucker speaks firmly. "Yeah. It's up to you kid. If you do it our way you get to go home and start from scratch. You go home to Brazil. No one even needs to know this ever happened. Not that you'd want to, but you can never come back here. But at least you'll be free, and alive."

Freddy keeps shaking his head, tears spilling down his face.

After a moment of watching the display, the two officers turn to leave the room. As the door opens, Tucker turns back.

"Make up your mind, Freddy. You don't have much time. This offer won't last long."

Outside the room, looking in at Freddy through the one-way window, Red and Jack high-five.

"Think he's going to go for it, Boss?"

Walking over to the soda machine in the corner, Red Tucker drops in a few coins, and punches a couple of buttons. A cold can of Coca Cola slides out onto the lip of the machine, and he pulls it out. He wipes his brow with the cool can. "He'll go for it. He knows there's no choice. Let's go back in there and sign him up. He'll roll." Opening the door to the interrogation room, they enter and Red Tucker magnanimously places the can in front of Freddy with a flourish. "If you work with us, you'll be home in a few days, and someone will be bringing you cold drinks on silver trays all the time. What's it going to be Freddy?" In a resigned voice, almost too soft to be heard, Freddy gives in. "I'll do it. Can I go home?"

Sighing deeply, Kelly responds. "You're making the right choice, kid. We're setting it all up right now. Chill out and someone will be in with the paperwork you need to sign, and to go over all the details. Just like a Harvard MBA deal."

Red and Jack step outside the interrogation room pumping fists, as the door slams shut behind them. Turning away from the room, they walk down the corridor to their office. As they pass by the open door of the Commander's office, he motions them inside, and exuberantly Kelly makes an announcement.

"Hey, Boss. We did it. We turned him. He's all yours. The Son Of A Bitch is going to cooperate."

THAT'S THE GOOD NEWS

LOOKING UP AT his two disheveled officers, the commander nods. "That's the good news. Here's the bad. You're both on unpaid leave. I've told you a thousand times, we can't get stuck with another IAD investigation or a law suit for that matter. Maybe you can come back when things cool off. Now get out of here. You're both relieved of duty. Leave your badges and your weapons and go."

Slamming their shields and weapons on the desk, Tucker and Kelly turned and walked out of the building. Jack fumes about doing their jobs and getting nothing in return. Walking away from the building, he grouses about how little money they make and why they even put up with the aggravation at all.

"I'm sick and tired of this shit. I can think of a zillion better ways to live, than dealing with scumbags like Freddy Lauria every day, putting our lives on the line, and then being put on ice just for pounding a prick like that around a little. What the fuck?"

Seemingly unperturbed, Tucker replies. "Relax, Jack. It's all good. Perfect in fact. I've got a plan that's going to get us out of this rat race and put us on easy street. You with me, pal?"

As they walk, Tucker reminds Kelly of a Brazilian investigator he met at Northeastern University. The two men had talked about what a nice guy he was, and how one day, knowing him might come in handy. Tucker and Kelly have always done their jobs well. Maybe they've done their jobs a bit too forcefully, for the current liberal policies being enforced in Massachusetts, but the important thing is, they've always done their jobs. They're both disgusted that they should pay the price, while a perpetrator like the rich kid they just locked away, will walk away unscathed.

A few blocks away, Red unlocks the door to his small Boston walk-up, crinkling his nose at the fetid smell in the hallway. Opening the door to the dingy cramped space, he thinks about how good it will feel to be out of there.

"I've wanted to get out of here for a long time. Now I'm taking my shot. Today my horoscope said I should seize the opportunities being offered to me. Well, that's exactly what I'm going to do."

Purposely walking to his desk, he sits down on a spindly-legged chair.

Kelly slumps dejectedly on the couch, hoping his partner can fix things, like he's always done in the past.

Rifling through messy desk drawers, Tucker pulls out a worn, torn address book. Flipping through the pages he stops with his finger on a name.

"Ah Ha. Here he is. This is the guy I was talking about. I couldn't remember his name. Knew it was some Jose, or Jobip or something. Anyway, it's been a while since I taught that Criminal Apprehension Techniques seminar at Northeastern, but I know he'll remember me. He said if I ever needed anything "South of the Border", that I should give him a call. Well, that's exactly what I'm going to do.

Fumbling with the phone he mumbles to himself.

"How in the hell do you make international calls, anyway?"

He dials, but slams the receiver down in frustration as a recorded voice repeatedly tells him that his call cannot be completed as dialed. Cursing under his breath, he tries again.

"God-damned thing. I need an operator." He fumbles with the phone some more, while Kelly skulks into the kitchen reaching into the refrigerator for a couple of beers. Standing there guzzling the cold brew, he listens to Red, who finally makes his connection.

"Jose? Hello?" He listens a beat then, "Shit. No. No. Jose Barros, please. English? Do you speak English?"

Gesturing in frustration, he seems ready to hang up the phone, when he hears a new voice and his friend comes on the line. From across an ocean, and six thousand miles away, the voice on the other end of the line is crisp and clear, though heavily accented.

"Alo?"

Excitedly, Tucker replies. "Jose? Is that you? Jose? Yes, yes. This is Red Tucker from Boston? Yeah, yeah, how are you, man? I never thought I was going to get you. Who was that who answered the phone? You shackin' up with some Spanish broad?"

Laughing, the foreigner answers him. "No. No, my friend. That was my maid. And we speak Portuguese here in Brazil, not Spanish, remember?" Shaking his head impatiently, Tucker agrees. "Yeah, yeah. Right. You told me that. We got a lot of Portuguese here in Boston, too. It all sounds the same to me." Turning the conversation to the real reason for the call, Jose presses on. "So, Red, how can I help you?" "I got a little situation here. My partner and I busted a kid for dealing drugs here at Harvard." Seemingly, not surprised, Jose replies. "So even the kids at Harvard are not such wonderful sons and daughters, eh?"

Tucker agrees. "Yeah, well, everyone thinks those kids are so perfect. We busted a real pillar of society. And here's the kicker He's from Brazil. He lives right there in Sao Paulo.

His interest piqued, Jose asks. "A Brazilian boy?"

Tucker tells him. "No. Actually, he was born in Boston. His Mom's a card carrying member of the Daughters of the American Revolution, and though his Dad was educated in the US, he was born in Brazil. His Dad owns some big Multi-National company down there. According to the kid, they're loaded. I'm thinking there might be a way for us to hone in on this kid and his family. You know. We could, ah "freelance" if you get my drift. Are you open to talking about it?

"What do you have in mind?"

After a lengthy discussion, Jose is convinced. The two cops instant rapport a few years before had helped cement the decision.

"That sounds good to me, my friend. How soon is this happening?"

"They're sending the kid home in a few days, and Kelly and I are going to follow him down to Brazil. We want to set up a sting. You want in?"

Jose encourages Tucker to continue. "Sting is my new name. How can I can help?"

Hearing the response he was anticipating, Tucker gives him more details.

"I'll send you an e-mail with my files. The kid's name is Freddy Lauria. Does that name ring any bells?"

Excitement building in his voice, Jose asks for more information. "Is his father's name Walther? I grew up with a guy named Walther Lauria, and you're right, if this is the family you're talking about, the guy is very rich."

A little unsure of himself, but wanting to keep Jose's interest, Tucker goes on. "Yes, that's the family. They live in Sao Paulo, and the father is a big shot." "Are you still close? Will your friendship, uh, interfere, with this project?"

Answering quickly, Jose tells him. "There will be no problem with my friendship. I've known Walther a long time. Our families were acquainted, but he has always been an arrogant jerk. There's no love lost, as you say, between us. Just mutual respect. He's a powerful man, but he also knows what I can do."

Sitting in his living room in Sao Paulo, Jose looks across the room at a silver-framed photograph of a smiling happy couple, arms draped around a young Jose. Even from a distance, Jose can see the puppy-dog look on his face as he looks into the eyes of the beautiful young woman.

Relieved to hear Jose's response, Tucker continues. "Maybe it's time to knock him down a notch or two. Kelly and I should be there in a few weeks. I'll call you when we're all set, and we'll discus how to proceed."

Happy to provide some assistance, Jose volunteers to do some research. "I'll look into the family a bit. I haven't socialized with them in years, but I'm anxious to see my old "friend" again. I'm looking forward to speaking with you again my friend. Call me when you have your flight arranged."

After discussing a few more details the men disconnect, and Jose wonders if there might in fact be a way to boost his conviction rate by making an example of the Lauria kid. This could be just the opportunity he's been waiting for. He thinks it could be time to stir the pot of arrogant Americans a little bit.

In Boston, Tucker grabs a beer from Kelly's extended hand, and turns on the TV. On the screen, two anchors jabber excitedly about the upcoming Olympic summer games. On the screen behind them, a beautiful young woman gallops a gleaming horse over obstacles in a ring. As they watch, the name Catlin Lauria scrolls along the bottom of the screen.

Slamming down his beer, Tucker raises the volume with the remote.

"Well, will wonders never cease? This is our lucky day."

HOME FREE

I N THE BRIGHT afternoon sunshine, Catlin Lauria gallops a
muscular chestnut gelding over a series of jumps in a soft dirt paddock.
To an untrained eye, Catlin makes sailing over six-foot vertical walls,
fifteen-foot water hazards, and huge tree-trunk hurdles, seem effortless, as
easy as floating a kite on a string. But controlling the two-thousand pound
animal, knowing just when to give him the signal to collect his front legs,
to leap over the obstacles, has taken years of dedication, hard work, and
training.

Knowing just when to coax her horse into giving her just a little more
speed, or a little more power; knowing when she can cut a corner a little
closer, or take the turn a little bit wider is second nature to Cat now. She
started riding when she was five. For the first five years she learned to
master her horse. Riding bareback for hours, using only her legs and the
slightest of signals with the reins taught Catlin to become one with her
horses. From the very first ride, she loved everything about riding. She
loved going to the club everyday. She loved the smell of the barns, of the
powdery fine dirt in the rings, the scent of the polished leather of the
saddles, reins and her boots. She loved the smell of clean hay and bedding,
and of the white foamy sweat that built up on her horse's withers and
neck after a hard workout. She loved the way the horses nickered and
nuzzled her, when she came to see them in their stalls. To Catlin riding
was her escape from demons no one knew about. When she was riding
she never thought about her father's drunken screaming, or her mother's
soft pleading. She never thought about missing out on boyfriends, parties
and school dances. And she surely never thought about the beatings she'd
endured on the few occasions she had stood up to her father's rule. Then,
as she got older, Catlin came to love the way she looked in her skin-tight
riding breeches and tall, black boots, and she loved being part of a special,
exclusive group. Every day of the week, except Monday's Catlin rode for
three or four hours after school. The club was closed on Monday's, and
the horses needed a break, but she would have ridden then too, if she were
permitted to do so.

As it was, she occasionally snuck into the club on Monday's, and took
a horse for a wild ride in the woods just a few miles away. No rules. Just her
and her horse. Nirvana.

She felt the most free when she rode there, going up and down steep
ravines, jumping over fallen trees and swift, clear streams. It was a break
from the daily grind of hard training, and she believed in her heart, that her
horses loved those adventures as much as she did. But her teammates and

The Colonel would be furious if they knew she risked injury to herself or the animals by breaking the rules that way!

At just a smidgen over 5'6" and weighing in at 118 pounds, Catlin looked small on her horses, but she rode with confidence, and ability that belied her size. She looked athletic and elegant atop her horse, her long, golden-brown hair whipping out from under her velvet black helmet, with her posture perfect, and her slim hands steady. Now at twenty-one Catlin was finally reaping the rewards of years of hard work and training. All those years of giving up time with friends at school, of passing up slumber parties and dances; all those years of giving up friends and boys, of missing the pool parties, and movie nights, had finally paid off.

Thinking about her accomplishment and of the new challenges it brought, hit her like a lightning bolt, and Catlin recalled how she'd felt when she first saw her name posted on "the list" on the club's bulletin board. The air had seemed to sizzle and pop when she saw her name on the list and a shot of adrenaline rushed through her body, as she realized she would be riding in the 2016 Summer Olympic games in Rio! She had made the National Equestrian Team! All her dreams were about to come true.

Early on, she'd learned to persevere, and never to quit. Even when it got hard. Even when she was in pain. She kept going. In her gut, she knew that someday, that perseverance would pay off. It would mean a ticket to an exciting new life.

Anyone looking at Catlin and her lifestyle, thought she had everything anyone could ever want. But she hid a dark secret deep in her heart, and she shared it with no one.

Her father was an executive to be reckoned with; her mother was a socialite with all the right friends and connections. They lived in a mansion with more servants than family members, but there was darkness there. Sometimes Catlin even feared that she'd inherited the "bad" genes from her father.

Cat shook her head in disgust, to ward off those memories and steeled her will to ride to excel.

She was almost there. What more could she ask for? She was happy, and now she was in love with Schuyler "Sky" Grant.

Thinking about him brought a smile to her glossy, pink lips. Strong, tall, beautiful, Sky. He had been one of the most coveted bachelors in Sao Paulo's "young-guard society" up until just a few short months ago, and now they were engaged! Engaged! With his slim, athletic build, devilish smile, sprinkling of freckles, warm brown eyes, and chestnut hair, Sky was a real catch. He wasn't just a pretty boy. Schuyler had endured some hardships himself, and though he was president of a thriving lumber business that had been in his family for generations, he'd made some sacrifices himself, and perhaps it was that which had initially attracted them to one another. A shared kindred spirit of hurt and pain.

Now, just six short months away they'd be married in December! Sky had just given her the best engagement present ever, and they were the talk of the town. She was certain this latest Olympic news would land them in the Sao Paulo society pages again. All she had to do was hang in there, and keep working hard. Soon she'd be able to put the lingering pain and hurt out of her life, and she'd start a fresh new life with Sky.

A slight vibration in her left ear brought her back to the present, and Catlin tapped the button on her tiny ear piece to connect the phone call. It was her brother Freddy, home from the States! She'd been expecting to hear from him after he'd cleared customs. "Hey Freddy! Hi! Welcome home! Is Dad with you?" Freddy, sprawled casually in the back seat of his father's black Mercedes sedan, laughed humorlessly.

"Are you kidding? Would the great Walther Lauria take time off from work to welcome me home? Get real Cat. Mom didn't come either. Just Nuncio showing up and driving."

Sensing his dejection, Catlin hurried to appease him.

"Oh Freddy, you know how he is. Work, work, work. And I know Mom is at the "Bienal" Art Committee meeting. She's chairing the show again this year, and she's super busy."

Freddy mumbles something as he gazes out the window while the town car glides past the poor neighborhoods surrounding the airport. The car seems out of place as it passes by mangy dogs, dirty, barely dressed children sitting forlornly in front of shacks made from scraps of wooden packing crates, corrugated tin roofs and dirt floors. This too common sight doesn't interrupt his conversation with his sister. Catlin apologizes.

"Sorry I wasn't there, either Freddy. I had to be here today. They announced the roster for the National Team. I made it! I'm on the Olympic Team! I'm so excited!"

Excited by her news he exclaims. "No shit! Wow! That's very cool. Congratulations Cat. You'll have to tell me everything. When are you coming home? What's going on tonight? Any parties?"

Calculating how long her workout will take, Catlin answers. "I'll be home around one or so. I still have to ride Strella, and I have a team meeting, so after that. But no parties, Freddy. I'll be beat. We can hang-out and catch up and you can . . . ."

Changing the subject, Freddy interrupts. "Hey, is Owen in town?"

Not surprised, Catlin replies. "Uh huh. God, Freddy I don't understand how you can be friends. It's hard to believe he and Sky are twins. They're so different."

Having received all the information he wanted, Freddy quickly ended the call. "Yeah, well I like him, that's why. I have to go. I'll see you later. Bye."

Catlin starts to respond but realizes that Freddy has already disconnected the call. She smiles thinking about her "big brother". All her life she looked up to him. In her adoring eyes, Freddy could do no wrong. He was her big brother. He was supposed to be her protector, yet somehow she'd never really been worthy of his attention. Maybe now that she was going to be a celebrity he would change his mind.

She laughed out loud then, remembering how he'd never even noticed her at all until she was in high school. It took Cat awhile to realize that even then though Freddy hadn't finally noticed her, he had really noticed her girlfriends. Catlin guessed they'd finally gotten cute enough or old enough to warrant his attention. But she didn't mind, she just wanted to be a part of his life. Once she was married and had her own beautiful home, and would be keeping her own elite company, Catlin was sure Freddy would be spending more time with her. Like the time he'd had a crush on her high-school friend Mel. He had crawled into Cat's bedroom late one night over Christmas break, when Mel was spending the night, and snuck into the twin bed with Mel. Cat had to hold her breath, pretending she was sound asleep. But that's what cool guys did, right? And wait until he met Monica. Monica had moved to Sao Paulo from Rio recently, and she was single, gorgeous, and smart. Monica's mother Inez, was a real Amazon Indian. Her father was an Italian actor. They'd met and fallen in love while he was filming a movie in the Amazon, and had moved to Rio after the shoot wrapped. Their genes combined beautifully to produce Monica, who was a real stunner! Freddy would fall head-over-heels in love with her, as soon as he saw her. Cat was always thinking of her brother, and maybe someday he would reciprocate.

Monica had just moved to Sao Paulo to start her own interior design and furniture company a few months ago. She and Catlin had met when Cat was picking out new furnishings for the house.

Sky had great taste, but everything in the house was too cold and masculine. He had every high-tech man-toy on the market, making the house interesting and unique, with it's voice activated doors and windows, it's smart heating and cooling controls to name a few, but it lacked a homey feel, a woman's touch. Catlin had enlisted Monica to add some softer, decorative touches to the house she would soon call her home. She loved Monica's sense of style, and together they were weaving the perfect eclectic mix of vibrant colors and fabrics, with old hand-tooled leather, and huge rugged wooden pieces that were being custom made and would be ready just before Catlin moved in, in six months. She could hardly wait.

Turning her thoughts back to the matter at hand, Catlin gathered up the reins, and continued her jumping runs with renewed energy.

Meanwhile Freddy slumped, dozing in the backseat, while Nuncio drove on in silence. The view outside his window had now given way to huge mansions almost hidden behind high walls topped with glittering shards of glass, or rough, evil looking spikes.

That kind of protection was the norm as the elaborate wrought iron bars on windows and doors. While the bars on the windows looked decorative, they served their purpose of keeping intruders out of the stately homes, although it was very rare indeed, to hear of anyone surviving the climb over the spiked walls, or the massive jaws of the vicious guard dogs that usually patrolled beneath those walls. Freddy ignored it all. He was used to all the trappings of his father's opulent lifestyle, and now was only interested in trying to figure out how he was going to get a piece of it for himself without actually having to do any real hard work. More than anything, Freddy was pissed off about his current financial circumstances, but he was determined not to let anyone in the family know what had happened. And he was determined to get back what he'd lost, as quickly as possible. By doing whatever he needed to do.

With that in mind, as quickly as he hung up from the call to his sister, Freddy dialed another number from memory.

Speaking in heavily accented Portuguese, he asked for Owen, but was disappointed when he was told Owen was not available. He'd been pleased to hear that Owen was in town, and knew he could reach him later.

Freddy slumped lower into the soft leather seat, and closed his eyes for the rest of the ride home.

In a few moments, the car slid to a quiet stop in front of fifteen-foot high stuccoed, white-washed wall. On top of the wall, hundreds of sharp shards of glass glittered their deadly warning. As Freddy reached for the door handle, the door was pulled open from the outside by Nuncio, the family driver. After offering Freddy a hand, Nuncio walked to the wrought-iron gate, pushed a code into the access panel, swung it open, and greeted the two beautiful German Shepherds who had silently taken up menacing positions as soon as the car came to a halt.

Speaking to the dogs in a purposeful tone, Nuncio soothed the two dogs. "Forca, Bruta," Nuncio said softly in Portuguese as he ruffled their sleek black and gold necks, "Mr. Freddy's home. You remember him, right boys?"

Nuncio stepped aside as Freddy walked past him, stopping only briefly to pet the dogs. Freddy walked up the driveway to the porticoed side entrance of the massive colonial house where he was greeted by a young black servant dressed in a discreet maids' uniform.

Freddy found himself slipping easily back into Portuguese, even though he'd been gone for over six months. Though he could speak it and understand it well, to a native he sounded like a "gringo". For some reason he'd never mastered an authentic Brazilian accent.

"Hey, Celia. Is my mother home yet?" "No sir, Mr. Freddy. She's at the museum meeting. She will be home this afternoon. She said you should do whatever you like until everyone gets home." "Great. Some welcome", he muttered under his breath and walked away.

Looking over his shoulder at Nuncio walking up the driveway with his luggage, Freddy wandered back into the big house, barely greeting Celia and Maria as they bustled around the kitchen. Looking around the beautifully decorated living room, Freddy felt lost.

With no one around, the house seemed a bit like one of the museum's his mother loved so much, and Freddy wandered from room to room slowly examining the heirloom silver, the priceless art and antiques, each object carefully placed to draw the eye without appearing ostentatious.

The silver gleamed, the glass sparkled, and the richly upholstered fabrics spoke to him of comfort and privilege he wanted to call his own. About to sink into the welcoming deep cushions, Freddy hesitated, turned around and walked back outside. Silently, the sleek dogs appeared at his side, and accompanied him as he walked instead to the apartment over the garage.

"This really sucks, girls". He muttered under his breath as he made his way from the beautifully appointed mansion to his new living quarters, the recently refurbished maid's quarters.

"I've got to figure out a way out of here soon." The dogs padded to a stop at the door to the apartment, then turned silently and padded back down to resume their patrol of the property's perimeter.

KAREN KEILT

MEET THE FAMILY

T HE SUN WAS almost setting by the time Freddy heard Nuncio putting the big powerful Mercedes away for the night, shutting the garage. He figured he'd just sleep a a few minutes longer, and suddenly Catlin was standing over him, shaking him awake and calling his name.

"Freddy. Wake up. Mom asked me to come get you. Dad's home and wants to have drinks before dinner. Are you awake?" Freddy groaned, rolled over, and buried his face in the pillow. Catlin, frustrated, shook him a bit harder. "Come on Freddy! Lazy Bones! Come on, come on, get up." Protesting, Freddy shouted at her, startling her. "Stop Catlin! I'm awake! Are you kidding me? I'm beat. I've had a rough few weeks. And a long trip."

Sounding a little miffed, Catlin turned to leave the room. "Yeah, well, get in the house. I'm going inside. I suggest you get your butt in gear, Dad's in one of his moods. He won't be happy about waiting."

Grumbling, Freddy responded. "Yeah, yeah, whatever. Go on, get out of here. I'm up."

Several minutes later, Freddy sauntered into the library, where the family was chatting about Catlin's upcoming riding events. He was sloppily dressed in baggy jeans, a torn and ragged Harvard sweatshirt, and flip flops. At the sight of him, Walther Lauria sat up in his leather chair, and Freddy knew he was in trouble. Freddy didn't know what he could ever do to please his father. Walther was dressed casually, but impeccably, in knife creased navy wool slacks, spit polished loafers and a gold cashmere sweater, over a parchment colored button-down shirt.

Freddy knew it was all custom-made for him, like all his clothes, at the finest tailor in Sao Paulo, with fabrics imported from Egypt, Italy and London. He looked down as his father's buttery soft leather shoes. They were impeccably shined and polished. His black hair was slicked back in a style made famous by Fred Astaire or some other long deceased star, and his good looks and surroundings made it seem like he might be a star, himself.

Colleen Lauria sat primly in a richly upholstered Queen Anne chair in her perfect, pink, Channel suit, complementing the fire-stitch design of her chair as if it had been custom matched just for this occasion. She looked like she should be having cocktails at the Paris Ritz.

"God" thought Freddy as he lounged on the sofa, "How would they react if they knew I've just been in jail?" Nodding demurely, Colleen asked. "What will you have Freddy?" "Whatever you're having." Freddy replied as he sullenly watched her expertly stir and measure the ingredients for a bourbon old fashioned. Obviously annoyed, Walther's voice exploded from his side of the room. "Goddammit Freddy, how in hell did they ever let you on a plane looking like that?" Without thinking, Freddy blurted out. "Jesus! Relax, Wally. I just got done with exams. I've had a rough couple of weeks. I'm just chilling out."

Catlin's hand flew to cover her small smile as she and Colleen exchanged worried glances. Walther's anger was palpable. When he answered his voice was controlled but seething.

"Don't you dare speak to me that way. I won't take your disrespect. You're going upstairs right now, shaving off that beard, and cutting off that hair. Then you're going to take a shower and change into something respectable before you sit down at my table. You look like a goddamned terrorist. I'm surprised I haven't gotten a call to bail you out of jail somewhere. You're back in my house, and if you want to stay here, you'll operate by my rules. Do I make myself clear?"

Slinking away, Freddy managed a last parting shot. "Yeah, yeah. I was going to get cleaned up anyway, you don't have to make a Federal case out of it."

Never one to let anyone else have the last word, Walther replied. "Yes, I do. Now get out of here. We'll continue this conversation later. Colleen see what you can do about that!"

Colleen gulped down half her drink and followed Freddy out of the room. "Wait, Freddy."

Catlin sighed and looked at her father's big desk. An ornate silver frame held a picture of the entire family during happier days on the beach in Guaruja. Her older brother Martin had his arm protectively around her shoulder as Freddy playfully tugged her long braids. Catlin smiled and wished Martin was still around to protect her. Glancing at the gathering gloom, Catlin thought it looked as if it might rain. On the patio a brightly feathered Amazon blue macaw, paced on it's perch, eyeing the gathering clouds. It obviously felt like it might rain too, and if it had not been chained to the perch it would have attempted to take refuge in the Royal palms swaying above the pool. Looking back at her Dad, and thinking that nothing ever really changed in this household, Catlin got up.

"I think I'll go make sure Nuncio gets Loro out of the rain. See you for dinner Daddy."

Without waiting for a response, Catlin left Walther swirling bourbon and orange slices in his glass. He dismissed her with a wave and nothing more. As she passed his chair she could smell the signature scent of his whiskey sour.

It almost made her sick. She remembered another tempestuous night long ago.

She was eleven-years-old, and cowered in her room at the family's East Hampton beach house. It was a great old place, set high on stilts on the dunes overlooking the Atlantic Ocean. That night the surf was pounding right along with teeming rain pummeling the roof and she wished it could drown out the battle being waged in the next room. She huddled in bed, listening, as her parents shouted in the living room.

By the time the fight had escalated to crashing china, Catlin managed to slip outside unnoticed, and had run to hide in the soggy dunes and whipping dune grass until the storm in her house passed. Sitting there shivering, feeling the grit and salt sting her eyes, watching the turbulent Atlantic thrash and crash on the shore a few feet away, was far less frightening than listening to her parents rage at one another inside. That was the night the sticky, sweet smell of orange and sugar muddled with whiskey imprinted itself forever in her memory. Crawling back inside much later, wet and tired, she had to step past a puddle of vomit that reeked of the mixture.

Shaking off the gloomy memory, Catlin called her fiancee, Sky.

"Hi Sky. Things are going about as well as I had expected. My father and Freddy are already at each other's throats. Freddy got home looking like a leftover hippie from the 60's in Haight-Ashbury.

"He's got shoulder-length hair, a real scruffy beard, and he's still wearing that ratty blue cashmere sweater he's had forever. Dad compared him to a raghead. I think if I had seen him get on a plane looking like that, I would have called Homeland Security myself."

As if asking for confirmation, Schuyler queried. "And he just graduated from Harvard?"

Sighing, Catlin answered. "Yeah, I know. He sure doesn't look like any business man I've ever seen. In his defense though, I guess he's been working really hard to graduate."

Wanting to change the subject Schuyler suggested. "Hmmm . . . I suppose so. Listen, let's not get involved. We have so much on our plates right now. Let's try to keep the dramas at a minimum."

Sounding instantly upbeat and excited, Catlin replied. "You're right. I'm still floating on air and I don't want anything to get me down. I still can't believe I made the team."

Without missing a beat, Schuyler enthusiastically ordered. "Believe it. You were a sure thing. Everyone said so. You've worked really hard to make it, and now with Olympus, you're sure to medal. I'm proud of you."

Catlin was grateful for her fiancee's unconditional love. "From your lips to God's ears, Sky! I'm going to work my butt off. Speaking of which I have a lot of paperwork to fill out, so I better get busy. Are you free for lunch tomorrow? Can you meet me at the club?"

"Sure. Call me at the office and we'll plan it."

"OK, Bibi. I love you." Catlin had a unique and endearing talent for mixing Portuguese and English. She thought in both languages simultaneously, yet had full command of English and Portuguese, causing both Brazilians and Americans to believe she was a native of their respective countries. She also made up many of her own combination words, and Schuyler loved that about her. He loved the BiBi nickname she'd coined, combining sounds and syllables from both idioms.

As she hung up, Catlin smiled. Her fiancee was always the voice of reason, and knew just the right thing to make her feel better. Schuyler Pierce Grant was her knight-in-shining armor, literally come to save the day. Catlin wasn't sure if she would have been able to keep up the happy, adjusted facade for too much longer if it hadn't been for him. He had won her heart by repeatedly showering her with love and attention. Though they'd attended the same American school since she was in eighth grade, they hadn't clicked instantly.

Schuyler had been a little distant and shy, and to Catlin and a lot of her peers that made him seem stuck up at the time. She smiled. Truth be told he was just a bit of a geek. He didn't seem to have any sense of style back then, but everything had changed after the tragedy in his life. Shaking her head to put aside any more unpleasant thoughts, Catlin started filling out the on-line forms for the International Riding Federation. She couldn't wait until she was married, and out from under her father's heavy hand. Living with Schuyler was going to be heaven.

YOU LOOK PRETTY GOOD
WITH SHORT HAIR

WALTHER, COLLEEN, FREDDY and Catlin sat down to dinner in the huge, formal dining room. The immense table was set with crisp Porthault linens, heirloom monogrammed silver, china and crystal. The Waterford glasses sparkled in the subtle lighting from the antique, amber crystal chandelier that hung over the always gleaming Carrara marble table.

French doors over-looked the spotlit gardens, and occasionally shadows of the sleek German Shepherds, Forca and Bruta, passed by the doors, as the pair made their endless rounds of the property perimeter patrol.

Only Freddy was watching the dogs and the night watchman, who also made repetitive circuits slightly behind the dogs. Having dogs and an armed guard was part of the landscape. It simply wasn't smart to be unprotected. Watching the dogs and the guard go by Freddy recalled a night of partying there three years earlier. Catlin and his parents had been on a trip to Europe, and Freddy had the house to himself. He had invited Owen and a few other friends over to try out the windowpane acid he'd brought from the States.

Several hours into the acid trip, he'd gotten spooked, and thinking he had to get rid of his stash, he'd foolishly taken it outside to the night watchman. He'd asked the guard to protect the bag with his life, and told him that it was a priceless treasure. The next day he'd forgotten all about it.

But the guard hadn't. A week later when the family returned to Brazil, the guard told Walther about the encounter, and presented the bag and it's contents to his boss. Walther had raged at Freddy in the library that night.

"Do you want to know what it feels like to us when we know you're doing drugs that could kill you? Do you care how much we worry about you?" Without warning, Walther had emptied the bag of pills onto the coffee table and scooped up a handful picking out a couple of the tiny flecks of the LSD soaked papers.

"I'll show you how we feel! I'll show you what it's like to worry!"

"Oh my God, Dad, don't!"

Completely shocking Freddy, Walther swallowed the acid, and for the next several hours he ranted and raved, and occasionally marveled at whatever was happening inside his brain.

Freddy stared blankly outside remembering the night, as Celia wheeled in the silver service cart and silently presented the family with their entree, a sea-salt and herb encrusted roast beef with thyme potatoes, and fresh roasted asparagus from the garden and a wonderful baby-greens salad.

Shaking Freddy back to the present, Walther spoke.

"Well, now you certainly look more like a recent college graduate."

Sullenly, Freddy replied. "I told you I was going to do it. I just needed a break."

"Let's not go there again, Freddy" Colleen interrupted gayly, "Your sister has some terrific news. She's been named to the Olympic Team. We're all so proud. Isn't that wonderful?"

Interrupting quickly to allay any arguments, Catlin continued. "I already told him about it on the phone today, Mom."

"We are so proud of you Catlina." Her Dad always reverted to his native Portuguese when he was pleased about something. "But you're going to have to work very hard. No more late nights out with Schuyler."

"Oh Dad. You know I work hard. I ride and work-out for five to six hours every day. I need a little break from that every now and then, and since Schuyler and I are getting married in six months, I have a lot of other things to do too. We need to spend more time together."

"Getting married? Who's getting married?"

"Freeedddyy!! Come onnn. I told you on the phone when I got engaged. Don't you remember?"

"Oh yeah, sorry. I was in the middle of exams when you called. When's the wedding again?"

"December twenty-eighth at five o'clock, at the big old stone Cathedral on Alameda Santos. The reception will be here afterwards. We have four hundred guests invited to the wedding and we'll have two hundred and fifty here afterwards. Oh, and of course, there's the rehearsal dinner at the Jockey Club the night before."

Somewhat impressed, Freddy gave his sister a huge grin. "Wow. Knowing you that'll be some party alright. I can see why you've been walking around on clouds. Congratulations Sis."

"Thanks Freddy."

As soon as he finished eating, Freddy stood up excusing himself. He was tired and wanted to get to sleep early. As he turned to leave the room, Catlin shyly implored him to come to the club.

"Freddy, Schuyler is going to come watch me ride at the club tomorrow. Why don't you come, too? You can see my new horse, he's amazing, he's almost 19 hands, and he's . . . ."

Surprised, Freddy interrupted her, speaking directly to his mother.

"You guys got her another new horse?"

Catlin was used to his jealous reactions, and again, spoke quickly to avoid a confrontation. "They didn't get me the horse. Schuyler did! He's an engagement present! He's so beautiful. Will you come?"

"Oh. Uh. OK. Sure I'll be there."

Pleading a headache and jet-lag, Freddy went back up to his quarters, while the rest of the family retired to the living room to chat about Catlin's future plans. Once in his rooms, Freddy picked up the phone and dialed.

"Sim. Sr. Owen, por favor."

Drumming his fingertips restlessly, Freddy waited for his friend to answer. "Hey! Owen, my man! How are you, man? It's Freddy. I'm baaaack."

Surprised, but pleased to hear from his buddy, Owen replied happily.

"Freddy? You're a stranger to my eyes. How are you? Better, WHERE are you?"

"I'm here in Sao Paulo. I just got in this morning. I graduated a couple of weeks ago, and I'm back for good. I'll be looking for a job, and for my own place. I'm staying at home for the time being, but I'm set up in my own apartment, out back."

Laughing, Owen couldn't resist a jab at his status-conscious friend. "Money makes a man act funny. Your own apartment? Where? In the maid's quarters?"

"Yeah, well it's not the best bachelor pad around. But it's private. Know what I mean?" Sensing Freddy's displeasure at Owen's remark, Owen quickly placated his friend.

"Sure. It's temporary, right? So I can't stop partying. Want to come over?"

Tired, Freddy just wanted to get off the phone. "Nah, not tonight. I've got to get some sleep. I'm pretty burned out, but how about tomorrow? I have to meet my sister over at the club. Schuyler's going to be there, too. If you join us, I won't be totally bored to tears. What do you say, man? Can you come bail me out?"

Owen agreed. "Yeah. Sure. I'll be there. What time?"

"I don't know. I'll call you. My sister's going to let me know in the morning. But I have another favor to ask. I had to come down "dry". Do you have anything? I'm dying, here."

"Of course, no problem, man. I'll have an unwrapped gift from me to you. Call me in the morning with the time. Hey, great to have you back. See you tomorrow." Freddy sighed deeply and hung up, reassured now. Things were starting to look up.

MOUNT OLYMPUS

LORO'S SCREECHING CALL woke Catlin from a deep sleep at six thirty. Jumping out of bed she pushed open the French Doors and walked out onto her terrace.

She hugged herself against the whisper of coming winter in the June air. The sky was gray and scudded with clouds. Looking over the elaborately carved wrought iron railing she sees Nuncio feeding and cleaning up the macaw's perch. The bird preens it's luxurious feathers as Nuncio places seeds and fresh fruit in the dish at the bottom of the perch. Catlin watches a few minutes longer as Loro claws his way down the five-foot pole to the ground where he picks up a banana with his lethal talon. Letting out a screech of joy, the macaw rips into the soft over-ripe fruit.

Settling into her morning routine, Catlin goes through a forty minute yoga practice, centering her heart and her body for the day ahead. She'd only been doing yoga for a couple of years, but had taken to it instantly, finding the profound peace that came with each meditation, was soon ingrained in her life; her strength and endurance, making her feel like she was exactly where she was always meant to be. After a quick shower Catlin settles at the dining table, and summons Celia with a push of the call button conveniently set into the floor at her feet. Celia, prim and smiling, appears instantly.

After exchanging a few pleasantries, the maid walks out of the room and quickly returns with a chilled glass of freshly squeezed orange juice, a platter of aromatic freshly baked rolls and breads, an array of soft cheeses and fruit spreads, a plate of eggs, bacon and toast.

In startling contrast to her trim athletic figure, Catlin ate a large amount of food quietly and efficiently, then headed to the kitchen door, stopping only to pick up a bag at the foot of the stairs. This is her daily routine, and she feels happiest when she's on her way to the club and her horses. After leaving messages for her Mom and Freddy, Catlin settles into the back seat of the chauffeur-driven car, and reads over team documents as Nuncio silently drives through the early morning traffic.

Concentrating fiercely, Catlin studies all the Olympic team rules and regulations. It's taking awhile for all of it to settle in. While she's worked hard, and is good at what she does, she sometimes lacks the confidence of an Olympian. But she vows to get over that! Soon they'll pull through the guarded gate at the club, where Catlin truly feels as if she's home. She knows she feels more relaxed here than she ever does in the big mansion she just left. Maybe soon she'll feel this way at home with Sky.

Her mind wandering, Catlin glances out the window as the car makes it's way slowly through increasing rush hour traffic. Thinking about the road to the club brought to mind the long journey she had started eighteen years before.

Catlin had been first introduced to horses in her father's arms as a nine month old baby. Over her mother's protest, Walther had taken the infant on a short ride, and if her glee was an indicator of her future love of everything to do with horses and riding, her father had been pleased that day. Catlin started riding ponies when she was just a toddler, and with the help of private instructors, and her own desire to ride as often as possible, by the age of five, Catlin was ready to move onto a horse and by the age of 8 she was competing and winning competitions with riders at least two years older.

She thought about the dedication and determination that had made her so successful, and swore she would continue until she had reached her ultimate goal.

Olympic Gold. Grand Prix Show Jumpers were the top athletes in their sport. Their competitions are the most challenging, and have the highest prize purses. The courses are very difficult and very fast, the jumps are higher and the riders are scored on faults, time and sometimes technique.

Usually a Grand Prix course has between 14 and 17 jumps or obstacles, made up of high and colorful fences set in patterns that require horse and rider to execute tight twists and turns at break-neck speeds, in order to make it over all the obstacles without refusing or knocking down a rail.

Every rider has his or her favorite type of jump, and as Catlin reviews them in her minds eye, she realizes she loves them all equally.

The Verticals are usually the highest with their rails placed on different stanchions one over the other as the name implies. An Oxer is comprised of two verticals placed at varying distances apart in order to make the jump wider. In an Ascending Oxer, the furthest pole is the highest, and in a Descending Oxer, the furthest pole or rail, is the lowest. In a Swedish Oxer the rails are slanted in opposite directions forming an "X" in the center. Triple Bars are spread fences that gradually get higher, but are usually easy obstacles for horse and rider. Catlin remembered a terrible fall she had several years earlier after a refusal at a five foot wall, but knew she'd learned a valuable lesson that day, and continued her reverie visualizing a Hogsback, in which the tallest rail is in the center.

If she had any favorites, it would have to be a combination jump.

In those, two to three different jumps are placed together, with no more than two strides between them, making precise timing necessary, in order to complete the jump. She also loved Open Water jumps over a simple wide ditch and Liverpools, which are larger ditches with an oxer or vertical jump, over them. Most horses don't like water jumps, as they have no way of knowing the depth of the water, so it takes special communication between horse and rider, for them to be trusting enough to let the rider to steer them up and over these intimidating obstacles.

Most obstacles have beautiful decorative fences on either side of the uprights that look like wooden fans, and some have planter boxers, called fillers at the foot of a jump, which help the animal judge height and depth. Some of the more difficult courses also have a "Joker" in the mix, specifically designed as a more difficult jump for the horses, with no filler, and simple, unpainted rails, which makes it extremely hard for the horse to gauge the real dimensions of the jump. Grand Prix horses and their riders must have the scope and courage to jump any high fence, and the athletic ability to handle hard, fast, very sharp turns. They must be able to execute bursts of speed, and be able to make decisions on a dime in order to navigate the difficult courses.

Whatever jump was before her, Cat loved the challenge, the ability to control the massive power beneath her, and the incredible sense of flight and speed.

Horses are usually huge investments for their riders, and often riders are sponsored. It's not uncommon for riders at this level to have several horses, and at a minimum of eighty thousand dollars for an "average" horse, only the lucky few are able to move ahead in the competitive field.

Catlin's inherent riding skills had brought her farther than most of the kids she'd first started riding with, but her father's bank account, her genes, her easy-going personality and her luck had all come together to make seeing her name on the roster of the Brazilian Olympic National Team a reality.

A new horse meant new equipment, and the Olympics mean the very best equipment and Cat made a list of things she would need.

She would get another custom made saddle, and this time it would be cut even smaller and lighter than a typical English saddle, allowing her to be closer contact with Oly.

A rider needs to feel her horses' muscles beneath her legs. She needs to be able to communicate with the horse through subtle, yet powerful moves with her legs and thighs, so Catlin was willing to sacrifice the comfort of a highly padded saddle for one that would let her feel closer to Oly. She'd also need a new saddle pad and girth, with a belly pad to protect the animal's soft belly from it's show studs wrapped around his ankles for protection, when he folded up his powerful legs to jump. She'd get a Cavesson noseband in a figure eight bridle, with a light bit for his soft mouth.

Putting aside her ever-lengthening list, Catlin collects her things and opens the car door as it pulls to a stop by the front entrance. Before Nuncio can open her door, she jumps out and races up the steps. Turning back to Nuncio from the top step, she tells him she'll get a ride home later. Nuncio smiles at his charge. He likes Miss Caty a lot. She's not like most of the spoiled kids his colleagues drive for. With one of them, he'd probably sit around waiting for hours only to discover the kid had already gone home with someone else. Not Miss Caty. She was always where she said she'd be, when she said she'd be there. She always has a kind word, and a beautiful smile. She was a rare one, and he felt lucky to work for the Lauria family.

It was a good job for him. Many Brazilians had nothing but grade school educations. They were the maids, and cooks, cleaning ladies, washer women, ironing ladies, and housekeepers. They were drivers, gardeners, houseboys and handymen. It was a stroke of luck to work for a family like the Lauria's. He was well paid, ate great food, had a nice room, and though his hours were often long, for the most part, the work was easy. He liked driving fancy cars. Mr. Lauria got a new car every six months, and if there was any serious problems it was taken care of immediately or it was replaced. Nuncio kept the cars looking like new.

He never wanted to go back to the favelas he had come from. Living there was hell on earth. He wasn't sure how he'd ever made it here from there, but one thing was sure. He wasn't going back.

Back in the car, he smiles, tunes the radio to his favorite Samba station, and drives back to the house, ready to take Mrs. Lauria wherever she needs to go once she's up.

Catlin scampers into the Ladies Dressing Room and greets the attendant, Claudia, with a warm hug. As Catlin changes into her riding gear, Claudia picks a pair of training boots from a rack of highly-polished boots, and brings them over.

"Will you be wanting these boots today, Miss?" Claudia asks in Portuguese. "Yes, Claudia, thank you. They look perfect. Beautiful as always. You always make them look brand new. I don't know how you manage that!" Beaming in response to Catlin's praise, the old woman begins folding Catlin's discarded clothing, placing everything neatly in her locker.

"You don't have to do that Dona Claudia."

"I know, dear. But I love helping you."

"Thank you. I'll make it up to you."

"You've always been a good girl. Excuse me for saying this, but things could get confusing for you now."

"What do you mean, Dina Claudia?"

"Just stay on your path. Some people will try to fool you."

Always amazed that the black woman still works at her advanced age Catlin turns around hugging her carefully, afraid for her brittle bones. She has no idea how old Dona Claudia is. She's worked in the locker room since Catlin was a little girl, and she was old and gray then. But her face is still smooth and unlined, dark as tanned leather, but ageless.

"Don't you worry, Dona Claudia. I've worked hard to get here. I won't mess it up now."

"I know dear, and remember I'm always here if you need to talk."

"Thank you." Giving the old cheeks a quick kiss, Catlin grabs her crop and helmet, takes a quick look in the mirror, sweeps her long curly hair into a neat ponytail, and leaves the room.

Walking quickly through the club house, Catlin stops to say hello to a few people offering her congratulations on her achievement. Smiling, she heads towards the stables.

Almost all the horses she passes are exquisite champions, most costing upwards of $80,000.00 each, many of them double that amount, or more. Each horse is meticulously groomed and cared for. When she reaches the row of stables housing her horses, she sees her groom, Pedro, scraping the hooves of her pride and joy. As her first soft step touches the ground there, both groom and steed turn in her direction.

The horse knickers softly perking up his ears. Running her hands over his sleek coat, Catlin praises Pedro for his care and attention to every detail. At nineteen hands the young Hanoverian gelding has a clean-cut head, large intelligent eyes, and a rich, deep chestnut coat, gleaming golden, seemingly lit from within by his fiery Arabian ancestry.

Walking away, Catlin turns to advise Pedro. "I'll be ready to ride in about fifteen minutes. When I'm done with him, you can bring me Strella and then Mach." Pedro keeps working, and the horse seems to revel in the attention and care. Moving from one stall to another, Catlin stops to greet each of her other horses.

At the first stall she stops to pet Mach, an unusual jet black Hanoverian stallion. Even though Mach is eleven-years-old, he is elegant and distinguished, and stands tall at 17 hands. Mach has been Catlin's horse since she was fourteen-years-old, and there is a special bond between them, like no other. Although Mach had been injured over seven years ago, and could no longer compete, she refused to part with him, and still rode him for pleasure a few times a week.

Though she hates to depend on any one horse, Catlin knows it's the larger Hanoverian, "Olympus", who will take her to the pinnacle of the Grand Prix Jumping circuit.

Catlin pauses at the stall of her baby, the silver Arabian mare, the regal, "Estrela Lunar". Her pure silver coat and white mane gleam, brushed to luster by Pedro. Catlin moves down the line of stables, but Estrela gently calls to her, nickering softly and stamping her polished hooves. Laughing, Catlin returns to the stall.

"Strella.... You didn't think I'd forget about you, did you girl?" Catlin reaches into her pocket and leans against her horse's long, sleek head, deeply inhaling the scent of horse, leather and hay, as Estrela happily gobbles the proffered sugar cube.

"I'll be back to ride you soon, girl." Catlin walks away towards the Olympic sized covered ring. She finds Schuyler waiting at the ring with his twin brother Owen and Freddy. Dismayed, Catlin wonders how it's even remotely possible that Schuyler and Owen are even related, let alone fraternal twins. They're nothing alike.

Schuyler is honorable and kind, Owen is a scammer and mean-spirited. Schuyler is committed to making a successful business, and Owen slips from project to project, bored with details, or simply unable to work hard at any endeavor. He's had too many failures to count. Once Owen had even attempted to start a Crayfish farm on the family's plantation near Savannah, Georgia. He had hired an excavation company to come in and clear out the centuries old rice fields. If Sky hadn't put in a lucky appearance on the tail end of a business trip, irreparable damage might have been done to the centuries old historic plantation. Sighing Catlin thought Owen obviously got screwed up when his parents were killed in a fiery car crash on the way back from a dinner party when the twins were seventeen-years-old, yet Schuyler somehow took charge of his brother and the family fortune. Somehow the teenager had managed to keep his head on straight, and not let all the money go to his head. Instead, he'd finished and graduated from Yale, expanded the family lumber business, and still managed to lead a normal, nice life. Yep. Schuyler was a keeper, and even

KAREN KEILT

if they had to constantly micro-manage Owen, her relationship with Sky was worth it.

"Hi Honey!" Catlin swung her arms around Schuyler's neck and as he pulled her into his embrace, they kissed passionately.

Clucking his tongue, Owen spoke under his breath. "Shawty got gifts. Get a room!"

Hearing him, Catlin turned to her future brother-in-law, "Oh Owen, you're just jealous. Can't you see we're in love? Aren't you happy for us?"

Like a spoiled child, Owen replied in a sing-song voice. "Ooh ooh, you make me happy for the rest of my days. Of course I'm happy for you Cat, it's just, Jeez . . . . don't you two ever act normal?"

Shocked, and not about to let him get to her, Catlin answers him. "This is normal Owen. If you ever settled down and found someone you really cared about, you'd see that."

Very familiar with breaking up these little family skirmishes, Schuyler diffused the argument. "OK. That's enough you two. It seems you're always at each other's throats. I can't have my best man, and my best girl bickering all the time now, can I?"

Not wanting to upset anyone, least of all Schuyler, Catlin agrees.

"You're right, Sky. He just knows how to push my buttons. I'll ignore him. How are you sweetie? Thanks for coming."

Under his breath, Owen turns to Freddy.

"I need to get me some of that. Your sister's hot, man. I wouldn't mind getting me some of that."

"Jeez, Owen, get a grip."

Anyone who knew Owen knew that he often subconsciously spoke in song lyrics. "Yeah, yeah, whatever. You can't always get what you want, but if you try real hard, you get what you need." It was actually quite a feat, and came from some corner of his brain that hadn't been affected by all the pot he smoked. He spoke the lines with no musical inflection, and it usually took strangers awhile to recognize a line he's used, but by then the conversation had already moved on, and so had Owen.

Freddy, Catlin and Schuyler all laughed. The tense moment was over. That was the thing about Owen. He always seemed able to diffuse things at the last possible second.

It was part of his charisma. His unconscious use of song lyrics usually had everyone in stitches, forgetting whatever rude or careless remark he'd made just minutes earlier.

The group stood together and watched the other riders in the ring, making silent comparisons with Cat and Olympus. A few people waved and called out to Catlin, giving her a thumbs up, and she blushed and waved back, with Schuyler hugging her close, and beaming, at his girl.

Feeling something bulky under Schuyler's jacket, Catlin reaches beneath it and tugs out a magazine. "Hey, what's this?" With a flourish, Schuyler unfolds a copy of the Veja magazine, that just hit the stands that morning. "Here, look for yourself." "Oh my God, that's me! Where did you get this?"

Looking over Catlin's shoulder, Freddy and Owen each grab for the magazine.

Almost tearing the magazine out of Schuyler's grasp, Owen shouts. "Yeah when you're a celebrity, it's adios reality. Check it out."

Putting a finger to her lips in an attempt to quiet him down, Catlin tries to grab the magazine back. "I'm not a celebrity. I hate being the center of attention. You all know that."

Not about to be undone, Owen insists. "Those magazine publishers know what sells. They'll write some awful stuff, but the more they run your name down the more your price goes up. This'll have all the men in Sao Paulo looking forward to the Equestrian Olympic events."

"Why just me?", Catlin asks ignoring Owen. "What about the rest of the team?"

Laughing, and still speaking loudly, Owen replies. "Come on Cat. Are you blind? And beauty is her name. The other two girls on the team look exactly like their horses, and the rest of the team are guys. No boobs. Sex sells, baby."

Any attempt at humor was gone, and Catlin grabbed the magazine, and handed it back to Schuyler. Her voice conveyed the strength of her conviction on the subject.

The Olympics is not about sex. It's about talent. Besides, everyone will forget about me soon anyway."

Putting his arm around her again, Schuyler looks into her eyes. "No one's going to forget you, honey. I'm proud of you. I bet you'll be in all the papers and magazines and on the news, too."

Feeling better, Catlin changes the subject. "Ugh, Sky, don't even think that. I just want to ride. Hey, look here comes my boy!"

Jumping down into the soft, specially sifted powder-fine dirt of the ring, Catlin rushes over to greet Pedro and her horse.

The horse is spectacular, everyone watching points, and whispers about the pair, obviously impressed.

Catlin mounts easily and sits crooning to the horse, as Pedro makes last minute adjustments to girth, reins, and stirrups. Ready, Catlin pushes him into a slow trot and proudly makes her way over to her family.

Beaming with pride, Schuyler smiles at horse and rider. "Wow, Cat. He looks terrific! You look terrific on him. Every time I see you two together I'm more impressed!"

"Thanks, honey. Freddy, Owen this is Olympus! He's a God among horses! You like?"

Owen bursts into laughter and turns to Freddy. "Are you kidding me? Now that we're here, you're so far away. Olympus? Why not just name him Captain Obvious? On a scale of one to ten for bad names, I'd say that ranks as a ten!"

Furious, Catlin responds.

"Ugh. Owen on a scale of one to idiot, you're a definite ten!"

Turning to Schuyler, Owen says . . . "I can't believe you bought him as an engagement present. Isn't that a bit unorthodox, bro? Just got paid, let's get laid, huh?"

Giving his brother a dark look, Schuyler speaks softly. "Knock it off, Owen. It may be unorthodox, but an engagement present is supposed to symbolize your future, and Catlin's future is in gold. Olympic gold, and I want her to know that I support her one hundred percent."

Uncharacteristically, trying to avoid a fight, Freddy intervenes.

"He's outstanding, Cat. I believe Schuyler really loves you. I'm doubly impressed."

"Thanks, Freddy. I knew you'd feel that way. Would you like to ride him?"

Seeing Owen has started to fidget, Freddy makes other plans. "Sure. But not right now. Right now, I'd like to see what you can do with him. He's big enough. Are you sure you can handle him when he gets going?"

Catlin gently nudges the big horse with the tip of her boot and together they move off as one. "He's like putty in my hands. He's so gentle, it's almost unreal. He has a really soft mouth, and he love's the training.

He seems to know exactly what I want him to do, before I want him to do it."

They all watch silently as Catlin puts him through a series of turning drills and then slowly starts warming him up on low, easy jumps.

Freddy interprets everything with dollar signs, and this gift is no exception. "So how much did that guy set you back, Schuyler?"

Scowling slightly, Schuyler answers him. "Well, Freddy, I did a lot of research. And I got him from one of the best German breeders. He's from all champion lines, so he cost a pretty penny. But he's worth every cent. Cat loves him, and I think they can win gold, so there's no telling how much he'll be worth in a couple of years. You can say he's a really great investment. He's worth much more than I paid, already. Besides I'd do anything for Cat."

"You really are in love with her, then." Freddy seems really surprised. "Yes, Freddy, I am. You have my word on that. I'll take the best possible care of your sister." Owen sighs and claps Freddy on the back. "Ah come on, enough of this romance novel, bullshit. I just need a drank. Want to join us, Schuyler?" "No thanks, not just yet. You guys go on ahead. I've got everything I need right here." Pretending to vomit, Owen sticks his fingers in his mouth, and he and Freddy turn and walk towards the clubhouse. Owen and Freddy slide into a corner booth in the nearly empty clubhouse bar.

Instantly, a waiter appears to take their order. Without making eye contact, Owen loudly orders a Bloody Mary, and Freddy does the same. Owen dismisses the waiter, who politely bows and leaves the table.

Looking over his shoulder towards the entrance, Freddy nudges him. "God. I'm about to lose it. I haven't had anything in days, man. Did you bring anything?" Speaking in song lyrics is almost an autistic trait and Owen doesn't realize he's doing it again now. "Some people call me the space cowboy, some people call me the Doctor of Love. I've got a little bit of everything. What do you need?" Relieved Freddy grins. "Oh man, a little "Vitamin C" would set me straight. I can barely keep my eyes open. Set me up. What've you got?" "Pure yay, brother. I've got about a gram on me, but I buy the drugs, I light the fire, I can get more later. "Excellent. Excellent. Pass it to me under the table. I'll go do a bump, then we'll talk."

Owen looks around the mostly empty room, and as no one seems to be watching him, takes a small packet out of his shirt pocket, and hands it discreetly to Freddy, who immediately gets up and moves out of the bar, towards the rest-room.

Owen sits humming softly to himself, and soon the waiter approaches with the two drinks. Again Owen dismisses him curtly, indicating that Freddy will sign the check when he returns.

With a jump in his step, absent just moments before, Freddy returns wiping his nose, his eyes bright, a smile on his lips. As he slides back into the booth, he passes the small packet back to Owen, who shakes his head dismissively.

"Go ahead and keep it man. I'm fine, I'm just fine."

Pocketing the small cellophane package, Freddy is grateful. "Thanks. This is great stuff, man. I'm feeling fine myself already."

"No problem. I'll be here. That's what friends are for."

They sip their drinks in silence, for a moment.

In a talkative mood now that the cocaine is having it's desired effect, Freddy probes. "So are you still in the import business?"

"Actually, it's Export business, as in "X". Ecstasy, what? It's my biggest product. EX, PORT, export business. Get it? I bring in a shipment of "E" every couple of months. Henri moves it for me with all his fashionista friends."

Freddy's surprised, and wants to know more. "No shit. How do you do it?"

"Call me the breeze. Ever since nine-eleven, it's been easy getting the shit out of the States."

Interested in all the details, Freddy continues to probe. "What do you mean?"

"They're checking everyone for bombs and weapons and shit, but no one's looking for paper. This stuff comes on blotter paper, just like that acid you used to get. I'm on acid. Acid. Chased around the car by midgets in the parking lot."

"So how do you get it through customs here?"

Proud of his entrepreneurial innovations, Owen divulges everything. "Shit, that's the beauty, man. Ring-a-ding-ding. I met a guy in a bar who works in customs. I got him a cheap laptop as an investment. The guy was stoked. Now, every time I come down I check his schedule and plan my trip to coincide with his work schedule. I bring him a few Hustler magazines, a few double x rated DVD's, a bottle of Johnny Walker Red, and when I get here, I pass him a couple of brand new "C" Notes. He pushes the "green" button, and I sail right through. Piece of cake. No one looks at me twice."

Freddy motions at the TV above the bar, silently showing footage of a demonstration in downtown Sao Paulo. "Yeah, well you better be careful. I sure as shit wouldn't want to get caught by any locals. You know what happens if you do."

"Shit. I'm not worried. I'm always prepared with cash in my hand yo. You know damn well you can bribe your way out of anything here."

"Wouldn't it be great if that's the way it was everywhere." Nodding at the TV, Owen sneers. "We got no worries in the world. It's not like the Lauria's would ever disappear like some of those poor saps will." Freddy motions signing a bill in the air, and the waiter rushes over with the check. Freddy quickly writes down his father's membership number and signs, leaving a hefty tip on his Dad's account. The waiter beams, and bows again as they leave the bar, and Freddy pats Owen on the shoulder.

"That's awesome. Bring me a couple of hits tonight, and I'll scope out a chick to try it out on. Now let's get back to the show out there, before someone takes offense."

WELCOME TO BRAZIL

LOOKING ANXIOUSLY AROUND the crowded airport Jack Kelly seems nervous as he glances at his wrist for the fifth time in the last two minutes.

"Are you sure he was going to meet us here?"

"He said he'd be here. He'll be here."

"Well, how are you even going to recognize him, or him you? You haven't seen him in years, and it's not like you've known one another forever."

Looking at his partner, Red was sure anyone would recognize both of them as American cops in a heartbeat. Kelly stood out in the vast room, head and shoulders above the average man, woman and child, but it was his white pasty skin, bright blue eyes, bulging muscles, and his air of entitlement that made him stand out like a beacon. Just as Kelly looked at his watch for the sixth time, Red caught a glimpse of a dark SUV with a flasher bar on top pull to the curb outside the automatic sliding doors. Picking up his beat-up rolling carry-on he gestured with his head.

"That looks like it could be our ride." Red and Jack head out the door, squinting against the bright sunlight, just as the SUV disgorges one of it's passengers. Jose Barros glances briefly at the doors, breaking into a huge grin as soon as he spots the towering Americans.

"Red! My old friend! I hope I'm not late. Traffic was a beast." Not waiting for a reply, he grabs Red's bags, while extending his hand to Jack. "And you of course are Jack! Welcome to Sao Paulo. How was your trip?"

"Uh, ok. We got here, didn't we." Jack checks out Jose's outfit, the sharply creased slacks, spit polished shows, and gleaming gold cuff links on an obviously hand tailored silk shirt. He looks toward Red, raising his eyebrows, but Red just smiles and shrugs.

"Here. Here. Let me help you with your bags. Get in the car. We'll take you to your hotel, and on the way I can give you some news. I think you'll be very pleased to hear what we've discovered." Jose speaks with a very heavy accent, but his English is quite good, and Jack is relieved he won't feel left out of any conversations.

The huge luxury vehicle stands out on the traffic-snarled streets of Sao Paulo. Most vehicles are small, many are smart cars, as the driver makes his way through traffic, as easily as a bull in a china shop. The first thing Red noticed about Sao Paulo as they maneuvered through the busy streets was that it bore no resemblance to Tijuana as he had expected. It was sophisticated, the architecture stunning and modern, and he was impressed. And it was huge. Larger than he'd ever imagined and teeming with well-dressed European-looking people.

"Take no prisoner's. That's Levy's motto when he drives." Jose guffaws loudly. "You have be aggressive to survive in Sao Paulo."

"So. You said you had news." Jack's impatience is wearing thin, after the long flight crammed into a tiny seat, and now crammed into the back-seat with Red and some minion of Jose's, who hasn't said a word, just smiles and nods at everything said.

"Yes. Of course. You Americans. I forget you're always so to the point. Business is business." Before Jack has a chance to pin him with his evil eyes again, Jose continues. "We already started to follow this Lauria boy and his friends. Did you know that his little sister is the newest star in Sao Paulo? She's beautiful, and she's gained celebrity status as Brazil's newest golden girl."

"Yeah. We heard. She's going to be an Olympian, right?"

"Yes. That's correct. I don't know how we can benefit from that just yet, but I'm sure we'll think of something." Jose smiles evilly at the men in the back seat and continues. "We've discovered that her fiance's twin brother is dealing ecstasy at the hot night clubs in Sao Paulo. We haven't figured out how he gets it in yet, but I've got men tailing him night and day."

"Are your men following the Lauria kid too?"

Nodding again, Jose looks at Red. "Yes, it's all been set up. My Captain, Eduardo Ramos, we call him Dudu, will have the pleasure of following that one with you. You'll find most Brazilians are known by their nicknames. He will report to you, and you can coordinate anything you need with him. My duties keep me busy in my office, so I regret I cannot participate in this adventure with you, but I am confident you will have everything you need at your disposal. How soon do you want to start?"

Red's been ready for a long time. "Right away. The kid's been back for a couple of days, and we want to be sure we catch him making his connections, and follow his associates too. This kid is bound to get involved in the drug trade again, and one way or another, I intend to profit from that."

"I agree. Dudu will be waiting for you outside tomorrow morning. Just give him your orders and he will deliver whatever you need. Call me if you need anything." Worried that the other tail might get screwed up, Red leans toward Jose.

"They won't screw up the tail, will they? I mean we don't want this thing to go in the crapper before we even figure out a plan."

"Don't worry. My men are very well trained. They meld into crowds like water in a stream, he'll never know he has a, how you say, tail. By the way, the fiancee has big money. Perhaps even more than Lauria himself."

"Excellent. It sounds like things are clicking right into place." Red looks at Jack with a smirk. "See. I told you things would work out."

And, even better this boy Owen has an accomplice. His errand boy is a, hmmmmm, social escaler."

Red interrupts. "I think you mean climber."

"Oh, yes. Climber. He is a social climber who wants nothing more than to fit in to high society with the Lauria's and Grant's. He is a small town crook from Paris, who left Paris after a dust up with the local police. He was caught cloning credit cards at some restaurant there, and rather than face jail time, he managed to get out and come to Brazil. He's reinvented himself as a semi well known fashion photographer. No doubt he has visions of winning some prizes for his pictures of Catlina."

"The sister, right?"

"Yes, Red. The sister. Any man in his right mind would like to get some of that. But enough business for today. Here we are at your hotel. Get settled, have a nice dinner, and tomorrow we will go over all our plans. Levy here will be at your disposal, and he will take you out tonight so that you can get a feeling for Sao Paulo. He will be back here to pick you up in about two hours. How's that?"

The SUV pulls to a stop in front of a small, old hotel. Levy opens the doors watching as both men grab their bags. Reaching into the glove-box, Jose pulls out two revolvers. "I thought you might like these."

Smiling, both Red and Jack feel the heft of the weapons, then place them comfortably at their backs in their pants waistbands.

"I had a feeling calling you was the right move. I knew you'd come through."

"You can count on me, Red. When you told me we might have some trouble here in town, I knew it was important for us to do the right thing and get the scum off the streets." Jose climbs back into the hulking car as Red and Jack head into the hotel, and the car pulls away from the curb.

"That went well."

"Better than expected. I feel good about this. You know you can always count on me to take care of us, pal."

Swinging his fist up high, tapping Red's knuckles, Jack agrees. "I'm sorry I ever doubted you. Now let's get some shut-eye. I didn't sleep on that flight at all, and I want to be able to take in everything this Levy guy is going to show us tonight."

SAO PAULO GINGA

CATLIN UP-SHIFTS AND down-shifts the gears like a race car driver, moving the little sports car through the traffic like a pro.

Freddy grips the "holy shit bar" above his right shoulder with bloodless fingers, too afraid to look anywhere but straight out the windshield, and speaks through clenched teeth begging Catlin to ease up.

"Jesus, Cat, slow down! You're going to get us killed! We're not late. Do you always have to drive like this?"

Quickly checking her side view mirror before accelerating calmly into the fast lane, Catlin reassures him. "Relax Freddy. I haven't had an accident yet. Even Dad says driving is one of the things I do best. I'm good." Then she blew past a slower driver, giving Freddy a "told-you-so" wink.

Not convinced, Freddy double checks his seat belt and replies while staring wide-eyed out the windshield.

"Yeah, well, you're no "Danika Patrick", and it makes me nervous, so unless you want my dinner all over your brand new Corinthian leather seats, you better take it easy. Will you slow down, please?"

"OK, OK, just for you. Let me just get around this slowpoke. Thanks for coming with me Freddy. Dad's been giving me a tough time about going out."

With inches to spare, Catlin guns the sleek car through a space that seems too small for it to fit through, into the next lane, then zooms up ahead of traffic, and finally, downshifts to slow down.

Freddy expels a pent up breath of air, and loosens his grip on the hand-hold. After taking a few deep breaths he comments on their father's continued belief that Catlin is still a child.

"For Christ's sake! You're twenty-one-years old. You're engaged, for God's sake."

Nodding in agreement, Catlin mimics her father. "You know how he is. As long as you're under my roof . . . blah, blah, blah . . . but I don't want to piss him off now. I want him to pay for this wedding."

Not fazed, Freddy replies. "Hell, Schuyler can buy this wedding a zillion times."

"That's not the point, Freddy. I just don't want to get on his bad side. You know how he can be. You should have seen him when Sky asked for my hand in matrimony. Dad actually chased him out of the house with a gun."

Astonished, Freddy finally turns his head and looks at Catlin. "What?"

"I kid you not. I was mortified. I thought Sky would dump me for sure."

"He really loves you. I saw that today. I don't think even Dad could scare him off."

"Thanks, Freddy. I know he loves me, and I love him too. I just have to stay on the straight and narrow, and not buck the system now. I don't want to blow this. Five months, seventeen days and seven hours from now I'll be married, and living with Sky. Can you believe it?"

A few minutes later they pull up in front of a trendy night club, where a valet rushes to open Catlin's door helping her out of the car. Without looking back, Catlin and Freddy ease past the long line of yuppies waiting to get in, as Freddy palms a hundred dollar bill to the doorman. Moving quickly inside, they're greeted by a multitude of Sao Paulo's trend setters, the subtle scent of incense, flickering lights, and loud music.

The Maitre D recognizes Catlin, and quickly leads them through the crowd, to a table near the dance floor.

Catlin spots Schuyler with Owen and a couple of their friends, and rushes ahead as Freddy peels another bill from a stack in his pocket ordering a round of drinks from a passing waiter.

Reaching out for her fiancee, Catlin kisses him passionately.

Twirling her at arms' length, Schuyler smiles. "Catlin! Wow, you look amazing!"

The slinky red party dress accentuates Catlin's sculpted body, the skirt flipping seductively, her long legs flashing in four inch spike heels as she hugs him tight.

"Thanks, sweetie!"

They join the rest of the group seated facing the dancers on the raised, circulating dance floor. Reaching across Schuyler, she kisses Bete on the on each cheek.

Catlin's known Bete for little over a year. Their completely different backgrounds would have assured they'd most likely never meet. Schuyler had met Henri at a photo shoot for a new product catalog. Liking the work, Sky had hired Henri to take some photos of Catlin riding, and then Henri had started tagging along to competitions, then to club events. At some point Sky had insisted he bring a date, and the next time she thought about it, Henri and Bete were everywhere. They both seemed nice enough, and Bete sure was rough around the edges, but the couples had become good friends.

Like many Brazilians, Bete was very short, but you would never call her petite. With her enormous breasts and colossal Afro-styled, dark frizzy hair, she was anything but small. She loved calling attention to herself

KAREN KEILT

with mostly clashing and flamboyant, vividly colored clothes. Usually the mostly unsuitable outfits did not compliment her pug-like features, and tonight was no exception. Cringing inwardly, Catlin hugs her friend vowing that one of these days, she's going to give the well-meaning brunette a makeover.

"Bete! How are you? Wow! That's some top! Where did you get it? It's wild and way sexy! I bet Henri can't keep his eyes off you!" She winks at Henri and blows him an air kiss. The Frenchman winks and blows kisses back.

Laughing, Bete responds. "Or his hands! I know. I love it too. I got it at that new store, Daisy at Iguatemi." She twirls. "It was a bargain, and I just love the colors. Do you think I got a good deal?"

"We certainly would never lose you in a crowd", Catlin replies, laughing.

The group settle down at a reserved table, and have to shout to be heard over the noise in the club. After two rounds of drinks, Catlin leans over to Schuyler and whispers in his ear.

"I hate to say it, but I'm beat. I wish we hadn't come. I'd rather be home, sound asleep."

Holding her close, and whispering in her ear, Schuyler is happy. "Than be here with me? Aw, come on baby. Make the best of it. Everyone's here. I know you've got a ton going on. We'll make it an early night, I promise."

"Arrgh. Alright. Let's not stay too late, though . . . . OK, make me feel good. Tell me how I looked on Oly today, BiBi." "You looked AMAZING. He's responding really well to you. You are going to make a winning team. I can tell."

"Do you really think so?

"Yes sweetie, I really think so. You're so in sync now, just imagine how you'll be in another year. We're talking gold baby."

Henri's been watching the couple snuggle and murmur, and finally shouts across the table. "Hey! You two love birds! What's with all the tweet, tweet whispering? You haven't said a a word to me all night."

Looking up sheepishly, Schuyler grins at his friend. "Oh hey, Henri. Sorry, man. We're just talking horse stuff. You heard Cat made the Olympic Team, right?"

"Yes, of course. Bete told me. Congratulations, Catlin! That's terrific news. Come on let's raise our glasses in toast to our star and the newest Olympian."

Henri raises his glass and the rest of the group follow suit. People close to the table turn to listen. Mimicking an announcer with a microphone, Henri makes a proclamation in a deep bass voice.

"May your future be filled with gold and many shining stars. Here, here! To Catlin Lauria, soon to be Catlin Grant, the newest member of the 2016 Brazilian Olympic Team! May she bring back all the gold! Chin Chin!"

The crowd joins in clapping and whistling, as Schuyler pushes Catlin, cheeks flaming, to her feet. "Thank you. Thank you." She sits down quickly as the Maitre D approaches with a bottle of Perrier Jouet, and pours glasses for the group. Beaming, Schuyler leans close. "See, aren't you glad you came?" Eyes shining brightly, and cheeks still flaming, Catlin buries her face in Schuyler's shoulder. "Sky! Did you have this planned?"

"I admit nothing. But you didn't think I'd let this moment pass us by without doing something. Come on let's dance. All eyes are on you now. Give the crowd what they want."

As they move off to the dance floor, Freddy, and Henri lean in to catch up.

"This is a new look for you, Freddy. Preppy? I never would have expected that."

Eavesdropping on their conversation, Owen chimes in.

"Darlin' don't you go and cut your hair. Cat said his dad gave him a TV style "Extreme Make-Over" when he got off the plane. Made him do it."

"Shut up, Owen." Freddy dismisses him and turns back to Henri. "I'm looking for a job. You know I just graduated, right? I was going to do it anyway. So what's new with you, dude?"

The photographer pretends to look through a camera lens and snaps pictures. "Same old, same old. Photographing the models, working the job." Butting in again, Owen pipes up. "They've got no horns but you must see some amazing tail, huh? How often do you score?" Shocked by his friends' inappropriate comment, Freddy turns to him. "Jesus Owen, you are so crude. Don't you see Bete is sitting right here? "Oops. Je suis desolee. Sorry, Bete. No disrespect meant." Sighing loudly, Bete, put her arm around Henri's croissant enhanced waistline.

"Forget about it, Owen, we all know you're just a pig. If it weren't for your musical talent and your good genetics, I don't think we'd tolerate you around here. You're lucky Schuyler stands up for you."

Not in the mood to be chastised, Owen replies. "Ha, I know another reason you "put up" with me. I'm the one that keeps you all in "Happy

Land". Don't forget that." Catlin and Schuyler return from the dance floor, and Catlin calls to Freddy.

"Freddy, I think we'd better head out. I've got another full day of riding tomorrow, plus all sorts of planning for the wedding." Schuyler looks dejected. "Hey, you can't leave now. If you do, I have to go home with Owen." "Oooh poor you! But you know how my Father gets. He'll be sending out an armed patrol if I'm not home soon. Better to placate the beast, than do battle." They kiss, then Freddy and Catlin move towards the exit, while Bete and Schuyler wave goodbye.

Henri and Owen head to the bar to settle the bill. Henri speaks softly. "So, did you bring the stuff?" "Oui, Monsieur. As promised. I am your main supplier. You got buyers lined up?" Looking around to be sure no one is listening Henri replies. "Of course, they've been asking for you. And I have some new guys interested too." "Hey, that's great. Who are they? "Cause I really want to know. Who are they?" "Some Americans. I'm working with some consultants from the States. They seemed pretty uptight at first. Typical corporate, straight-laced guys, but they're good guys, and really gung-ho on getting into the Brazilian party scene." Owen seems pleased. "Cool. As long as they pay cash. Cash is God." "Excellent. I'm sure that won't be a problem at all. It seems money is no object for these guys. Why don't you come to my studio tomorrow and we'll set it up." "Sounds good. Call me. Call me. Call me, call me anytime. Call me!"

PAY ATTENTION

S CHUYLER AND OWEN drove away through the nearly empty streets, each engrossed in his own thoughts. Schuyler maneuvered the sleek, powerful Mercedes gingerly, like a man who knows he's had too much to drink.

"So, how long are you staying this time, Owen?"

"You know, the usual. Feel the city breakin', everybody shakin'. A week or two, I guess." "Well do me a favor, will ya? Try to think before you open your mouth. That wasn't too smart tonight with Bete and Henri. Or with Cat, at the club today, either." Sheepishly, Owen replies. "Yeah, I know. Oops, I did it again. You know I don't mean any harm."

"Right. We know that Owen, but it's tiring. Can you just think first?"

"Yeah, yeah, yeah whatever."

Twenty minutes later the car bumped off the main road onto a less travelled dirt road at the entrance of a remote, exclusive neighborhood. Schuyler slowly and carefully turns the car in between two tall stone pillars. It's an inconspicuous driveway, and gives no hint to what lies beyond the simple cattle guard set in rough cement. As the car noses onto the property two sleek Doberman's appear out of the shadows, following silently as the car wends it's way down the long hill, past a perfectly groomed regulation clay tennis court, exquisite landscaping, and an extensive vegetable garden.

From the top of the hill, the ten-thousand square foot modern construction of glass and stone seems to glow softly, lit from within and with the intermittently twinkling outdoor light. The house is a one story, long, rectangular edifice, with lots of gleaming floor-to-ceiling glass walls, and a large swimming pool set in the center of the mammoth "U" shape.

Under a portico at the bottom of the hill, Schuyler guns the cars' engine before turning it off.

He loves the way the car performs, and though paying the three hundred percent import duty on the ninety thousand dollar automobile was an indulgence, it's one he can afford.

Massive wooden doors are flanked by floor-to-ceiling etched glass panels, welcoming all visitors with a chimera of radiant soft light. An enormous amber crystal chandelier glows comfortingly, in the center of a simply decorated atrium. The black and white marble-tiled floors gleam. Schuyler pulls open the door and enters the house, the two powerful dogs alert at his heels and Owen tagging sluggishly behind.

"I'm going to crash, bro. G'night."

Still jacked up from celebrating with Catlin, having had several drinks and driving the powerful car, Schuyler heads to the kitchen. "I'm grabbing a little bed-time snack. I probably won't see you in the morning Owen, I'll be out of here before you're up."

"You got that right. Any plans for tomorrow? The wild night is calling."

Smiling patiently at his "younger" brother, Schuyler replies.

"Tomorrow is poker night. Someone's got to make some money. Henri, Bete and Cat come over every Thursday to play. You and Freddy can join us. The more the merrier. I can whup you all."

"Don't count on that. I hear Freddy's a mean card player, not an imaginary player."

"Whatever, good night."

Dismissed in his own home, Schuyler makes his way to the antiseptically, spotless kitchen with the dogs following closely at his heels. They sit silently at attention watching their master, as he moves from the Sub Zero refrigerator, to the stainless steel and butcher-block prep table, with all the fixings for a cold roast beef with fresh horseradish sandwich and a tall glass of milk. I've got to stop drinking so much, he promises himself. The kitchen is a chef's dream, with all the latest equipment, comfortable cork flooring, blue granite counter tops, multiple ovens, and a walk-in pantry the size of a modest kitchen.

Smacking his lips and licking crumbs off his fingertips, Schuyler places his utensils and dishes in one of several stainless steel sinks, and turning out the lights, walks back through the eerily empty house.

For a brief moment, he hears a melancholy melody echoing down the hallway. For the millionth time, he wonders why Owen hasn't done more with his musical abilities. Owen may be the family black sheep, but he's a genius when it comes to music.

And everyone knows it, but Owen. If only he would concentrate on doing something with his ability, instead of wasting his life. Dejectedly shaking his head, Schuyler continues through the library, past the formal living and dining rooms, to his sanctuary in the master wing.

Automatically switching off adverse thoughts about Owen and thinking about more pleasant things, Schuyler silently wonders how much of his painstakingly decorated bachelor pad will be changed once Catlin has moved in.

In the large master bedroom, a fire has almost burned itself out in the worn brick and glass fireplace. The immense bed is turned down, crisp linens, pressed and inviting. The only thing missing is Catlin.

Grinning, Schuyler thinks about how he'll be holding her soon, and knows that it won't matter at all, if she wants to rip out every old leather chair or sofa, and put lace drapes up on every floor to ceiling window throughout the entire house. She can do whatever she wants. He's completely lost and in love. But he wonders what he's going to do about Owen. He knows Cat won't put up with his antics once they're married.

THE SET-UP

WHILE SCHUYLER PONDERED what he should do about Owen, several miles away, Red Tucker and Jack Kelly are standing side-by-side at the front of a strategically spotlit stage.

They're both completely absorbed by the performance taking place on the stage inches away from their glazed, sweaty faces. They guzzle beers trying to maintain their composure as they watch two beautiful mulatto women perform oral sex while a large, naked, black man stands over them masturbating. In moments, the women bring one another to climax, then focus their attention on the enormous man.

On their knees, the women now take turns sucking and licking, fondling his sculpted ebony skin, all while rubbing themselves against his legs, thighs and each other.

When it seems no man could endure another moment of their attentions, he shoves one of the women to the ground impaling himself, while the other one squirms around the thrusting couple, alternately licking and kissing them, while masturbating.

Shortly the man explodes in orgasm, and the crowd of mesmerized viewers sigh and murmur appreciatively. Standing next to Red and Jack, an elegantly dressed stranger politely wipes his lips with a starched white handkerchief, then places it back into his sport coat pocket. "You can have the pleasure of a private session with any of them, or all of them, if you wish my friends. Just say the word. Your friend Jose has made it all possible."

Aching to participate, Kelly moves toward the stage.

"No shit! I'm ready, where do we go?"

Grinning enthusiastically, the stranger steers Jack toward a curtained exit. Passing one of the young girls, he tells her that all expenses have been taken care of. His guests should pay for nothing, and should have anything they want.

Jack's brow is sweating in anticipation. He waves at a young woman, who smiles happily at the big American's lap. She knows she'll get a big tip from this guy.

Red places a restraining hand on his partner's arm.

"Thanks, not tonight. We're here to appreciate the show, and I appreciate your offer, but we'll come back another time to enjoy the spoils."

Nodding appreciatively, the stranger replies. "Ah, typical Americans. You're all business. Here in Brazil things are different. Sex is part of our every day lives, and it can be had anywhere, any time, in any fashion you prefer. But I will admit, a lot of my friends and colleagues get side-tracked, and then do not take care of business at all. So, enjoy, watch the show.

Then when you have concluded your business come back and you can have your choice of delights."

They make their way to a table in a darkened corner of the room where two exquisite, and mostly undressed, young women stand eager to do their bidding. Jack Kelly slumps in his seat momentarily sulking until the two women smile and place ice cold beers on the table.

"Shit. What the fuck was that about?"

"Look. We still don't know the lay of the land. I'm lookin' out for you buddy. You'll probably thank me for this later. And if everything's kosher here, we'll be back. You know what they say about anticipation, don't cha?"

Grabbing is crotch suggestively, Jack frowns. "Anticipate this."

Surreptitiously watching Jack who sways side-to-side while attempting to keep his red eyes open, Jose wonders if he can trust these two American misfits. Unable to hold on any longer, Jack lurches to his feet and staggers into the adjacent bathroom. Shrugging his shoulders, Red slams the bathroom door shut behind him, but nothing can mask the sounds of retching behind the flimsy door.

"He's a good guy. Loyal, you know? But he can't hold his liquor." He shrugs again and continues. "Here's the plan. Your guys keep watching the group of kids. Have them get some pictures too. My job is gonna be to put the screws to Freddy. He's gonna have to trade."

"How are you so sure he will work with you?"

"I told you that before. He won't confess to his old man. And that's the only way he could get out of this."

"What if he tells his friends about you and they simply stop their uh . . . activities."

"Not gonna happen. Trust me on this Jose. I know this guy. He'll want to save his own skin."

Distaste etched on his features as another loud bout of retching erupts from behind the door, Jose wrinkles his nose as the tell-tale offensive odor of vomit seeps into the room, and he gets to his feet. Jose extends his hand to Red and they shake. "This is going to work. The kid'll crap his pants, and we'll nail 'em."

WEDDING BELLS

COLLEEN LAURIA IS the perfect image of a corporate trophy wife, in her sleek gray sheath, fitted ivory blazer, sensible low heels and "Mikimoto" pearls. She speaks to her daughter in dulcet tones, as cultured as her pearls.

"Good morning, Caty. Are you ready for a fitting?"

"Hey, Mom. Yep, I can't wait. I'm so excited to see what my dress looks like! It was one thing to see the design on paper, but to actually put it on . . . . I'm ready! I can't wait."

"OK, let's go. Nuncio is waiting, and I have an appointment at 11:00."

As the car drives through the busy city streets, Catlin and Colleen chat about all the preparations being made for the reception.

By the time they reach the seamstress' atelier, Catlin's "Blackberry" to-do-list has been e-mailed to her wedding planner. Commenting on how much easier it is to coordinate a wedding with the high tech gadget, the two women enter the designer studio arm-in-arm, where they're greeted like honored guests, by a beautiful young attendant.

"Madam Sandra will be with you shortly. Please sit down, and let me bring you a cafezinho."

Catlin and Colleen nod in agreement, and soon they're sipping, steaming aromatic coffee in the delicate porcelain demitasse cups and munching on tiny, sugary pastries. Away from Walther's fierce control, Colleen is a different woman. She is elegant and confident, and Catlin loves seeing her this way.

A few moments later, an elegant, very tall, very thin woman in her late fifties enters the room. Two trailing attendants follow behind her, carrying a sparkling white gown. With a flourish, they hold it up for inspection. Setting down her coffee cup, Catlin jumps to her feet to touch the fairytailesque, ivory silk dress. Reverently, Catlin addresses the illustrious seamstress.

"Oh, Madam Sandra. It's exquisite. It's more beautiful than I had imagined. You certainly outdid yourself."

In a surprisingly deep voice, the seamstress responds. "Well, dear, go try it on. Sofia, and Paula will help you."

A few minutes later Catlin returns to the room where her mother and Madam Sandra are chatting. As she makes her appearance, the women stop chatting, mesmerized. Madame Sandra is especially moved.

"Catlina, I see beautiful brides every day, but you, my dear are absolutely stunning, That dress is indeed fabulous, but on you, it is magnificent."

Choking back tears, Colleen agrees. "Oh darling, you look incredible. I'm tearing up just looking at you, here. I don't think I'll be able to watch you walk down the aisle without making a scene. This wedding and this dress will be the talk of Sao Paulo."

Proudly, Catlin spins around. "It is gorgeous, isn't it?"

Catlin's hair cascades down her shoulders and framing her face.

Clear blue eyes sparkling, her neck looks regal and incredibly long in the gently plunging neckline, which accentuates her breasts with it's lacy trim and delicate seed pearl beading. Hugging her tiny waist, it flares to fit snugly over her hips, then flares out again in a swirl of tule, and silk, that shimmers and floats with each step. Catlin turns slowly on the dais, showing off the back of the dress, a sexy surprise. The gown plunges revealingly to the gentle curve of her hips. It's demure and sweet in front and sexy and daring in the back. Madame Sandra makes a few tiny adjustments, while her mother and the attendants ooh and ahh over the bride-to-be.

Breathlessly, Catlin thanks her. "Madam Sandra, I couldn't be happier. This dress is exactly what I dreamed of. Schuyler will be blown away. Thank you."

Humbly, Madame Sandra accepts the praise. "So will every other man in that church, my dear. I'm certain that there will be many broken hearts in that church. I make beautiful gowns, but not many women have the bodies to pull off a dress such as this."

"Madam Sandra, you're very kind. Thank you."

FRIENDS FOREVER

S EVERAL HOURS LATER, after riding all three horses, Catlin hangs up her riding britches in her locker, and steps into the shower. As the steaming water cascades down her back Catlin thinks about the wedding dress, and how sensual it made her feel. Hurrying to be with Schuyler, she shampoos her hair, and quickly dries off, slips into a pair of faded black jeans, a turtleneck sweater, and Frye boots.

Shaking out her hair, she runs a comb through it to untangle the jasmine scented locks, turns on the blow-dryer for a few minutes; just long enough to get most of the water out.

She knows the cool air will dry her hair into soft curls, so after applying a hint of blush and a dab of faint pink lip gloss, she waves goodbye to a few other riders and runs down to her car.

Pammy Oliver is walking into the club just as Catlin is rushing out. With her long, wavy black hair, olive complexion, smoldering eyes and athletic figure, she could be Catlin's dark alter ego. Almost colliding, they laugh and hug.

Happy to see her friend, Catlin exclaims. "Pammy! I haven't seen you in days! Where've you been?"

"I was in Rio with my Mom. She wanted to pick up a new bathing suit for our trip to Italy next month."

Cat mockingly taps her forehead with her palm.

"Right. I forgot you were going. I've had serious brain drain."

The two friends continue catching up and Pammy congratulates Catlin on her accomplishment.

"Hey! Congratulations! I heard the big news while we were in Rio! You made the team! That's too awesome! You better not go getting all high and mighty on me. Will we still be friends?"

Hugging her Catlin intones seriously. "Are you crazy? Of course we'll still be friends! You've been my best friend since first grade. Has anything ever come between us? Anything other than Matt Larson?" They both shake their heads, and laugh in unison calling out together. "What were we thinking? Ewwwww. Matt Larson!!! I guess that's eighth grade, for ya!"

Catlin reassures her friend once more. "Seriously. You know you mean the world to me. Our friendship means more to me than anything. You know me better than anyone on this planet, and I don't plan on ever loosing that!"

Catlin quickly hugs her friend again, and in typical Brazilian style, kisses her on both cheeks. Looking over her shoulder as she races to her car, she shouts to Pammy. "I'm running a little late or I'd stay and chat. I've got to get to Sky's. Are you riding tomorrow? Want to get a massage together after you're done? We can catch up then." "That sounds great. See you tomorrow around 11:00. Bye.

The sky is quickly darkening from gray to navy blue, and as night sets in after a long busy day, Catlin is anxious to get to Schuyler's side and fill him in on all the events of her day.

Pulling the car to a halt under the portico, Catlin happily greets the two dogs she's come to love as her own, and who, happy to see her, cover her face with warm wet kisses. Picking up two saliva covered tennis balls deposited at her feet by the dogs Catlin flings them down the driveway toward the pond. Dodge and Dart hurl themselves down the incline, snatching them together, before they can roll down into the water. Tails wagging joyfully, they drop the balls at her feet again, wriggling and bouncing with energy as they wait for her to toss them again. Over and over, Catlin throws the balls for the dogs. She is so caught up in the game, she doesn't notice Schuyler watching her from the doorway. Rubbing his arms against the evening chill, he comes outside and wraps Catlin in his embrace.

"Hey you, get inside, before you catch a cold. Your hair is still wet. Let me warm you up."

Looking up at him seductively, Catlin smiles. "Hah! I bet I know how you want to warm me up."

"Well, come on then, time's a wastin'."

Scooping her up in his arms, Schuyler steps inside. The dogs follow happily behind as Schuyler carries Catlin through the house, and then slams the door to the bedroom shut on the bewildered dogs, and deposits her on the giant bed. In the soft glow of the crackling fire, Schuyler pulls off her boots, and slowly peels off her jeans. Laying down beside her, he cradles her head in his arms, and they kiss, softly at first, then with increased passion.

Quickly now, Catlin removes her sweater, T-shirt and jeans, and Schuyler undresses too, dropping his clothes in a heap on the floor.

Thirty minutes later they lay exhausted and sweaty, and Catlin covers Sky's face with soft kisses. Schuyler reaches over to the bedside table and takes a long swig of scotch from a tall glass, speaking in breathless gasps.

"Oh baby. That was awesome. You really are amazing, you've worn me out." Touching him, Catlin laughs. "Are you kidding me? Look at you, I bet you'd be ready to go again in just a minute if I do this . . . or this . . . ." Catlin slowly starts to slither down his torso, but Schuyler pulls her up, giving her a pat on her bare bottom. "No time, now." He says. "The guys'll be here in an hour. You've got to take a shower and get dressed."

Giggling, Catlin replies. "Oh come on, don't be such a party-pooper, looks like I'm not the only one who wants to play some more. And I can be ready in a flash, anyway." Sliding down his body again, Catlin quickly has Schuyler aroused, and no longer protesting. Several minutes later they lay satiated, again, breathing deeply, both quiet.

Catlin jumps up, and Schuyler watches as she skips into the shower, peeking around the bathroom door.

"Want to join me?"

Nodding in agreement he says. "Yes, but if I do, we'll never get out of here. I won't be able to keep my hands off you, if I go in there. Now scoot."

Catlin showers quickly, while Schuyler slips into jeans and a pale blue Balantyne cashmere sweater. Stepping out of the shower, Catlin flashes him, laughing before she vigorously dries off her glowing pink skin.

"Tell me why you'd rather play cards than get some more of this."

"Ah, no fair" he exclaims. "You know how I feel about Poker Night. Besides, tonight Freddy'll be here, and you know how he always says he can whip my ass . . . . well in a little while we get to see just who can whip who's ass."

Resigned, Catlin continues dressing. "Ugh . . . . you guys just always have to be so competitive. Win, win, win, that's all you think of." "Are you kidding me? Look who's talking about winning!" "Touche."

HOLD 'EM

CATLIN, SCHUYLER, FREDDY, Owen, Bete and Henri sit laughing and talking at a supple leather and green felt, card table. A few feet away the bar has been set up, with glasses, ice, sliced lemons and limes, a vast array of bottles, including vintage wines, private label aged scotch, soda, and designer waters. The pleasing aroma of small canapes, nuts, and cheese tempt the group as they chat congenially. Anxious to get on with the card games Schuyler picks up a deck of cards.

Acting as "Pit Boss", Schuyler intones in a deep voice.

"OK, you all know the rules. Minimum bet's a Franklin, that's five hundred reais to you Henri, and it's dealer's choice. That means me. Since I'm starting off, we'll go with Texas Hold 'Em. Everyone in?" Grousing, Henri mumbles. "Yeah, yeah, five hundred, I got it."

Pretending to be a little bored, Henri answers. "Schuyler, of course we're all in. You don't have to say that every time we play. We're not in Monte Carlo. Deal."

They play several hands with Schuyler repeatedly taking the largest majority of the pot every time. They drink a lot, and as hours pass, Catlin begins to lose interest, and Schuyler chastises her.

"Hey Cat, you just threw out a pair of aces! And you threw out a pair of eights last hand, too. Are you sure you know what you're doing?" "Oh. Uh, yeah I guess I wasn't paying attention, Sky." "Well come on, honey get your head in the game. That's no way to play." Pushing away from the table, Catlin starts to get up. "I think I'm calling it a night. I'm beat. Come on, Freddy. Let's go home."

The rest of the group groan, and make it clear they all want to stay longer, but Catlin seems resolved, saying she has too much on her plate, with the wedding plans, shopping, and duties at the riding club.

Freddy looks meaningfully at Henri and Owen, and they shake their heads in agreement. Holding on firmly to her wrist, Freddy looks at his sister.

"Hey Catlin. Come on. Everyone wants to play some more. This is "Poker Night"! You're always complaining lately that you have too much to do. You're no fun!"

Catlin reacts as if she'd been slapped.

"What do you mean? I'm fun. But I ride and then work out in the gym for hours, I'm planning a wedding for four hundred people. It's a lot of work. It's already eleven O'clock, and I'm beat."

Still holding her wrist, Freddy is happy to see she's wearing the bracelet he gave her about eight years ago, when she won in Nationals. She had been ecstatic when he gave her the bracelet. One of her friends had given him the tip about Hermes. The bracelets were "all the rage" with riders, and so he had picked out the gold and navy blue bracelet embossed with horses' bits, and it had been a favorite ever since. Catlin had hugged him tightly, and apparently never took it off. Smiling conspiratorially, Freddy looked directly in her eyes.

"Well, I think I have something that might help you get some energy back."

"What are you talking about?"

Reaching into his jacket pocket he pulls out a Zip Lock baggy filled with cocaine, and places it on the table in front of Catlin.

"Here you go. The very best Columbian Marching Powder. Try it."

"Are you kidding? Is that cocaine?" She looks at the faces around the card table, but no one else seems shocked or surprised.

"Yep."

Catlin is astonished.

"Are you kidding me? Is this the latest thing from Harvard?"

"Don't be such a prude, Cat. Everyone does it."

Catlin looks at Bete and Schuyler, who both nod.

Shocked, Catlin she turns to Schuyler.

"Sky! Have you done this before?"

Slightly embarrassed, but too drunk to really care, Sky replies in a low voice.

"I've done it a few times. It's really no big deal."

"Isn't it supposed to be really addictive?"

Schuyler starts to reply but Freddy quickly interrupts him.

"Oh come on, Cat. That's all hype. Do I look like an addict to you?" Cat looks around the table at Freddy, and the rest of the group, who are well dressed, and have great jobs, then stops and stares at Owen. "How about you Owen? Do you use cocaine, too?" "You know it. But it's no big deal. Actually, I prefer some other party favors, like the stuff that make the ladies go "Ahhh". Hold on tight. It's a crazy night." "God Owen. You always have sex on the brain. The truth is you probably wouldn't get any without your drugs." "Yeah, well whatever." Then in typical Owen form, he answers with an old Lionel Ritchie lyric "All night long, oh yeah, all night long. All Right." Slurring his words, and getting up for a refill of scotch, Schuyler leans over Catlin. "It's OK, honey. Really. Just try a little toot. You'll see it's not all bad." Catlin looks at Bete, who nods her encouragement, and Catlin looks decisively at Freddy.

"OK. OK. I'm not a prude. I've done other stuff before."

Getting up to pull a small antique hunting print from the wall, Freddy spills some cocaine onto the gleaming glass, then chops it into thin lines with a razor blade, and quickly rolling a new hundred dollar bill into a straw, snorts two lines, then places the frame down in front of Catlin.

"I just can't believe you've never done this before." "Well, I haven't. I've seen it around, but anyway it always seems like there's always some kind of shit around you and Owen." In a condescending tone, Freddy pushes some more. "Oh come on, Cat. Try it, you'll love it. Would your big brother steer you wrong?" Looking at him adoringly, she replies. "Of course not, but you all know I don't even smoke pot. I hate feeling out of control. I hate feeling paranoid." Nudging the picture frame, Freddy hands her the rolled up bill, and reassures his sister. "This isn't anything like pot. Come on, Cat. Just do one line. If you don't like it, that's it. At least you'll have tried it, then you'll know for sure. But I bet you'll love it." Looking over at Sky, Catlin twirls the bill in her hand, and asks him again.

"How come you never told me you'd tried it, Sky?"

"It was no big deal. I did it a couple of times in school, and now and again with Henri and Owen. It's no big deal."

Catlin's always felt a bit of an outsider with her brother, and more than anything she's always wanted his approval. Though she has serious doubts about trying cocaine, in her heart she knows he would never steer her wrong, so when Freddy touches her shoulder, and speaks again, Catlin makes up her mind.

"Come on, Cat."

Through his alcoholic haze, Schuyler has second thoughts. "Hey! If she doesn't want to do it, don't force her. You don't have to if you don't want to honey. We can call it a night."

"Who's forcing? If she doesn't want it, that just means more for me." Half serious, Freddy continues making finger quotes as he speaks. "Maybe you're right. Maybe I shouldn't start my little sister down a scary, dangerous road." Freddy reaches across to pick up the picture, but Catlin stops him.

"Whatever. Give it to me. I'll try it. I know I won't like it anyway."

Watching his little sister, Freddy feels a brief flash of guilt. He reaches for the frame again. "Shit. Never mind. You should just stay your little old innocent self. I kinda like you dorky like that."

"Forget it Freddy. Now you know I'm gonna try it."

Putting the bill to her nostril like Freddy did, Catlin pinches shut the other side of her nose and inhales deeply. Sputtering and gagging, she whips her head from side-to-side in attempt to stop the stinging in her nose.

"Uck. That's gross. It burns. Is it supposed to do that? It tastes horrible."

Watching feverishly Owen chimes in. "You've got to give it a second. Free Your mind, don't deny, try the other side. Go ahead."

She quickly inhales the other line, again shaking her head from side-to-side, and everything changes. She feels a rush of electricity in her veins, then everything is brighter. Alive. Catlin winces as she watches everyone each snort a couple of lines.

"OK. Well, I don't feel anything. And that was gross. You guys like this? I'm never doing this again. OK. Come on, are we playing or what?" Laughing, Freddy deals another hand of cards. "Hmmm . . . . we'll see what you think in a few minutes."

The group gets back into their game, and talk animatedly about all the excitement in their lives, smoking cigarettes, drinking and playing several more hands. Obviously affected by the cocaine, Catlin plays feverishly, jabbering about this and that, everyone is constantly talking as the speed factor of the drug kicks in. The piles of chips shift from Schuyler to Freddy, then briefly to a large pile in front of Henri. But by two thirty, the pile has grown significantly in front of Schuyler again. Stretching and catching a glimpse of the clock, Catlin is shocked to discover the time.

"Oh my God! It's two o'clock. Freddy we've got to go! Dad's probably having a having a conniption fit! I can't believe it. How did it get so late?"

Henri, Bete, Owen and Freddy look knowingly at each other and smirk. They each understand that although Catlin doesn't know it, yet she's enjoying the high, and they think that's pretty cool.

Getting up, Catlin wipes her runny nose, and quickly kisses Owen, Henri and Bete on the cheek.

Pulling a very drunk Schuyler to his feet, Catlin makes her way to the front entrance, and calls back to Freddy. "Let's go Freddy. Let's go! See you tomorrow Sky. I'll call you at work."

Quickly kissing Schuyler, Cat grabs her purse and jacket, then Catlin races out the door, shouting to Freddy as she goes. She jumps in the car and revs the engine. Freddy waves goodbye to the group, and joins her. She guns the motor again, and the speedy little car jumps up the hill, and across the cattle guard. Dodge and Dart sit and watch as the car stirs up clouds of dust, and moves off into the darkness.

Swirling tendrils of smoke seep out the window of a beat up, dark blue "Fiat" parked on the side of the road, under the low hanging leaves of a giant Poinciana tree. Inside the car, two shadowy figures duck down in their seats, as Catlin and Freddy zoom past. Still in motor-mouth mode, Catlin tells Freddy how much fun the night turned out to be.

"That was fun! I don't usually like playing cards, but I had a blast. Schuyler loves poker night. Of course he always wins, but I didn't even mind that, tonight. I'm glad you were there."

Freddy puts a lightly restraining hand on her wrist. "Slow down, Cat. And pipe down, too. You've been motor mouth all night."

"Jeez, Freddy, just when I think you're going to be a nice guy, you say something mean. What crawled up your butt?"

Looking at his sister, Freddy grimaces. "Sorry, sorry. I just have a headache and I'm kind of tired. Don't make a big deal out of it."

They drive the rest of the way home in silence, and when Catlin parks the car in the driveway, they barely say good night. The house is in complete darkness, and quiet, but Catlin can sense her father lying awake in bed, looking at a clock. She tip-toe's up the stairs almost bumping into Walther staring down at her. "Do you have any idea what time it is?"

"Oh, sorry Dad. I fell asleep, and Freddy didn't think there was any big deal."

"No big deal my ass! You're still under my roof. And if you want me to pay for that fancy wedding of yours you better toe the line. I won't have any one saying my daughter is sleeping around!"

"I'm not "sleeping around"! I'm engaged to be married, and I am in love with Sky. I'm twenty-two Dad, not twelve. I've had enough of you being such a freaking control freak!"

Walther's eyes blaze and he raises his arm. Colleen steps up behind him grabbing his arm, as Catlin cowers on the steps.

"Walther, calm down dear. Cat, apologize. I know you didn't mean that. She's just overwhelmed with everything going on, dear. You know she would never talk back to you. She fell asleep, and Freddy doesn't think. Let's all go to bed. I'll talk to Freddy in the morning."

Fire still blazing in her eyes, still high, Catlin opens her mouth to respond, but the scared look on Colleen's face silences her on the spot.

Mouth set tightly, Walther stalks off muttering and disaster averted Colleen follows, shaking her head "No" at Catlin who slinks slowly into her room and shuts the door softly. Laying in bed, her mind racing, Catlin replays the evening's events over and over.

She's so sick of being treated like that by her father. She didn't feel so great about trying the cocaine, but she's pleased that at least she's shown

Freddy she isn't the square he thinks she is. She probably won't try it again. It really wasn't as scary as she thought it would be, in fact, she felt pretty good, and that was a surprise.

Rolling over, she punches up her pillows again, and looking at the clock on her bedside table, she sees it's four thirty. Mind racing, Catlin wonders if she and Freddy will ever be close. She thought about special brother and sister relationships she'd seen in high school. One of her good friends Nancy, had a twin brother David. Cat smiled wondering if she'd always be connected to twins. Forcing herself to focus, Cat pictured another night she'd tried to buck her Dad. Nan had been bugging her to come spend the night. Cat had asked permission, but of course Walther had said no. Cat couldn't understand. Nan's Dad was the American Consulate General at the time, and her Mom was on the Art Board with Colleen. Only a few people knew that Cat and David were a bit of an item at school, and she could think of nothing more wonderful than spending the night at Nan's house, and maybe sneaking a few minutes alone to make-out with David. She'd made up her mind and would go spend the night and deal with the consequences later. How bad could it be, right? So she'd be grounded for a few weeks. She was never allowed to do anything anyway, and he never stopped her from riding, how bad could it be? So after school, Cat rode the bus home with Nan and David. Everything was wonderful, Catlin was ecstatic to be part of a "normal" family meal. She loved watching Nan and David interact, teasing one another, and making jokes, but always sticking up for one another too. She wished she could have a bond with Freddy just like that. But then the night plummeted into a Lauria nightmare when the phone rang at the Taylor residence and the maid quietly informed Mr. Taylor he had a call. Face burning, Cat somehow knew it was about her, and when Mr. Taylor returned to the dining room just a few moments later the somber expression on his face told her she was right.

"Catlin. That was your Dad. He says you disobeyed a direct order by coming here tonight." The expression on Mr. Taylor's face when he uttered those words made Catlin feel he understood her pain. I mean after all, who issues a "direct order" to a sixteen-year-old. Catlin broke down. Sitting at the Taylor dining room table she cried and told them about how her Dad could be brutal, and how she was never allowed to do anything. She could tell the Taylor's were shocked by the revelations, and as she cried in Mrs. Taylor's arms, Mr. Taylor left the room once again to call Walther, to try and reason with him.

But soon enough, he came back again, sadly shaking his head "No", and told Catlin that Walther was on his way to pick her up, and that she had better be ready. Catlin went out onto the patio twenty-eight floors above the ground, and she and Nan waited for Walther's dreaded car to pull up. When they saw it, Catlin briefly considered flinging herself over the railing, but knew that the family she had come to love so much more than her own in such a short time would pay the price, and reluctantly she bade them all goodnight, taking the long elevator ride down to the lobby alone.

Colleen was in the front seat and Walther was red-faced, livid. Walther ordered Cat to sit behind him, "so he could reach her", he'd said. Tires squealing he drove away, stopping whenever there was a red light to turn around and slap or punch her, his anger overwhelming and escalating. When they finally arrived at the house, Walther dragged Catlin from the car, kicked her all the way into the house and up to her room, where he'd made her strip, then he beat her with his belt.

"No more." Catlin thought. No more guns being waved around, no more embarrassing moments with prospective suitors running for their lives, climbing over the front gate. Finally, as dawn was breaking Catlin drifted off to sleep her last thought a remembered image of herself and Freddy hovering over the opened hood of her father's Mercedes. Freddy had scissors in his hand, and they both wore pained expressions as they tried to figure out where on earth in the middle of that jumble of tubes and wires were the brake lines. They'd never figured it out of course, but Catlin felt so good about doing something, anything, with her big brother.

Forgetting all about the plans she'd made for the next day, and her date with Pammy, Catlin finally drifts off to sleep thinking only that for once, she might just take a day off and sleep in late.

FORGET IT

THE MILD WINTER months passed by seamlessly, one gray, rainy day at a time. Freddy started working at Lauria Enterprises but rather than move out on his own, he remained in the service apartment above the Lauria's garage. I mean after all, how could he rationalize giving up no rent, no expenses and maid service?

Together, Olympus and Catlin thrived under the tutelage of "The Colonel" and the team trainers, and usually they placed first or second in the bi-weekly trials of the Grand Prix circuit.

Most days Catlin kept to her rigorous schedule, and managed to keep all the preparations for the big wedding and her riding duties on track. Catlin and Schuyler spent more and more time alone together, and it seemed that even Walther finally backed-off and gave his daughter some space.

Occasionally, though, she was over-whelmed. On those days she seemed short tempered and not herself. She was feeling out of sorts when she practically bumped into Pammy in the locker room. Surprised to see her, Pammy grabbed her in a bear hug.

"Catlin! I've missed you. You're always rushing around. Want to grab lunch?" Softly, Catlin replied. "Oh, hey, Pammy. How's it going?" Surprised by Catlin's stiff reception, Pammy went on. "Pretty good. We had a super time in Italy, and I can't wait to tell you all about it. Come on, let's go grab a salad."

"Sorry. I can't make it today. I've got a ton of stuff to do and I'm really not that hungry anyway. How about next week?" Sullenly, Catlin attempts to disengage and walk away.

Stunned by her friends' indifference, Pammy reacted stridently. "You know, just forget it! You're always too busy. You've always got these big plans, or you're never hungry. Forget it!"

Pammy rushed past her into muttering under her breath.

"Oooh. Don't worry. I'll never change. You're my best friend in the whole world! Yeah, right."

Grabbing her arm, Catlin spins Pammy around, and they face off.

"If you have something to say to me. Say it to my face."

In tears, Pammy shouts at her friend. "Fine! You said you wouldn't let making the team or getting married change our friendship. But you've been a real bitch. You never have time to spend with me or any of our friends anymore. You're always rushing off to be with Bete and Henri! You always have some big night planned at one of the clubs! I'm tired of it!"

"Hey, I can't help it if I get asked to go places. If you ever got a boyfriend, maybe you'd get asked too. Plus, you're such a square. No smoking! No drinking! You're no fun!"

Eyes widening in shock at Catlin's words, Pammy sputters and turns away.

"Fine!"

"Fine!"

Watching quietly from across the room, Dona Claudia catches Catlin's gaze while almost imperceptibly shaking her head "no". Shamed Catlin's cheeks flamed red, but it's too late. The damage had been done.

Catlin knew she'd been on edge ever since the poker game when she'd snorted cocaine. She'd tried desperately to put her finger on what had been going on with her since then. Her nerves had been on edge, and lashing out at Pammy was another perfect example of that.

Heading toward the stables, Cat wondered if the stress of wedding planing, her disagreements with her Dad, feeling like she was on a stage every day and wanting so badly to be perfect was getting to be too much. She also wondered, not for the first time, if perhaps trying cocaine again might help smooth out the rough spots. She had told Freddy she hadn't really felt much, but she had. It had been a pretty powerful feeling, and she had to admit, she'd kind of liked it.

PARTY PREP

FREDDY AND HENRI drive through stop-and-go traffic as the Sao Paulo rush hour winds down. Insulated from the pollution, the cacophony of street noise, and honking horns in Henri's beat up silver Corolla, Freddy sounds edgy and nervous.

"I hate doing this, you know. Can't Owen get us the stuff for the party?"

Placating him, Henri responds. "I already asked him. He said he's too busy. Besides he doesn't know Ricardo. It's no big deal. You can wait in the car if you want. I won't be long."

"Are you kidding? That's even worse. I'd be a wreck. Just let's do this quickly. I want to get home." "Jesus, Freddy. You've been so uptight since you got home. You need to relax man, you're back in Brazil. Good life, remember? Henri's cell phone rings, and he turns off the tinny radio to accept the call.

Ricardo's voice fills the car through the speaker.

"Henri?"

"Oi, Ricardo! How are you, dude?"

"Fine, man. Where are you?"

"We're just a few blocks away. We should be there in a couple of minutes."

"OK, well good, I'm glad I caught you. I have some friends who were supposed to be here earlier, but they're running a bit late. They just called and said they're almost here. How about if you come by in thirty minutes. Is that OK?"

Causing Henri to quickly mute the call, Freddy shouts angrily.

"Damn it! See? This is what I mean! This SUCKS!" Quickly un-muting the call, Henri puts a finger to his lips, and responds to Ricardo.

"Sure, sure. No problem. We'll just stop in and grab a quick bite to eat. We'll see you in thirty minutes. Call me if there's any problem." As he disconnects the call he turns to Freddy.

"Freddy. Dude! This isn't like shopping at Carrefour! We have to do this on Ricardo's schedule. If we piss him off, he won't deal with us anymore. Then we'll have to find someone else."

Remorseful now, Freddy sighs. "Right. You're right. Sorry I snapped. My Mom read me the riot act this afternoon about not participating in the big wedding plans, and I guess it got to me. I'm a little edgy."

"Don't worry about it. Let's grab a beer and a bite to eat. As soon as we meet with Ricardo you'll get that edge off." "Yeah. It's not a big deal. Everyone's freakin' out about the big wedding. She'll get over it. I already have." Thirty minutes, a couple of grilled steak sandwiches and a few frosty brews later, they park in front of a stately colonial house in the Jardins neighborhood of Sao Paulo. The house is the archtypal TV series, modern family home; it's an average looking, well cared for home, and Freddy feels a little more relaxed.

With another nervous glance at Henri, they approach the front gate together. Henri reaches for the bell, the front door opens and a good-looking, athletic young surfer, with curly long brown hair and a winning smile beckons to them.

"Hey guys. Come on in, but we have to keep it down. My Mom's sleeping."

As they slip in the door, and start walking down a dimly lit corridor, a groggy voice drifts towards them down the stairs.

"Who's there? Is someone there? Ricardo is that you?"

Ricardo, puts a finger to his lips and answers his mother in Portuguese.

"It's OK, Mom. Go back to sleep. Some friends just dropped by to pick up some DVD's. They'll be leaving in a few minutes." Smiling and pushing them ahead to an open door at the end of the hall, Ricardo explains. "She's a little out of it. My Mom just had some surgery a few days ago. Lipo, you know? Anyway, I've got what you need."

Down the hall, Ricardo's room is decorated like a surfer's paradise. Three ornately designed surfboards hang from racks above the bed, which is neatly made up in ocean-print sheets. All the furniture is made from rough hewn wood, that looked like it had been reclaimed form a ship wreck. The room even had a slightly salty scent, and even Freddy wrinkled his nose walking in. Ricardo closes the door, and turns on a "Bose" CD player.

From high on the walls the surprisingly loud seagull calls and crashing waves, echo in the room. The wall opposite the bed is a full scale photographic image of a palm tree lined beach. Ricardo points proudly at the wall sized photographic reprint.

"It's Praia do Forte. My favorite place to surf. When I go to sleep, and play a CD of waves, it's like I'm there, you know? Henri told me you surf, right Freddy?" Glancing sideways at Henri, Freddy rolls his eyes. "Uh, yeah, I used to. I don't much anymore. When we go to the beach we mostly scuba dive now." Looking at Freddy with renewed admiration, Ricardo answers. "That's great! Anything to do with water is great, right? So, alright then, let's get this done."

Ricardo moves over to a large antique armoire which seems incongruous in the otherwise beach themed room, until he opens it and pulls out a Davey Jones style lock box. Opening it, he pulls out a large Ziplock baggie filled with pale urine-colored crystal rock formation, and opens the baggie holding it out to Henri. Taking the baggie from Ricardo's outstretched hand, Henri breathes in the pungent, slightly chemical scent of the cocaine, and offers the bag to Freddy.

"Wow! That's some rock. How much is that?"

Smiling like a proud Papa, Ricardo replies. "It's just a bit over twenty five grams. We'll weigh it. Looks good, huh?"

Ricardo holds out a sinister looking switchblade, and takes the bag back from Freddy causing him to flinch. Inserting the tip of the blade into the baggie, he offers some of the cocaine to Henri.

"Here, go ahead and try it, while I weigh it for you. How much do you want?"

Holding the dangerous point of the blade just beneath his nostril, Henri inhales deeply.

"Whoo. Good. How much for the whole thing?"

Ricardo grins, and nodding his head to music only he can hear, weighs the baggie on a small jewelers scale set-up on a shelf of the armoire, telling Henri the weight and price.

"See? I told you it was twenty five grams. It's actually closer to twenty eight, but I want you guys to be good customers. I'll give it to you for twenty five hundred U.S. Cash. How's that?"

Freddy and Henri exchange a quick glance, eyes gleaming and nod at one another. Henri extends his hand. "That sounds great. We'll take it." Henri pulls out his wallet and counts out twenty five crisp, newly printed one hundred dollar bills. Clapping Henri on the back, and pocketing the bills, Ricardo leads them out of the rooms and back down the hallway. "Man, I wish all my buyers were like you. The guys who just left here, they're pretty scary dudes. I thought I was going to get knifed right here in my own house!"

He laughs a bit nervously and looks over his shoulder at Freddy.

"But you guys are becoming my favorite customers. As the song says . . . "*don't go changing*. Don't you have any more friends you can send my way?"

Humming tunelessly he opens the front door and watches as Freddy and Henri get in the car and drive away.

As they pull away into traffic, the beat-up, blue Fiat pulls away from the curb, following them at a safe distance.

SPRING EVE

GATHERING HER THINGS, Cat speaks to Sky on her "Bluetooth" head-set, as she wanders around her bedroom. "Everything's set for the party. It's going to be a blast. The place looks really great, and the chef is already there. I've got everything set up. What time will you get home?"

"Oh, I don't know. The usual time I guess. Depends on traffic. What time will you be there?"

Smoothing back her hair, she looks at her reflection in a mirror, and answers. "Around five I guess. I'll bring my stuff to the house, and get dressed there. I want to be sure that everything is "just" right. I'll be there when you get home."

Tapping off the phone, Catlin smiles to herself and picks through the section of floor length gowns, removing a simple taupe halter-top dress and holds it up to her face. Though it doesn't look like much on the hangar, the dress was custom made by an up-and-coming Brazilian designer, and fit her like a second skin. Not unlike the world renowned Brazilian bikini's, this designer obviously believed that "less is more". And, Catlin knew it made her look flawless.

"This'll do."

Carefully draping it over her arms, Catlin quickly picks out a stunning gold and diamond necklace to go with it. Rather than wear the same things everyone else was wearing, Catlin often designed her own jewelry, and Schuyler had just had this piece made for her. It too was a simple design, looking like an ancient gold coin embossed with cave drawings. Imbedded in the coin were several tiny sparkling diamonds. It was strung on a soft leather cord, and would draw all eyes to Catlin's prominent collar bones and decollete.

Next, she picked out a pair of strappy gold sandals, and snatching her over-stuffed overnight bag, rushed downstairs to find her mother. "Mom. I'm leaving in a few minutes. Do you need me for anything?" "No dear. Oh. Is that what you're wearing tonight?" "Yep. I'm all set. What do you think? This dress with gold sandals and the new necklace Sky had made for me." "Perfect choice. Simple and stunning. That dress will look great with your tan! Have fun and don't stay out all night. You know how your father gets." "I can't wait until I'm married, and I don't have to come home at all!" Seeing a flash of pain in her mother's gaze, she covers up the insensitive remark, by apologizing. "I'm sorry. You know I don't mean that has anything to do with you, Mom. I'm just so excited about having my own home. And don't worry, you'll still see me all the time."

Looking proudly at her beautiful daughter, Colleen tells her to go on. "Of course, dear. Don't worry about it. Every bride-to-be is excited about her first home. Go. Have fun. See you tomorrow."

A short while later, Schuyler's houseman, Ronaldo, carries Catlin's things into the master bedroom. "Please let me know if you need anything else, Ms. Catlina."

Catlin replies politely. "I'll come find you when I'm ready Ronaldo, and we'll go over everything again. I want this party to be perfect. It's officially the start of the season, and I want everyone to remember this night. I'm going to take a short rest now. Please have Rosa wake me at six thirty."

Bowing slightly, Ronaldo leaves the room, softly puling the double doors closed behind him. Minutes later, snuggled peacefully in the crisp indigo sheets, Catlin is sound asleep.

After waking from a restful short nap, Catlin is pleased to see tiny white lights and lanterns twinkling in the gardens and trees, around the infinity pool, and set on the sweeping lawn above the lake. Catlin makes her final rounds of the kitchen, patio and bar before her guests arrive.

A Japanese chef and an assistant huddle together by the cooking station, speaking softly while Ronaldo and Catlin make certain everything is in place. Checking last minute details Catlin asks the houseman about the dogs.

"Are Dodge and Dart locked up?" "Yes, Ma'am. I'll let them out after the last guests leave." "Good. What about the bar? Do we have enough mixers? Did the Sake I ordered from Domo arrive?"

"Yes, Ma'am. I've checked it all twice. Everything you asked for is prepared. The waiters are in the kitchen and will be out serving drinks and appetizers as soon as the guests arrive. Everything's just as you requested. Will there be anything else?"

"No, Ronaldo. Everything looks perfect! It looks like you and Rosa have got everything under control. Great job. Thank you."

Back in the spacious master wing, Catlin showers quickly. Shaking out her hair, she quickly blows-dries it into billowing curls, then slips her dress on over her head, and peeks into the bathroom, where Schuyler is spritzing on her favorite cologne.

"Mmmm. Dangerous. I love that Cristiano Fissore. It's the sexiest cologne I've ever smelled, and it always turns me on." "Why do you think I'm putting it on? I want you thinking about me all night. Sure we don't have time for a quickie before everyone gets here?"

"Sorry, Sky. I'm already dressed. Can't mess up the look." She does a little pirouette as Sky looks on with a gleam in his eye. "We've got to get out there, now! You're going to have to wait until later. Come on, let's go."

Arriving guests are greeted by waiters bearing trays of sake and perfect sushi and Sashimi appetizers.

A giant wok sizzles and smokes aromatically, as the chef prepares a spicy shrimp and vegetable tempura combination. Guests mingle by the pool, watching pale aqua twinkling lights shimmering under the water, and inhaling the fresh scent of the newly mown lawn, the elusive herbs and jasmine artfully planted close-by. Catlin and Schuyler greet their friends, and make their way from one small group to the next.

A beautiful, petite young woman, grabs Catlin in an affectionate hug.

"Wow! You picked a perfect night for this party, Catlin. And you look fabulous. Being engaged sure agrees with you."

Quickly kissing her on both cheeks, Catlin admires her friend at arms length, thanking her for the compliment.

"Alix. You look divine! I cannot believe you've just had a baby! How do you manage to look so fabulous?" The two chat for another moment.

"Thanks, querida. Lucky for me I inherited my Mom's great genes. She always looked great. The only thing that gives it away, is when it's time to breast feed. Then I leak!"

"That sounds embarrassing! But I'm happy you risked discovery to come tonight. It's so great to see you!" "Oh don't worry. Once you have a baby, you'll get over any embarrassing moments fast. Nothing fazes me anymore. Or Mario either." "I'm really glad you came. Go on, enjoy. I'm going to mingle. See you later!" "I wouldn't miss one of your parties for the world. We can't stay long. Patricia is home with the nanny, and I only have about three hours until her next feeding."

"Why don't you bring her over one day next week? I want to find out everything about having babies. Sky won't want to wait long before we have a couple! We can sit by the pool and catch up, now that the weather is finally perfect again."

"That sounds great. I'll call you and we'll pick a day. Now, I've got to get over to that wok. Something smells wonderful, and I'm still famished all the time." "OK. Enjoy. I'll call you Monday."

Spotting Henri and Bete across the patio, Catlin waves then heads over to greet them. "Hey Guys! How are you? Bete, you look incredible, as always. Come on. Let's find Schuyler. I haven't seen him in a while."

"We brought some great "party favors" for you guys, and I could use a little bump to get me through the night." "What are you talking about? Are you bored by my guests?" "No. No. Everyone here is so interesting! This is Sao Paulo's Creme de La Creme. I wish I had my camera!" "Oh, Henri. You don't fool me. You're bored. I know it."

Wrapping his arms around their waists, Henri and the two girls wave to Schuyler, and head toward the other side of the pool. On the way, Henri motions for Freddy to join them, as well.

Holding an empty glass above his head, Freddy points at the glass and heads towards the bar.

"Two minutes."

In the quiet dark corner, Henri pulls a tiny glass vial out of his pocket. It's filled with cocaine. He shows it to Catlin.

"Check it out. We got it from a guy I know. He got it straight from his contact in Medellin, and it's by far the best stuff I've ever had. This is what real "hielo" looks like. It's not cut at all."

Holding her palms up facing Henri, Cat replies. "Great thanks, Henri. But I really don't want it."

"Come on. You had a blast at the poker game. You really let loose that night. You should do that every now and again."

"Oh. I really don't know. It's not my thing."

"Come on. You know you want to. Its' no big deal."

"God. I feel like you'll just keep buggin me until I agree. You're reminding me of Owen. That's not a good look for you." "Too bad Owen is still in the States. He'd a loved this. He's been missing out on all the fun. When does he get back?" "Actually," says Schuyler, "He's coming in on Tuesday. He'll be here for a week." Winking, Bete continues. "Great. Much as your brother can be a pain in the ass, I find myself missing the guy. He's really quite amusing."

Leaning in close to her boyfriend, Bete laughs.

"We'll have an excuse to have another party when he gets here. That sounds good to me."

Looking out across the pool, Catlin pipes up. "I don't know how many more of these parties I can take. I'm not used to staying up all night like this."

Henri looks over his shoulder at her, shaking the vial of white powder.

"We'll have plenty of Marching Powder to keep us going. You only have a few more months 'till the wedding. You can't wimp out now. It's going to be party central for the next several months."

Finally acquiescing, Catlin nods her head and the small group steps into the greenhouse, where they all do a couple of lines. Hiding the vial behind a stunning orchid they wander back to the party, which is now in full swing. Small cliques have formed all over the patio. Some are lounging comfortably by the artfully lit pool, others are laughing and talking by the wok and delicious finger food. A few guests have wandered out to the croquet court to see a baby ocelot Schuyler recently rescued, during a hunting trip in Mato Grosso. Though the animal has been hand-fed, and is used to seeing people, it's still a wild animal, and Schuyler has cautioned them to keep their distance.

No one notices two men standing in the dark distance by the wall near the tennis court. Deep in shadows, they scan the group below through binoculars for several minutes, then climb down from the wall, light up cigarettes, and walk to the waiting blue Fiat.

NOT WHAT IT'S CRACKED UP TO BE

TIGHTLY GRIPPING HIS telephone handset, Freddy looks up through the wall of glass, checking to see who might be listening. He wants everyone in the office to know he's a tough negotiator; not someone to be trifled with.

"I told you that's not going to happen! You'll have to accept our terms or we've got no deal. Go back and look at your numbers again. If you can't come up with the figure I gave you, I'm sorry you'll have to find someone else."

He slams down the receiver, and looks out toward his secretary once more. Earphones on, she's typing busily, and missed his great performance. Sighing deeply in frustration, Freddy leans back in his chair and swivels it around to look out the floor-to-ceiling glass wall. For as far as he can see, tall buildings cram into every available square foot of space. This building is one of the tallest, and sitting there looking at the view Freddy knows he's landed the perfect job. He realizes he's got a great chance to start again.

But he better not fuck it up either. That call could signify a huge deal for him, but if he loses it, it could also mean egg on his face as the new guy. Freddy silently vows to take whatever steps he has to, to make sure the deal goes through.

A few minutes later worried that he could have blown the biggest deal of his life, Freddy decides to clear his head with an early lunch and walks down the busy street to the Brazilian version of Chili's, "Um Dois, Feijao com Arroz". It's Freddy's favorite lunch spot. But the telephone call has him rattled, tormenting him now, wondering did he push too far? Arauja and Sons have been preferred clients at Lauria Enterprises for twenty years. What an asshole, sticking to last years' prices, he's just yanking my chain. Man, I hope I didn't screw this one up.

Questions continued to plague Freddy throughout his lunch, and he's glad he's alone. How on earth could he enjoy his meal thinking about the commission he'd lose if he didn't make that sale? And Walther would probably ream him another one if he lost the sale. Shit!

Without realizing it, Freddy finished his meal wiping his plate clean with a hunk of bread. Deciding to order dessert Freddy raised his arm to summon the traditionally dressed waiter.

Holding his menu arrogantly over his shoulder, Freddy speaks to the person hovering at his shoulder.

"One Pudim de Leite and a cafezinho. Bring the check, too. I'm in a hurry."

A deep voice resonates inches from his ear. "Yes, Sir. Whatever you say, Sir. At your service, Sir, right away."

Beyond shocked, Freddy looks up at the source of the voice he'd hoped never to hear again.

Red Tucker, and Jack Kelly look down at him, smiling. Freddy attempts to stand up but powerful arms shove him roughly back into his seat, the two men crowd into the small booth, one on either side of him, effectively pinning Freddy.

"What the?" Freddy sputters.

Red Tucker closes a steadying arm around Freddy's shoulders. "Shhh. Pipe down Freddy. Take it easy. Aren't you glad to see us? We're glad to see you, buddy."

As if in a flashback, Freddy finds himself unable to speak clearly. "I'm not your buddy. What the Fuck . . . . Let me out . . ."

Laughing Jack Kelly tells him. "Freddy. You've got a bad habit of not finishing your sentences. Do you do that with everyone? Or is it just me?"

"Yeah." Think before you speak. Freddy."

Picking up the menu Jack calmly pretends to read the choices in Portuguese.

"What looks good?"

Red Tucker raises his arm to summon the waiter. Freddy squirms and tries to get up again, causing a brief look of concern on the waiter's face.

But the restaurant is very busy, and Red smiles engagingly at him, then leans over to whisper in Freddy's ear and the waiter carries on dismissing whatever might have spooked him.

"Smile, Freddy. That's a 357 Magnum pressing into your kidney, not my dick. Make a scene though, and you'll feel something hotter than this barrel. And it'll be the last thing you feel. Relax pal. We're just here to talk."

Stunned speechless, not believing these guys could be anywhere near him, let alone in Brazil, Freddy slumps back, in surrender.

Red calmly explains to Freddy that they've followed a lead to Brazil and that now they need Freddy's help to apprehend a suspected narco trafficker. Reassured that he is not in any trouble, Freddy sighs deeply and speaks urgently.

"Look. I'm not in that life anymore. I can't help you."

Holding out his arms to indicate his surroundings, the upscale restaurant, and pointing at his well cut custom suit, Freddy smiles at the DEA agents and continues speaking.

"I work at my father's company, the largest supplier of chrome auto-parts in Brazil. I can't help you. There's no way I can jeopardize my life again. I don't know anyone in Brazil who's in that business. You'll have to find someone else to help you. Now if you'll excuse me, I have to get back to work."

Freddy pushes the table away, immediately wincing in pain as Red shoves the gun even harder into his kidney again, forcing Freddy to sit and listen.

"That's not polite at all, now is it, Freddy? We've come all the way to Brazil, just to see you. But here's the deal, loser. We've been following you, your cute little sister, and all your friends. No more bullshit. We know what you're doing, and if you want to keep all this, this is the way it's going to be. You're going to sit here and listen to what we have to tell you, and then you're going to tell us how you're going to help us out."

Trying to summon a little bravado and courage, Freddy responds harshly but his quavering voice gives away his fear.

"This is bullshit man. I already helped you back in the States. You got what you wanted, and you let me go. What more do you want from me?"

With anger seeping into his voice, the agent smugly replies. "Because of you, we were relieved of duty, asshole. We lost our pensions and our pay. But you get this! You get to start a new life, and you're a scumbag! I figure why not me? So, here we are. You're going to help us, and this time, we're going to benefit financially, or you end up dead. Am I making myself clear enough for you asshole? Now shut the fuck up and pay attention."

In the next ten minutes Red carefully outlines a plan to arrest and detain a wealthy American, and to extort money from his family in exchange for his freedom. He tells Freddy that they've got the Brazilian DEA involved, that the plan is already in place. He explains to Freddy, that Freddy has no choice. He can help set-up their mark or it's Freddy who goes down. His choice. But someone's gonna pay.

Making sure Freddy understands, Tucker repeats himself. "You got all that, Freddy? This isn't a request." Visibly shaken, and pale, Freddy excuses himself to go to the Men's Room.

A few minutes later he returns to stand by the table.

A wet brown stain on the placket of his otherwise pristine white shirt, plus the green tinge to his face, indicates that Freddy gets the picture.

"Fine. I'll set it up. Who is this poor sap?"

Secretly relieved that Freddy is cooperating Jack pipes up. "Your pal Owen. But don't worry about that yet. It's him or you kid. And we'll reach you. Now get back to work. You don't want to be late. Lunch is on me kid. Have a great afternoon."

Without looking back, Freddy walks out of the restaurant and back to his office. Nodding his head back and forth to himself, Freddy tries desperately to think of a way out of this mess.

HANGOVER

MONDAY MORNING CATLIN had driven over to Sky's house with Nuncio. It was a weekly trip for the two of them, bringing the exquisitely wrapped wedding gifts that accumulated all over the Lauria house. Arms-full of boxes, they walked down the long corridor to the guest bedroom they were using for storage. Suddenly excusing herself, Catlin placed her packages on the ground and told Nuncio she'd be right back.

Panicked Catlin realized they had left the glass cocaine vial among the orchids. Racing outside she hoped Mr. Sakamoto, Sky's Japanese gardener hadn't already found it. Entering the greenhouse she raced up one of the aisles to the spot she thought they'd left it. It wasn't there! Panicked Cat knocked over a prize Jade Siam, and collapsed in tears on the ground as she attempted to collect the delicate blossom. Looking up she saw the small vial on the shelf and pocketed it, just as Mr. Sakamoto walked in.

"Miss Catlina! You OK?"

"Yes. I, uh, I broke the orchid, and I feel so bad. I'm sorry."

Mr. Sakamoto bowed assuring Catlin everything was all right. Feeling badly about lying to him, and bowing briefly, she excused herself, and walked back toward the house wondering for the hundreth time why she was acting this way. In her heart though she knew it was the cocaine.

Saturday night she'd lain awake for hours again, her mind in turmoil recalling vividly some of the tortured moments of her relationship with her Dad.

That night she'd recalled an incident that had been a turning point in her life. She'd met a great guy at the University of Sao Paulo, during her first year there. He was an artist and though he was several years older than Catlin, they had clicked. Cat knew her Dad would never approve of any relationship with him, so she kept her meetings with Roberto secret, blowing off a simultaneous interpreter class at the end of the day to spend a few hours with him. But of course somehow Walther found out. She never knew how he'd discovered it, but he did, and they had a huge blow-out when he forbade her from seeing the young man.

Walther calmly informed Catlin that Roberto was a nobody, that his chosen profession would never support her, and pursuing anything with him was foolish. And then he dropped a bomb. He told Catlin that the artist probably smoked pot and used drugs and that he would have his friend Jose Barros arrest him if they persisted in meeting, and that way no one would ever have to deal with him again. Horrified, Catlin knew her father's threat was not an idle one. She called Roberto and told him she never wanted to see him again. But she also made the mistake of telling him why.

The next morning Catlin was still in bed, listening to the hustle and bustle of the household gearing up for another day. She heard Tica knock on her parent's door to inform him that a young man was at the front door insisting to speak with Mr. Lauria.

Walther's booming voice sent a bolt of fear throughCatlin.

"Who on earth is here at this ungoldly hour? I'm not expecting anyone."

Meekly Tica continued. "He says his name is Roberto and he just wants a minute of your time."

Catlin was suddenly wide awake, and had sprung to her door, and pressed her ear against it so she could hear everything.

An argument ensued with Walther at the top of the stairs, and apparently, Roberto at the foot of the stairs explaining he was just a friend of Catlin's, that he was from a good family, and on his way to becoming a renowned artist.

Walther told him he didn't care who he was, he wanted him to stay away from his daughter. The argument escalated and Catlin heard what she'd feared from the start.

"Get out of my house and off my property before you get hurt. I can shoot you now as an intruder and no one would ever ask any questions."

By this time, Catlin knew Walther had his gun out. Unmindful of the consequences, she bolted from her room. Standing at the top of the stairs as Walther waved his weapon she begged Roberto to leave and never come back.

"Get out of here. He'll kill you. He really will!"

His face a mask of fear and confusion, Roberto turned and fled even as Walther started running, gun raised after him.

"Daddy! Stop! Please stop. He's gone. I'll never see him again. I promise!"

Walther turned and pushed past by Catlin who was on her knees crying at the top of the stairs.

"Don't you ever defy me again."

Walther returned to his room, finished dressing and left for the day. Catlin returned to her room, mortified and desolate, listening to the sounds of normal activity resuming. Once she'd heard her father leave and Colleen go downstairs, Catlin tip-toed to her parent's room, where she stood in front of her father's dresser shaking. After a few moments she pulled out the gun, and returning to her own room, closed the door.

She sat cross-legged on the floor, and looked at the gun.

"My life will always be this way." she thought. "I can't keep causing this kind of turmoil."

She lifted the gun slowly and pressed it to her temple. She had no idea what she was doing. But she'd seen movies that showed people shooting themselves in the side of the head. *Above the ear, behind the ear? Oh God. Would it hurt? I can't screw this up. I don't want to end up paralyzed.*

Looking across the room, Cat saw a photo of her riding Mach. Pammy had taken the picture one sunny afternoon. Cat had been practicing jumps over a a a scary obstacle. The huge tree trunk was about eight feed wide, and was intimidating all on it's own. If Mach ever hit that he could be severely injured. Unlike most of the other jumps in the ring that would fall apart on contact, this thing was solid. It wouldn't budge. It wasn't going anywhere. On top of it there were two verticals in ascending order, making the entire jump just about 5 feet high. It was scary, but that day, Cat had known they were both in the zone, and Pammy had captured a look of complete joy, and total confidence in both her eyes and Mach's. As they flew over the jump, Cat had her head tucked in right next to Mach's sleek neck, holding the reins ever so lightly, Cat was an appendage to Mach, you could see their bond. *How can I give that up? Maybe if I just follow the rules, maybe I can get away one of these days.* Gingerly fingering the trigger, Cat slowly lowered the gun to her lap, tears streaming down her cheeks.

Shaking her head to clear her mind of that image, Catlin knew she'd be free soon. She'd made it this far. She only had to hang on a bit longer, and then she and Sky would be married. She also knew she didn't want to relive moments like that one again and knew that was the reason that little glass vial was in her pocket. And she vowed to throw it away someplace where no one would ever find it.

FOCUS!

TIRED AND CRANKY, Catlin steals a glance at her watch. The stainless steel and diamond Tag Heuer reminds her she's only been riding for forty five minutes. God, I've got at least another two hours to go. Her instructor's insistent voice brings her back to the moment, intruding on the fantasy of laying out by the pool in the warm afternoon sun.

"Catlina! Pay attention! You've missed your timing four times straight! What's wrong with you?"

Mind drifting and struggling to keep her voice level and amiable, Catlin looks over at her instructor and coach, "The Colonel", and tells herself to be civil. He's such an old goat sometimes. And why on earth does he always have to wear that uniform?

It's not like he's still in the army or anything. He must be at least seventy-five-years old. He stinks and his breath is enough to knock anyone on their ass; she can almost smell his breath from across the ring as he shouts to her.

"Catlina! Pay attention! Again! Take that jump again." Throwing his arms up in complete frustration, the old man waddles out into the center of the ring, and stands expectantly by the small oxer. "Come on, now Catlina. Concentrate. You'll never make it past the first round, if you ride like that." Ignoring The Colonel, Catlina rides over to her groom, and effortlessly dismounts, handing him the reins. "Here. Hold him. I'll be right back."

Leaving Pedro, and the Colonel standing open-mouthed, she rushes past the spectators toward the clubhouse. Running into the ladies room, she quickly enters a stall, and quietly pulls a small glass vial from her hip pocket.

Pouring a bit of cocaine on her carefully manicured fingertip, Catlin inhales quickly through each nostril, and feels the power in her nerves.

Wiping her nose with tissue, she inhales deeply as she flushes to mask the snorting sound, in case anyone is in the rest room, Catlin shoves the vial back in her pocket and rushes back out to the ring.

Quickly grabbing the reins from Pedro, she gets back up on the horse, and rides over to the still dumbfounded Colonel, who looks around the ring in disbelief. He starts to say something to her, but Catlin quickly apologizes.

"Sorry Colonel. I've had so much excitement going on, my stomach has been a little queasy. I feel much better now. I can do better. Let's get back to work."

With a grin she rides off, and "The Colonel" looks around blankly, then shrugs, as Catlin gets back into the rhythm of her ride, but is over confident, miscalculates the jump, and everyone watches in horror as horse and rider tumble end-over-end, smashing to the ground sending wooden rails crashing. Olympus shakes himself to his feet, and Catlyn sits unhurt but dazed and afraid as everyone rushes to her side.

KAREN KEILT

A FEW DAYS LATER

A TRENDY ROCK AND roll band is setting up on a small stage in a dimly lit night club. Owen and Henri stand pressed up against the bar sipping cocktails and watching the band. Sitting quietly, across the room deep in the shadow, two men watch the two friends.

Looking bored Henri asks. "So these guys are your customers, Owen?"

"I can always tell when you're feeling no pain, Henri, your accent is really thick. I can barely understand you. Yeah, every body's got a drug dealer on speed dial man, and these are cool guys, I think you'll like their music."

Ignoring Owen's remark, Henri continues. "How much do they spend with you?"

Getting serious, Owen replies. "These guys always buy everything I have. They got credit cards with no limit. I mean, think about all the chicks that come on to them. They bang them all. Speaking of which, check out those two bimbos at the end of the bar, they're checking us out."

Henri looks toward the bar, and tries to steer Owen back to the matter at hand. "Don't get side-tacked, man. We're here to talk business. Did you get everything through customs, OK?" Focusing again, Owen responds. "Yeah, yeah. I got something strong. Something extra-strength. We're golden. How much do you want?" "My buyers say they'll take as much as I can get them. Can you bring it by my apartment tomorrow night?" "Sure I'll be there. Now let's say we have some fun. Let's get this party started."

Owen walks towards the end of the bar, where he insinuates himself between the two scantily clad women. He whispers into the ear of the woman on his right, then ducks his head and whispers into the ear of the woman on his left.

The two women giggle loudly, and Owen signals to the bartender, who prepares two fresh drinks and places them on the bar in front of the women.

Boldly cupping their asses with his hands, Owen steers them over towards Henri. The foursome move into a dark corner booth, and make introductions. The men across the room continue to watch from the shadows, as Owen slips his hand into his pocket and pulls out a small vial of pills.

Laughing, he hands the vial to the women. "What do you think, girls? Come and party with me. One-two pump it up, one-two back it up." In halting, heavily accented English the shorter brunette loudly replies that they came prepared to meet some other friends.

Sensing that the women are trying to make a better deal, Owen pulls his wallet from his hip pocket extracts a hundred dollar bill, which he places on the table. Feeling dejected he continues.

"That's too bad. Nothin to do. Nowhere to go. Just put me in a wheelchair and get me to the show. I can't control my fingers, I can't control my toes. I want to be sedated."

The two women look at one another in confusion, and whisper for a moment, then the short brunette quickly palms the bill, and looking at Henri says.

"I think our friends are supposed to meet us here tomorrow night. Maybe we can party with you after all."

Smiling at Henri, she bats her eyes and adds.

"Besides, you're pretty cute."

Wondering how Henri always manages to score first, Owen shakes his head and speaks up. "He's not cute. He's French. I'm good. Like what you see?" The girls get up laughing and head to the rest room, taking Owen's pill vial with them. Giggling and waving, they signal that they'll be right back. Offended, Henri asks Owen. "What kind of crack was that? He's not cute . . . he's French."

"Shit, Henri. That accent of yours always gets you laid. What about me? What am I, some kind of has been? I give them a wad of cash and a hundred bucks worth of ecstasy, and you're the cute one? Come on, shawty need to choose me."

"Don't worry about it, man. You know we're both going to score."

They high-five and signal to the bartender for another round. Having seen enough, the two men in the corner, inconspicuously pay their bill and leave the bar. As they walk to a waiting car, one of the men pulls a cell phone from his jacket pocket. Speaking softly in Portuguese, he makes a call.

MOVING RIGHT ALONG

SITTING TOGETHER AT a small cafe table, Jose, Red and Jack are strange companions. Elegantly dressed Jose could have stepped out of a men's fashion catalog casually sipping his cafezinho like he'd been born with a silver spoon in his mouth rather than in the slums of Sao Paulo, while Red and Jack look the part of the proverbial bull in a china shop. The delicate coffee cups disappear in their gigantic paws, and they look as if they'd be more at ease handling meat cleavers or axes.

Spread out on the table in front of them are various photographs of Owen and Henri drinking in bars, of Freddy and Henri exchanging money, of Owen handing an envelope to a customs agent and one of the group of friends snorting cocaine at Schuyler's house.

"Your men are sure getting the goods. These kids are so stupid. They're being watched all the time, and they act like they're invincible."

"Which is exactly what we want. There were even a few times when my men thought they'd been spotted, but they keep right on doing whatever they're doing."

Laughing out loud Jack gives his opinion. "They probably think your guys are paparazzi. They're all pretty oblivious to anything but themselves and their own little world."

Picking up the photograph of Catlin, Jose's brow furrows slightly. "At first I was surprised by this one. But she's been kept on a very short leash. It looks like she's finally cut the cord."

Getting back to business, Red covers the pictures with his laptop, booting it up to a banking web site. Jose and Jack lean in.

"I've got a measly $1,000.00 in this offshore account. It's numbered and untraceable. When we get the kid, we'll give his brother this number. Once the funds are wired and that number doesn't look so small anymore, I'll transfer it to our individual accounts and you can let him go home."

"Perfect. But first perhaps he might like to tour one of our little facilities." Jose nods at his men sitting a few tables away. "Those guys would love to show him some of our, uh . . . how do you Americans say it? Amenities?" The men all laugh and Jose raises his demitasse cup in a toast. "You've done a great job putting this deal together my friend. I applaud your vision and international business skills."

SNAP JUDGEMENT

HENRI ADJUSTS HIS camera, focusing on the platform at the back of his studio. As he fiddles with the camera's focus mechanism he can hear the model, hairdresser, and his assistant, Paulo, getting ready for the morning shoot.

He feels great. His life, like his work, seems to be clicking on all cylinders. He's just landed a major new client, and this shoot can make or break him in the hugely profitable, Sao Paulo advertising industry.

Henri adjusts the fan, thinking about how far he's come from Montmatre, and how strange it is that his dreams are becoming reality in, of all places, Brazil. Yet, so many of the world's top models, like Tom Brady's wife, Giselle Bundchen are Brazilian beauties, and there are so many exotic locations to shoot, he really shouldn't be too surprised. It seems like it was a great decision to move so far from home after all.

Out of the corner of his eye, Freddy sees that Paulo and the gorgeous model are ready, and waiting for him. Cranking up the volume on the newest "John Mayer" CD, Henri points to the backdrop, and the bikini-clad beauty strikes a pose.

Who'd a thought? Pudgy, geeky Henri getting to hangout with all these sexy women. Ah . . . I must be dead and in heaven. All those years of struggling as a waiter for the cheap tourists paid off. Here in Brazil he was close to fame of his own.

Henri thought about what his life had been like before he came to Brazil. He'd been living in a broken down, rat infested apartment building on the outskirts of the glitzy streets of Paris. He'd barely gotten by waiting on rich American Tourists for years in a popular bistro and had hated it. One night he'd watched a tourist gloating about getting great shots of a fashion photo shoot on his digital camera. Looking over the customer's shoulder, Henri thought, I can do that. The next day he'd bought a ticket to Rio and a really good digital camera with his rent money.

He fabricated a portfolio for himself, scanning photographs from fashion magazines at a local copy shop, and hadn't looked back once. Smiling smugly, in his version of sexy, he encouraged the model. "OK. Come on now. Give it to me baby. You look perfect. You are perfect!" Pursing her lips, and turning this way and that the tall, svelte model works the camera, and Henri clicks away, capturing exquisite image after image. "Paulo! More wind. Turn up the fan. I want her hair blowing out behind her! Yes, that's it. That's it, Come on baby, give it to me. More. More. Like that. Yes. Yes. You're so hot."

Henri's so into his work he doesn't hear the phone ringing, or notice Paulo running to pluck it off a table. Paulo stands quietly watching Henri work for another moment before coming over to nudge his boss. He hates interrupting him, as he's seen that French temper kick into overdrive.

Everyone says the Latin temper is hot. They should see this guy!

"Ah, excuse me Boss. The phone. This is that call you've been expecting. I think it's the American."

Reluctantly, Henri stops shooting and motions the model off the platform.

"OK. Take a break. And get her some more lipstick."

"Right boss. We'll be ready when you are."

Paulo loops his arm through the model's to keep her from breaking her neck on her high, spiked heels, and they head back to the "green room."

Henri puts the camera down, grabs an icy bottle of Perrier from the small fridge, sits down, and swings his legs up onto the couch. He picks up the phone.

"Hello? Yes. This is Henri." Happily, Henri recognizes the Americans he met at the club the night before. "Hey. Yeah, man. How are you?"

In the next room, Paulo tries to eavesdrop on his boss, but the Frenchman speaks too softly and too quickly for him to make out much more than a word or two of Henri's side of the conversation.

"Of course. Yes. I told you it was a sure thing. I'll be able to deliver tomorrow night."

Henri pauses, swallows half the bottle of water, wipes his mouth with the back of his hand, and listens for a moment, then laughs as he adds.

"Sure. I can tell you all the hot spots. But let me make another suggestion. One of my best friends is getting married this weekend. It'll be a hell of a party. Anyone who's anyone, will be there. How would you like to join us?"

He listens a beat, then continues.

"No. I don't think they'll mind at all. It's a huge wedding and a couple more people won't make a difference. I'll ask them tonight, and bring you an invitation when I see you tomorrow."

After a quick goodbye, Henri hangs up the phone and calls out to Paulo to bring in the model. "Paulo. Let's get going. We haven't got all day. Let's go before she cools down." Rolling his eyes at the sultry girl, Paulo reacts quickly. "What a jerk. We're sitting here waiting for him, and he acts like I'm tweezing my eyebrows or something."

Moments later the model and Henri are back in sync.

"That's it baby. Give it to me. That's the way I like it. Hmmm. You're so good. Lick those lips. Open your mouth a little more, like that. Yes, lick your lips. Mmmm. Like that. Oooh baby. I love it. You're so good."

MATINEE

A FEW MILES AWAY Catlin and Schuyler are sweaty and naked on his giant bed. Catlin licks a bead of sweat from Schuyler's brow, lowering her head like a panther ready to pounce.

Beads of water pool and drip down the sides of a short crystal glass next to the bed. Reaching over, Schuyler picks it up, and takes a long swallow of the mellow amber liquid and sighs contentedly.

"Mmmm baby, that was good. I can't get enough of you. Let's go again." Teasing him, she purrs. "Sorry to be so vulgar but that's the last time you ever fuck Catlin Lauria. Tomorrow I'll be Catlin Grant. Mrs. Catlin Grant!" "Whoo Hoo! You mean I get a new broad? Every man's dream." "That's right, Bibi. Just wait 'til you get a load of your wife. She's gonna make your head spin." "Are you kidding me? If it spins any more than it is now, I'll be christened as a planet. How can this possibly get any better?"

As he takes another swig of scotch, Catlin gets off the bed and pulls on a slip dress.

"I better get going. We don't want my Dad freaking out on the night before the wedding. He's been pretty good so far, but there's still time for him to wig out and ruin everything tonight." Reaching out and snaking his icy, wet hand up Catlin's leg, Schuyler pulls her back to him.

"Aw come on, baby. One more for old time's sake? Besides, I really like fucking a Lauria. I think I'm going to miss that. How about one last time? And lookey here, you're still wet. Can it be Miss Lauria still wants me?"

Laughing, she falls onto the bed and eases her dress teasingly over her head. Her hair is tangled and cascades down her back as she turns back on her knees and looks over her shoulder at Schuyler. He reaches for her then stops. "I wish we had a bit of cocaine right now."

"You know, Bibi. I'm glad it's gone. It was fun, but it's brutal stuff, and messed with my head and my riding. I'm all done with that."

"You're right baby. I'm not thinkin' straight. What do I need with drugs when I got this?" He reaches for her and they embrace passionately once again.

As she kisses him, Catlin flashes to the image of the glass vial she'd quickly placed in Sky's top dresser drawer. She'd forgotten to throw it away, and reminded herself once more that she had to get rid of it. It was bad karma.

PART TWO

THE WEDDING

CATLIN WOKE UP to the screeching call of Loro the macaw on the patio beneath her bedroom. Any other day she would have run out on the terrace, but today she languishes in bed and thinks about the day ahead. It's going to be a great day. It's going to be the best day of her life. Getting out of bed, she walks slowly into her adjoining bathroom, and looks in the mirror. A little puffiness under her eyes, and a smudge of darkness there too. Nothing four hours at the day spa can't fix.

Listening to Billy Idol's "White Wedding" play through her Ipod's surround sound system, Catlin splashes her face with cool water, thinking about how her Dad always told her she washed her face like a cat. She piled her hair into a loose knot on the top of her head and quickly threw on a tank top and loose fitting comfy shorts, then headed downstairs where the house was already buzzing with activity.

There are flowers everywhere, and beautiful white satin ribbons trailing along the bannister of the curving staircase. Walking through the large rooms, Catlin marvels at the transformation. The furniture and Aubusson rug have been removed from the dining room, and it looks like a lavish ball room. Through the massive leaded glass French Doors, Catlin can see workers bustling about as they erect a massive white tent out by the pool. Dainty white gauze, tiny lights and perfect white roses decorate the patio, where dozens of small tables, overflowing with massive floral arrangements, and chairs have been set up to accommodate guests.

Walking quickly from room to room Catlin scouts for her Mom. They have an appointment for several relaxing treatments at Mizuki, her favorite Japanese Day Spa in a little under an hour. Catlin's looking forward to a sea salt body glow and Vichy shower massage, before they meet up with the rest of the women in the bridal party. On her way to find Colleen, Catlyn examines one of the perfect silver flutes, each engraved "Cat and Sky in Love In Life", each one a token gift for each guest, smiles approvingly and continues on through the house.

Colleen and Cat have appointments for an morning of manicures and pedicures, make-up, and hair, before she returns home to get dressed, and gets to the church for a day she'll remember for the rest of her life.

Catlin feels excited and drained, apprehensive and impatient at once. Her life is about to change, and suddenly Catlin needs reassurance that this is the right thing to do. Spotting her mother at the end of the long drive-way in the midst of delivery vans and caterers, Catlin skips across the yard.

"Come on, Mom. We have to leave in five minutes. You can leave all this in Celia's capable hands. Everything will get done perfectly."

Colleen starts to protest but Catlin gently tugs her towards the waiting car and Nuncio.

"But."

"No buts. Just think of Shiori-san's hands, and that warm water cascading down your back. Think Jasmine, hot rocks and green tea. Come on, Mom. Come relax with me. We both need this. Come on, it'll do us good."

Smoothing her hair back from her damp brow, Colleen agrees.

"You're right. Let me grab my bag and we're out of here."

A few hours later Catlin and Colleen enter a peaceful lounge wrapped in traditional, cotton yukata robes. Taking careful, delicate steps in their zori sandals, they settle down on tatami mats, and sip green tea from perfect porcelain bowls as they listen to water sluicing peacefully through bamboo tubes into a pond nearby. Their faces are flushed and their skin is glowing from the attentions of Shiori-san and her assistants.

"That was perfect. That was exactly what I needed. Thanks for insisting I come."

"No problem, Mom. Now we can enjoy a nice light lunch and then go meet the girls for "Step-Two-To-Beauty.""

Giggling and whispering like young girls, they wait for their lunches to arrive. Much later, after all the women were softened and scrubbed, perfumed, painted and coiffed, they left as a group, to dress the bride.

The excitement was palpable, and a quiet videographer captured the feelings as well as the images, so Catlin could look back on this day over and over, for years to come, to breathe in the essence of her wedding day.

Finally, an hour before they were to arrive at the church, Catlin descended the curving, flower laden, and beribboned staircase, intently watched by family, friends, and servants alike. Eyes sparkling, cheeks flushed, a tiny vein beating visibly in the hollow of her throat, Catlin cleared her throat.

"Well, what do you think? Will he still want to marry me?" She twirled at the foot of the steps, and heard murmurs of appreciation. Walther approaches his daughter with tears in his eyes. "Catlin. You look beautiful." He sighed deeply and reaching into the inner pocket of his tux pulled out a small black velvet box.

"I've been saving this for you, since the day you were born. I really never wanted to give it to you, because it would mean you were no longer my little girl, but now I see that you haven't been for quite some time. This belonged to my mother. Her father gave it to her on her wedding day, and now I'm giving it to you."

Fingers fumbling nervously, Catlin opened the box, and squealed in delight.

"Oh Daddy! It's gorgeous. Thank you. Thank you. I'll treasure it always." She spun around and carefully lifted her curls. "Here, put it on for me. Oh my God, Dad, it's gorgeous. How come I've never seen this before?"

This was a sparkling, rare, three carat tear-drop shaped ruby, surrounded by pave diamonds, set simply and elegantly in a gleaming platinum bezel. As he fastened the delicate chain around her neck, Walther told her it was meant to represent a father's sadness when he gave away his daughter's hand in marriage.

Catlin spun around and hugged him, a small tear escaping her eye.

"I'll always be your little girl, Daddy, and I'll always make you proud."

In a few moments the wedding party, was whisked away in several cars, forming a caravan as they drove from the house to the church. As part of a tradition in her family, Catlin rode alone in the back of a white limousine, while the rest of the bride's party followed behind.

Taking a deep breath, Catlin thought about the new journey she was about to embark upon.

She thought of all the gifts she'd received over the years, thought of her friends and family, and of the natural talent she'd been given, and of all the dreams about to come true. Catlin was glad she hadn't done any cocaine last night with Schuyler, She knew it had messed up her head and she was glad she'd decided to stop the craziness before it took control of their lives. They had everything to live for, and no reason to throw it away so casually through foolishness and drugs and drug use. Confident and happy with all her decisions, Catlin closed her eyes, and listened to her heart beat as the car made it's way towards the church and her future.

FLASHBACK

L OOKING VERY SELF-ASSURED, the tiny eight year old trotted purposefully into the ring on the smallish black gelding. Dressed in tall black boots, white breeches, and a white shirt, Catlin snapped the buckle on the chin strap of her black velvet riding helmet.

As a toddler she'd watched as her Daddy rode the big beautiful horses over the big jumps at the Hipica. Today would be her turn to show off. She'd already been riding for three years, at first with an instructor holding the reins as the horse trotted in small circles around the ring, then on a lunge line with no reins, riding around in bigger circles using only the strength of her little legs to hold her upright in the saddle. She'd loved every minute of those rides, but waited impatiently for the day that she would be able to ride a real horse, not just a pony, like a big girl.

With a helpful leg up from her groom she'd grasped the reins, and led Skyjet around the ring in a slow trot. The "Colonel" was standing there watching his protege as she made her way toward him. He gave her a few last minute instructions and then she was on her way, this time in a slow canter, then up and over the low vertical bars.

She made it over! She was flying. It was everything she knew it would be, and as she sailed over the jump she leaned her small body close to her horses neck, just like she'd seen all the big kids do. She loved it, she wanted more. She wanted to go faster. She wanted to go higher.

All those exciting images of her youth and her horses flashed before her eyes and Catlin recalled the exhilaration she'd felt at her first competition. Once again she felt the excitement of the crowd murmuring in the bleachers. She remembered how she'd blocked out the sights and sounds of the crowd and the other young riders.

She was sitting tall in her saddle looking toward her Mom and Dad, then turned to face the judges, as she bowed, her left hand sweeping out in a curtsey. She'd gathered the reins in both hands, and nudged Skyjet into a slow canter and to the start of the course she'd memorized only moments earlier.

The gong sounded, and she spurred the horse to a gallop, heading for the first jump. She sailed over it, and urging her horse forward, she sailed over the nine remaining jumps with the speed and ease of a seasoned pro, then she bolted to the finish as quickly as she could.

Catlin smiled as she recalled her pride that day, receiving the first of many trophies. Holding it up for all to see she trotted victorious, around the ring. She could hear the applause again as if she were there, she could feel her blood thumping in her veins as heart slowed, and she could feel

Skyjet's big heart beating beneath her. She could taste the fine powdery red dust coating her lips and smell the sweat cooling on Skyjet's withers. There was no feeling like it in the world, and Catlin knew it would always be a part of her life. Grand Prix jumping was a dangerous sport, but she'd mastered it, she'd been born to ride, and soar over the jumps. This was one of the few sports in which women and men competed on the same level.

In this country where women were revered as goddesses in it's notoriously sexual society, they were also humiliated by men, and rarely perceived as competent. Catlin was beyond proud that she could knock the socks off most of the men who competed against her.

Starting all those long years ago, all her hard work and dedication had been leading her to this precise moment, and today, with another Sky in her life like she'd had thirteen years ago, as she stepped delicately from the limo, gathering the folds of her stunning gown around her, standing in front of the resplendent cathedral, she knew her destiny was taking her exactly where she was supposed to be. To Sky and their future.

SHOWERED IN LOVE

T HE CATHEDRAL WAS ephemeral, glowing softly with the warm lights of hundreds of candles.

The wedding ceremony was an out-of-body experience for Catlin. Gliding down the aisle on her father's arm, Catlin barely saw the multitude of elegantly dressed guests, the flowers or the white bows. Her eyes locked on Schuyler's, which guided her to him like a heat seeking missile. Without knowing how she got there, she was suddenly standing at his side, barely aware of the pomp and circumstance surrounding them; his warm hands holding her steady and coaxing her though her well rehearsed lines. It was only after they had said their "I Do's", as scores of translucent ivory and pale pink rose petals drifted onto their heads and shoulders from above the altar that Catlin really, really realized they were married. Her skin tingling, her eyes sparkling, she finally managed to look around the church and see her family and her friends. She was ecstatic. She was Mrs. Schuyler Grant. With tears of joy in her eyes, Catlin lifted her veil, and they kissed.

Laughing, the happy couple made their way slowly down the aisle, now and again stopping briefly to throw a kiss at this friend, or to shake hands with that distant cousin. Outside Schuyler picked her up and swung her in a circle as applause echoed behind them. They were married!

SHE'S ALL YOURS

THOUGH CATLIN KNEW there would be a "Sweet Station" set up to tempt the guests at the reception, she and Schuyler had stopped at a small doceiria for an espresso and a tiny, sweet pastry to kill some time, so that when they pulled up in front of the gates of her father's house, the guests had mostly all arrived. Cars lined the streets and drivers mingled in small knots smoking and catching up.

They got out of the car, and were amazed to see armed guards dressed in official parade uniforms posted at the gate, along the driveway, and at every entrance to the house. Looking like a scene from a movie, the house was lit up with twinkling lights, and strategically placed spot lights that made the giant palms look even taller and more majestic then they already were. The sultry night air was gently perfumed by barely perceptible incense being released every few minutes from diffusers carefully hidden at bases of the trees.

As Walther and Colleen stood at the door waiting to greet the young newlyweds, Walther commented under his breath. "It's over. Finally. No more bills, no more decisions, no more crying jags from either of you! I didn't think we'd get through this." Squeezing his arm to silence him, Colleen stepped through the doorway, as Catlin rushed into her arms. "Mom! I'm married! Can you believe it? Was it beautiful? I felt like I was in a movie!"

"Oh honey! It was gorgeous. You were gorgeous! Schuyler let me hug you!"

Catlin slipped into her father's arms, as Schuyler took her place with Colleen.

"Daddy! Everything looks so great! Thank you. Thank you for everything. But you sure went overboard with those guards, didn't you? How on earth did you get them?" "Oh, they weren't my idea. You'll have to thank Jose Barros for that touch. Those are National Guards in full parade uniform." Raising his eyebrows as he looked over his shoulder at the guards, Schuyler appeared dubious. "Wow! I don't get it. That's some strange gift." Playfully punching Sky, Cat pipes in. "As if we need any more china or crystal! I love it! And you should talk, you've never given me a traditional gift yet!" "Hmmm. You've got me there."

Opening his arms to escort Catlin and Colleen into the house, Walther turns back to Schuyler.

"You don't know José well, but he's always been an "over-the-top" kind of guy. He's always trying to impress your mother-in-law. And he told me he wanted to be sure no unsavory characters tried to crash your party. Now come on, let's get inside; all our guests are dying to see you two!"

"We'll be sure to find him and thank him personally. First, I need something bubbly and cold. Come on Cat, I see Freddy and the gang."

As they enter, the guests break into applause and cheers. Catlin and Schuyler bow and curtsy in good humor, stopping to chat with guests as they make their way towards their group of friends. Schuyler deftly grabs two glasses of champagne from a passing waiter, and moments later they're standing with their friends.

Henri tilts his glass towards the couple, and the others follow suit. "Here's to our very dear friends, Catlin and Schuyler, may they always have new shoes, and live long healthy, happy lives!" "Always have new shoes? Henri what on earth are you talking about?" Catlin exchanged a puzzled look with Bete.

"Don't worry about him Catlina. He's already had a few too many glasses of champagne. He keeps saying something about how your souls looked so very new and shiny at the church. I couldn't figure out what he was talking about."

"Your soles. Your soles." Henri balances precariously on one leg and lifts his foot, so that everyone can see the bottom of his shoe.

Leaning on Schuyler and lifting her foot, Catlin glances quickly at the sole of her shoe then nudges Schuyler to do the same. Sure enough they're both wearing brand new shoes, and the soft leather is shiny and clean.

"Oh. Henri. New soles. Is that what you were looking at while we were kneeling at the altar? You were supposed to be paying attention to what Father Fernando was saying."

Laughing and raising his glass, Owen piped up. "Are you kidding me? You were supposed to be looking at the back of her dress! Devil in a white dress, white dress, white dress, devil with the white dress on!"

Rolling her eyes at Owen, and laughing, Catlin raises her glass and they all take long swallows of the bubbly champagne. Schuyler reaches to kiss her again, but Freddy grabs her arm and pulls her away from the group.

"Hey you two. Follow me. Come on everyone. I have a wedding present for the happy couple, up in my apartment. Let's go. I want to give it to you."

The small group of friends thread their way through knots of guests, make their way through the jasmine scented gardens, to the service building. Along the way they nod and smile at the guards stiffly posted along the drive way.

Upstairs, in typical paranoid fashion, Freddy checks the windows and empty rooms, then pulls a small box from his jacket pocket and with a flourish, hands it to Schuyler.

"Here you go, you two. Don't ever let it be said that I was stingy. There's enough pure marching powder in there for all of us to do the samba all night long! Plus there's enough for you to take on your honeymoon, too! Congratulations, and enjoy!"

Carefully ripping open the beautifully wrapped box Schuyler holds up a zip lock bag filled with cocaine. Catlin and Schuyler quickly exchanged winces, and Catlin grabbed the box, handing it back to Freddy.

"Uh. Thanks, Freddy, but no thanks. Sky and I are keeping our heads on straight. We want to remember this night. But if you guys want to party, go ahead. You just better be careful with all those cops out there."

Miffed, that his gift was not accepted, but looking forward to doing cocaine and seeing if he could bed a bridesmaid, Freddy shrugged and taking the box back from Catlin proceeded to carve out lines of cocaine on a glass table-top for the rest of their group.

"I know you said you didn't want to do this anymore. But it's your wedding night!"

"Yes. And that's precisely why we don't want to do it."

"OK, I guess. But seriously, you're missing out on some great shit."

Linking arms and smiling at the group, Catlin and Schuyler make their way back to the party that's just kicking into high gear.

SPEAK OF THE DEVIL

A SHORT TIME LATER one of the guards makes his way to the front door, and stands a moment, anxiously scanning through the crowd. Spotting Walther Lauria chatting with Henri, he smiles amicably and walks over.

"Mr. Lauria. I'm so sorry to bother you sir. There are two gentlemen at the gate. They do not speak Portuguese, and they do not have invitations, but they say they are friends of Mr. Desjardins."

Walther looks questioningly at Henri, who nods his head and the two men walk towards the door.

"I hope it's OK, Mr. Lauria. I've invited some colleagues who are here from the States on business. They were on their own for the weekend. I meant to get invitations from Cat, but I forgot, I hope it's not an imposition."

Almost imperceptibly slurring his words, Walther claps Henri across the back. "That's no problem, Henri. If you can vouch for them, that's good enough for me. The more the merrier, I say!"

As Henri and Walther watch, the two men walk up the driveway. One carries a large bouquet of flowers, and the other an elaborately wrapped bottle. Henri steps towards them, and putting his arms over their shoulders, guides them to Walther who is smiling magnanimously.

"Hello, fellas. I'm Walther Lauria, father of the bride. Come on in and make yourselves at home."

Awkwardly shifting the huge bouquet of flowers the first man grips Walther's extended hand, he turns to look back at the gate, over his shoulder.

"Thank you, sir. Boy, I thought we'd never get in here. That's some welcoming committee."

Henri laughs and claps his guests on the shoulders.

"Don't be surprised by all the guards. Mr. Lauria went to school with the head of Sao Paulo's CNE. That's Center for Narcotic Enforcement. Sort of like the DEA. The guards are a wedding gift."

"They look good, don't they? It's kind of nice to have friends in high places. And they keep out the riff-raff. Lucky for you two, Henri vouched for you. Come on, come on let's get inside, grab you boys some drinks, then you can meet the bride and give her the foliage."

Easing through the tightly packed guests, they make their way to Bete, and a group of bridesmaids. Henri signals to a waiter who approaches with a tray of canapes. A wandering photographer is taking candid shots of the guests, and seeing him look their way, the two men quickly turn to face away from his lens. Spotting Catlin on the edge of the dance floor, Henri grabs her, propelling her toward the small group.

"Hey, Cat. I hope you don't mind. I brought two guests. These are some really great guys."

Over her head, Henri spots Freddy across the room, and waves to get his attention. Freddy doesn't see him, and wanders off in the opposite direction. Smiling Catlin reaches out her hand to the two new arrivals.

"Oh, no problem at all. Any friends of Henri's and all that! I'm Catlin Lau . . . Oops . . . I'm Catlin Grant. It's nice to meet you."

Just as she reaches for his hand, Schuyler pulls Catlin out of the small circle and spins her out onto the dance floor.

"Oops. Excuse me. We'll be right back. They're playing our song. We'll be right back."

"No problem. Go dance. We'll talk later."

Then Freddy spots Henri as he is frantically waves him over. Photographer at his side, Freddy begins to make his way towards the group from across the room. Henri points at him urging Bete and his friends in Freddy's direction through the dancers.

Conscious of being watched, Freddy stops for a second looking towards the group, but the photographer spins a young woman towards him, blocking his view, and asks them to smile for the camera. Distracted, Freddy smiles and puts his arm around the waist of a beautiful young woman and they both pose for a wedding album shot. Henri, Bete and his two guests step up behind Freddy and the posing woman spinning them around quickly. Freddy's face registers surprise, as Henri claps him on the back.

"What's the matter Freddy? You look like you've seen a ghost? Are you alright?" Quickly trying to cover up the shocked expression, Red Tucker reaches across and takes Freddy's hand, pumping it in his own. "Freddy Lauria? Wow! Freddy!" As he continues enthusiastically pumping Freddy's arm, Red briefly narrows his eyes in a look of warning. "Can you believe this? I don't believe it! This is Freddy Lauria. We met at Harvard. What a small world. I never knew you lived in Brazil, man. How are ya? Wow! Freddy Lauria. What a surprise."

Just then Catlin and Schuyler rejoin the group, smiling and laughing.

"Hey, Freddy! You know these guys? Close your mouth, you'll draw flies."

Red puts his arm around Freddy's shoulder making a show of squeezing him close to his side.

KAREN KEILT

"Of course he knows me. How great is this? Hey I gotta get a copy of that photo?" Pulling out his cell phone he quickly snaps a shot of Freddy. "Wow. Is this great or what?"

Creating a distraction, Red turns to Catlin reaching for her arm.

"So Catlin, congratulations! What a great wedding party! And I just can't get over the fact that I've flown half-way around the world, and I know your brother. This is awesome."

Feeling at ease now that the ice has been broken, Catlin and Red talk like old friends.

"It is amazing, isn't it? Talk about six degrees of separation. That theory is so true. You'll have to tell me all about Freddy's antics up in Boston. I'm sure you have some good stories!"

Exaggeratedly, winking at Freddy, Red continues. "I'll tell you anything you want to know. But first I want to hear all about you. What you do. Everything. Freddy never told me he had a sister! And such a beautiful one at that."

Red has turned on the old Irish charm, Cat is captivated, and eager to share.

"Oh, you're too sweet. Well where can I start? I'm a rider. You know, horses. I was born and raised right here in Sao Paulo. I just graduated from USP. The University of Sao Paulo, and I've lived here my whole life."

"You don't look Brazilian, and your English is perfect. I'd never have guessed in a million years that you're not American!" Henri points across the dance floor to Walther and Colleen Lauria.

"You met Walther when you came in. He's Brazilian too. Born and raised, just like Cat. His family connects back to the US somehow though. I've heard stories about clipper ships and gold mines and fortunes. Their oldest son is in the US making his fortune there. I've never even met him." Henri continues pointing across the dance floor. And that's Mrs. Lauria. She's a native New Yorker. They're both pretty hot, eh?"

Blushing in embarrassment, Catlin nudges Henri.

"Henri, stop! You're embarrassing me. Stop it!" Wanting to change the subject, Catlin continues. "I learned English and Portuguese at the same time. I'm bilingual."

Not wanting to be excluded from any conversation about his bride, Schuyler places his arm about her waist possessively and leans in to the conversation.

"Most Americans who come to Brazil don't bother to learn the language. They figure they're here for a year or two, then they'll be heading back to the States. Catlin has her own language too. We call it Portingles. It's our version of Spanglish. She makes up new words all together, and she'll switch syntax now and again. You'll notice it more once you get to really know her."

Winking suggestively again, Red responds. "Well, I hope you'll let us get to know you both a lot better then. I want to hear this. And your riding, too! Tell me more."

The group of friends laugh and raise their glasses. Anything is an excuse for a toast. No one seems to notice as Freddy chugs his champagne and quickly grabs another from a passing waiter, chugging that one, too. From across the dance floor a distinguished gentleman watches the group of young friends. Colleen Lauria approaches him and struggling to be heard over the band's loud rendition of "You Start Me Up" leans in close to whisper in his ear.

"Jose, my dear! Thank you so much for coming. And the guards! Only you could think of such an impressive gift. Thank you."

"Ah Colleen. You look lovelier than usual. And you're quite welcome. I hope I have not embarrassed Catlina."

"Don't be silly dear, she's thrilled. Come with me, I'll take you over to speak with her, and introduce you to Schuyler as well.

Taking his hand, Colleen begins to lead Jose around the room. Watching from across the room, Red nods his head at Jose indicating Jose should bring her over to meet him, but Jose leads her to the dance floor instead.

"Come on, let's dance! This is a night to celebrate. There will be much time to talk to the younger generation later. Walther won't mind. This is one time, I can feel like I am "King of the World" like him."

Shaking her head and laughing, as if she finds him charming and silly, Colleen let's him lead the way. Across the room, Red and Jack walk through the garden doors. The lights are twinkling, and another group of revelers are mingling at dining tables under the tent. The two men slowly walk away from the house to stand and admire the view.

"What a way to live. This sure isn't what I had envisioned when you talked about us coming to some third-world country. Hey did you see Freddy's face when he saw us? He almost pissed himself."

"I know that was great wasn't it? He didn't know what to do. He's got to be scared shitless that we'll tell his sister all about his little adventure in Boston."

They continue to walk around the grounds until they settle next the macaw, who is sleeping peacefully, wings tucked in, on it's perch. Jack reaches over to pet the bird, but Red quickly moves his hand away, as the macaw quickly jabs at him.

"Whoa! I thought that thing was sleeping! That was quick. He almost bit my hand off."

Jack starts taunting the macaw, just out of reach, by swinging his arm back and forth. From nearby tables, guests turn to watch the boorish American. The macaw weaves and bobs back and forth on it's perch, squawking, feathers ruffled, beak open.

"Come on. Leave it alone. Macaw's are vicious. They look beautiful and all that, but I've heard they can be really nasty. Let's go back inside. I want to get closer to Catlin." Shrugging, Jack smirks. "Yeah, yeah. Macaw, parrot. Same thing. It sits on a perch and squawks doesn't it?"

Owen and Henri have wandered outside for a smoke, and watch. "Haven't I seen those guys before? My eyes have seen them." Sounding just a little nervous, Henri replies. "Yeah. When you came by my studio last month they were there." "Right. Memorize that alley on an endless roll. I knew I'd seen them, but I couldn't quite place where. Freddy knows them too?" "Yeah, it looks that way. Forget about it. Don't worry about them. Let's work out the details for the next shipment." "I can bring in as much as you need on my next trip, but I'm raising the price. It's goin' up. It's goin' up." "No problem. If you can deliver, my buyers will take it all. Have prices gone up in the States, or have your margins?" "What do you think? My feature price is goin' up." Laughing they high-five and return to the party. Catlin and Freddy are standing together speaking quietly. Freddy has a worried look on his face as he scans the room, looking for Red and Jack. Having forgotten all about her vow not to do more cocaine, Freddy presses Catlin to go upstairs and do a line with her. "Come on Freddy. I told you I'm done with that."

"Ok! Whatever."

"See? You're a mess. This is my wedding night!"

"They'll be watching you. That's all I'm going to say."

"Freddy, what are you talking about? Who'll be watching me? What's going on?" "I'm not paranoid. Just trust me." Angry, and fed up, Catlin starts to walk away, but Freddy grabs her arm. "Look, I have to tell you something." Glancing nervously over his shoulder, and then at the ground, Freddy lowers his voice even more. "I was busted in the States. Just before I came home. I'm on some kind of international watch list."

"What? Are you kidding me!?! You got busted? Where? For what? Does Dad know?"

"You don't need the details. And you can't tell anyone. I thought it was over. But now. Well, it's a long story. I don't want to go into it right now, but trust me. It's a mess."

"My God, Freddy. Dad will kill you. What do you mean you thought it was over?"

Anxiously looking around Freddy answers. "Nothing. Nothing. I just meant, uh, shit. Look forget I said anything."

"You lay a bomb like that on me then tell me to forget it? What happened exactly?How come you're not in jail?"

"You can't tell anyone about this. Swear to me! It'd be the end of me. The end of my job. The end of everything. I was busted for dealing coke, and in order not to go to jail I had to turn "State's Evidence" against some Colombians. Then they got busted."

Pulling out his wallet, Freddy unfolds an official looking piece of paper and hands it to Catlin. "Holy shit. Holy shit." Freddy reaches over to pull the document out of his sisters hand, but not before she had a chance to read the bold type. *The United States of America, VS Frederick M. Lauria* "Yeah. They think I'm dead. But. Look. Shit. I don't want to talk about it. You don't need to know everything." "Are you kidding me Freddy? Don't be stupid. You're an ignoranus. You need to tell me everything. You're out of control."

Before he can respond, Freddy sees Red and Jack approaching them. His eyes widen and though he tries to control himself, he inadvertently stiffens, when the two men join the siblings.

"Ignoranus? Is that one of your made-up words, Catlin? That's a new one on me. But I like it." "Oh, hi Red. No. I don't think I coined that one, it's just a combination of ignorant and anus!"

"So who's the jerk? Anyone I know?"

Dismissing them, and preoccupied, Catlin turns away.

"No. Uh. We're just talking about someone I know. Hey. I gotta go. I think the waiters need more champagne."

Catlin smiles as she walks away leaving Freddy with the two rogue agents.

"You're mine you Son of a Bitch. Screw this up, and Daddy in there will find out all about his little Harvard boy. Don't forget, you work for me now! Don't fuck this up."

ON THE ROCKS

CATLIN AND SCHUYLER stood side-by-side, facing into the wind on the bow of the SweetSeaDream, a one hundred eighteen foot Banetti, Schuyler had chartered for their honeymoon, marveling at the sights of the Straits of Magellan. They'd just enjoyed an incredible brunch featuring freshly caught Chilean King Crab, a bottle of Veuve Cliquot, freshly baked pastries and croissants, both satisfied and looking forward to the day's adventures.

Catlin was ecstatic when Schuyler told her about the extended trip.

She'd thought they were just spending a week in Buenos Aires with a quick side-trip to Mar del Plata, but after a few days of shopping and fine dining, in the world-class city, Schuyler surprised her at the marina. Pretending to "just take a look" on-board the gorgeous yacht, Sky led her to the Master cabin where their suitcases had been magically unpacked and a bottle of champagne cooled alongside a platter of fresh fruits and flowers. Soon the large ship had been underway.

Catlin had always wanted to visit Patagonia, and with all the terrible implications of global warming Schuyler agreed it would be best to get a look at the wonderful scenery at the ends of the earth before some calamity destroyed it all.

They were looking forward to spending time in Punta Arenas, the southern most city in the world. They had plans to take a helicopter ride to the Torres del Paine National Park which was historically known for it's glacier lakes, penguins and incredible scenery.

Cruising slowly through the narrow straits, they were amazed to see long-tailed green parakeets flying along the banks, even as they watched agile, small penguins diving and darting into the icy waters below them. The dichotomy that was Patagonia had intrigued Catlin for years, and Schuyler had struck a home run by surprising her with this trip.

As she marveled repeatedly about the brilliant aquamarine blue glaciers, and giggled over the antics of penguins, Schuyler snapped photo after photo of postcard images of his wife and the sheer, frozen backdrop.

Suddenly there was a horrific grating sound, and Catlin was nearly thrown overboard. If Schuyler hadn't quickly pulled her to his side and wrapped the other arm around one of the stanchions on deck, they might both have ended up in the frigid waters.

The large ship shuddered and rocked for several minutes and then all hell broke loose, with sirens, alarms, and horns blaring.

After a quick glance over the side of the ship that didn't give any indication of a problem, Catlin and Schuyler ran to the bridge, where all seven crew members had gathered around the various instruments and screens, peering intently at an image on one screen. It looked like a jagged piece of metal. Schuyler quickly determined that it was a picture being sent up from an underwater camera, and it showed the ships' ravaged hull. From stem to stern the ship's hull was pierced and ragged, and the ship appeared to be taking on water.

Catlin screamed in fear. "Oh my God! We're sinking!"

"No. No, Madam. We're alright. We're alright. We have a double hull, and what you see is the first hull that is pierced. Don't worry, I've already radioed for a helicopter, and it will take you to Ushuaia, while we make repairs. Please Felippe, I think I hear the rotors now. Take them to their cabin and get them underway."

Turning back to matters at hand the Captain started giving orders to the rest of his crew, and Catlin and Schuyler moved down the hallway to their suite, to gather a few personal belongings.

"Felippe? Have you ever heard of anything like this happening before?"

"Well, Senhor. It seems we either hit an unchartered rock of some kind or a piece of an iceberg. Probably the latter. Pieces are breaking off all the time. The "SeaDream" is OK. But someone is going to be in big trouble. Someone should have seen that."

"Even if it was underwater?"

"Sure whoever's on duty on the bridge is supposed to monitor everything in the water through these straits. It can be treacherous. It was probably a section of ice that broke off and was below the surface. I can just hear the Captain now!"

Sure enough, as Catlin and Schuyler gathered up a few personal belongings, while being reassured by Felippe that the rest of their luggage would be safe, the Captain and the navigator were at one other's throats. It was going to be a costly mistake, and someone would lose their job.

Looking down at the ship, from her safe perch on the sleek helicopter, now a few feet off the deck, Catlin was disappointed that their trip was so suddenly cut short.

"Well, we'll never forget this moment. Not many people can say they had a shipwreck on their honeymoon. It's like the mate said. This must be like some sort of reverse curse. We're getting any bad luck that could ever come our way out of the way right now. That way our marriage won't end up on the rocks, too."

"No kidding. Look, let's just make the best of it. We can still enjoy the rest of the trip, and improvise as we go along. Come on, let's get over this, and go face another adventure."

KAREN KEILT

COFFEE BREAK

"**I** COULD GET used to this. The weather's perfect, all these women are really hot, and like to show their stuff, and no one ever seems to work."

Jack takes a sip of the aromatic, steaming "cafezinho" while doing some serious people watching.

It seems there's a coffee bar every few feet along the busy downtown streets, each one more dilapidated than the next, yet they all do brisk business. Patrons stop just long enough to get a jolt from the strong, rich, espresso blend, and then move on into the flowing crowds.

Wiping his sweaty brow and anxiously looking at his watch, Red doesn't seem quite as enthralled.

"Those guys were supposed to be here ten minutes ago. This place is filthy. I'm sure we'll both catch some weird tropical disease, then waste away in that rotten hotel room."

"Oh, chill out. Enjoy. Man look at the ass on that one."

A curvaceous brunette walks by and smiles at the big Americans.

"What's the rush, anyway? They said they'd be here, they'll be here."

Tapping his fingernails on the grimy counter top, Red looks up and down the street.

Almost ten minutes later a blue Fiat pulls up and stops right beneath the No Parking sign. Two men get out of the car, and approach Red and Jack. They greet them in halting, heavily accented English.

"Ola, Chefe. Senhor Jacky, how are you?"

"Fine. Fine. You guys are over 20 minutes late."

"Twenty minutes? That's not late, my friend. That's how long it takes me to squeeze my dick." He laughs a loud booming laugh and claps Red on the back. Slamming his hand on the counter top, he shouts at the young attendant. "Ai, moleque. Mais dois cafezinhos ai, pronto."

"Sim, Senhor." Carefully the young boy places two of the small shot glasses filled with syrupy, steaming hot coffee, and a sugar dispenser on the counter. "Estao na casa para os Senhores e seus amigos. Fiquem a vontade."

"What's he saying?"

"He says it's on the house, and that we should be comfortable."

Red and Jack listen intently as the officer flips open a spiral notebook, and reading from his scrawled notes, gives them a detailed accounting of their week-long surveillance.

After several minutes Red nods and tells them they've done a good job. He refuses another of the potent pure caffeine shots, and tells the men to continue their surveillance and arranges to meet with them the following night in a small park on the east side of the city.

HAVEN'T I SEEN THAT CAR BEFORE?

WEARY, AFTER A fast-paced photo shoot, Henri parks his battered, red, VW bug on the street in front of his apartment. He'd had an uneasy feeling all day, and as he unfolded himself from the front seat of the small car he noticed a Fiat that he'd recalled seeing several times over the past few weeks. It was a distinct dark blue, and though it was an ordinary enough car, it had caught his eye. Perhaps it was the back quarter panel on the driver's side covered with silver gray primer rather than paint that had caught his attention. Or the shiny new dual exhaust on the otherwise aging vehicle.

Jingling his keys as he walked through the building's front entrance, he looked back over his shoulder at the car, and tried to commit the license plate to memory. Y27 G54 Bete greets him at the door, and soon her amorous attention makes him forget all about the worrisome car. A few hours later, when Henri leaves the building for his meeting with Owen, he never even thought about the car again, even though it was still there.

As he pulls into the busy nighttime traffic, Henri thinks about how much extra cash he had made in the last couple of months selling ecstasy for Owen. If things kept going at this pace, he might finally be able to dump Bete, and maybe start dating one of Catlin's friends. Her friends were all rich like she was, and Henri had a feeling that pretty soon, he'd be able to pay for all the fine things those girls were used to. Bete's mannerisms were getting too "Redneck" for his taste. She didn't "get it". Her hair always looked like a wild mop, and her sense of style was appalling. He'd seen the way Catlin had raised her eyebrows a few times, when Bete made an entrance in one of her color clashing outfits. She'd been putting on a few pounds, too. What was once pleasantly plump, was quickly becoming downright obese. She didn't have any social skills, and had even embarrassed him a couple of times with some gross faux pas.

She had served her purpose when he was a nobody, and needed her help to pay the bills, but now he was moving on. Lately he'd been surrounded by "the beautiful people", Henri was starting to get some flirtatious vibes from some of the models. Yep, it was time to move on.

There were four empty shot glasses on the bar in front of Owen, when Henri walked in. He had a glazed look in his eyes when Henri clapped him on the shoulder.

"Hey, Man. How are you doing? What are you drinking?"

Looking a little confused, and slurring his words as he tried unsuccessfully to figure out the right answer, Henri beat him to the punch and raised one of the empty glasses to his nose.

"Ah, Cachaca! No wonder you look like shit!"

Signaling a busy bartender with the raised glass, Henri ordered another round for them both.

"Who looks like shit, you fat Frog? Let me introduce his frogness. Lady kiss that frog! Sit down here, and have a couple of drinks with me, and we'll both look like shit. Oh no, wait. I'll still look good, and you'll look shittier!"

Owen laughed loudly causing several other patrons to turn and look in his direction.

Not wanting to attract any attention Henri didn't respond, but filed away Owen's comment, and spotting a small table in a dark corner, helped Owen relocate. In a few minutes they were both settled, then the conversation turned serious.

Instantly Owen seemed sober and made the mathematical computations of their deal. Henri knew Owen really was a smart guy, but he was a total fuck-up; he'd never get ahead. Of course with Schuyler taking care of him, the prick didn't ever have to do anything like real work. Well, Henri was only in this for the money. He'd be getting out in a few more months as soon as he had a good nest egg.

"OK. Your cut of this deal is $6,000.00 US. That's pretty good, buddy. In no time you'll be living in hilltop houses driving fifteen cars. Not that piece of shit you drive now."

Biting his tongue again, Henri swallows his anger with a slug of the Brazilian fire water and nods.

"So when are you coming back again? My buyer said he wants to triple his purchase. He's gotten really well known in the club scene, and everyone loves this stuff."

"I hope he's spreading the wealth all over the city, because we don't want to hear about some string of rapes or something happening at one club. 10 minutes, 20 minutes, feeling funny butterflies."

"He's not stupid Owen. And neither am I. I know that the police would take an interest in him if anything negative went down. Don't worry. Rio is a happening place. Don't you worry about my buyers. I know what I'm doing."

Raising his hands in mock surrender, Owen backed off.

"Fine. Fine. Forget I said anything. I'm staying a few more days. When Catlin and Schuyler get back from their honeymoon I'm going to split, I have a feeling the newlyweds are going to want their privacy for a couple of months. I'll be back in April, though, with a full load. Yeah, full speed."

Fitting right in with the hip crowd, Henri and Owen have several more drinks and flirt with the single women in the club for another hour or so, before Owen calls for a taxi, and Henri stumbles out to his car.

Neither of them noticed the blue Fiat parked at the curb again, or the two burly men inside watching their every move. The taxi drives away into the night with Owen slumped up against the back door, and Henri cautiously pulls his car onto the busy street.

Though he drove slowly in the right lane, Henri had trouble staying in his lane. A car next to him veered away from him and honked his horn, gesturing wildly at Henri.

"Fuck you! Can't you see I'm drunk?" He gestured back at the other driver, but the car was long gone.

CARNAVAL!!!!!

A FEW WEEKS LATER, inside "Oba Oba" a trendy night spot, the volume is loud and getting louder, as the revelers sway to the thumping Carnival music. Over the resonating deep bass and drum beat, Catlin shouts to be heard.

"Wow! This place is packed!" Next to her, Bete is comically jumping up and down, trying to see the dancers over the heads of people in front of her. "I know! But I'm so glad we came. This place is the best! I LOVE your costume. Let's move closer to the front! I can't see!" As she tries to muscle her way through the crowd, Henri obviously fully recovered from his encounter with Red and Jack, nudges Catlin. "Whoo Hoo! This is some party. Sexy! This is what I'm talking about. I'm going for drinks. Who wants what?"

Bete shouts back over her shoulder as the four friends nod in agreement. "Caipirinha! What else?"

Unceremoniously pushing Bete aside, Freddy follows Henri towards the crowded bar.

"Henri. Wait up. You're going to need extra hands!"

Catlin falls back against Schuyler's rock hard stomach, and they sway sensuously to the pulsing beat. Catlin's costume is drawing appreciative looks from most of the men around her, and a few of the women too. Around her neck, Catlin is wearing piles of feathered and beaded necklaces, which give the illusion of her bare breasts beneath them. But it's only an illusion, she has on she a skin colored leotard. It's her concession to modesty. Tied loosely at her hips is an authentic Amazon Indian sarong made from hundreds of brilliant blue, red, gold and green Macaw feathers strung on palm cords, woven tightly with tiny red seeds and pearly shells.

The tiny skirt is only a few inches long, but covers her well enough, fitting in easily with the rest of the colorful and mostly immodest Carnival costumes. In front of them, Bete keeps bouncing. She's wearing a bikini top that's at least two sizes too small for her, and her breasts threaten a wardrobe malfunction at any moment. Sweat drips into the folds of her belly above her knee length Hawaiian-style grass skirt, making her look a bit like a gnome on a local travel agent's posters. Her beautiful eyes are glazed and wild, as she struggles to keep from being knocked over by the pulsating crowd.

Many of the women in the crowd are topless, and most of the men wear only tiny bikini briefs or shorts, as is custom during the rowdy, hot Carnival nights. Having finally reached the bar, Henri and Freddy stand surveying the undulating crowd and ogling the women. Opening his arms as if to encompass all the women, Henri toasts the room. "This is crazy. I love Carnival! Where else can you see so many beautiful women, just letting it all hang out?" Wanting only to steer the conversation to Owen's drug deals, Freddy replied. "I know! It's the best. I'll bet half the people in here would love to try some EX."

Distracted Henri replies. "Tonight no one is going to need anything extra to get laid. Look at 'em! I'm fresh out of E, anyway, but Owen's coming back in a week, and I'll be back in business again."

"Do you and Owen have a deal in the works?"

"Yeah. You know everyone loves the "E" he gets. We're making tons of cash. Why? You want in?" Thinking that this might be exactly the way to get out of the predicament he's in with the two rogue agents, Freddy nods. "Who can't use extra play money? If I had some buyers he could bring in more shit?"

Sensing a way to make his portion of the proceeds grow a few points, Henri agrees.

"Sure! If you can guarantee the buyers ahead of time, I can e-mail him and he'll bring in more. All you have to do is let me know how much you want."

Freddy looks up for a moment as if making calculations in his head.

"Sure. Why not? Some of the guys I've met through work are serious party animals. I could unload a couple hundred hits at any of their parties."

"Well, if it's a sure thing I'll e-mail Owen. He's headed back tomorrow. Whatta ya say?"

"Yeah! I'm in. Ask him to bring an extra 500 hits for me."

"You got it. For now, let's party!"

They pay for the drinks the bartender has set down in front of them. Henri and Freddy each pick up several of the infamous Brazilian cocktails, then holding them high over their heads, shoulder their way back to Schuyler and the girls.

Several hours later, the group joined thousands of onlookers jamming the sidewalks as elaborate, colorful flotillas of costumed dancers make their way up the long avenue. They watch, scream and shout along with the other revelers, at the progress of the different Samba schools, while passing a small glass vial of cocaine back and forth.

Catlin and the group are having so much fun, that again, not one of them notices the two men sitting in the blue Fiat, parked in the shadow a towering glass and steel high rise building, watching every move the group of friends make through the zoom lens of a high tech video recorder.

FLYING DOWN
DOWN DOWN

HAVING RECEIVED HENRI'S message, Owen loads his illicit contraband into his carry-on. After carefully examining the ream of paper he determines that no one would ever notice a few thicker sheets mixed in with the rest. Fanning a few porn magazines over the top of his clothes, Owen expects the laughter and jokes he'll hear at customs, and knows all eyes will be on that rather than anything else. Pulling the zipper closed, he smiles at his badass self laughing out loud. "Ain't no manicures on board. Baby switch your plane."

The flight was crowded with mostly young travelers looking forward to the last few days of Carnaval, and a flight crew that was eager to get to their home base so they could party too. They passed out free drinks, and appetizers, and played Carnaval videos and music in each seat at no charge. For once Owen was glad he was flying coach. Everyone was loosening up, and he couldn't wait to get out tonight and really celebrate!

After making his way through customs with no issues, Owen flags a taxi and gets inside. Giving the driver the address he settles in his seat dialing Freddy's number. "Got your stuff." "Great! You're here?" "Baby I know how to fly." "I'll call you later and we'll set up a meet."

Hanging up, Freddy nervously paces his office but then picks up the phone again. "Owen's here with the stuff. I'll set it up for tonight." "I'll be there." Red's steely voice sends a shiver through Freddy. He doesn't trust anything the dirty cop has said and knows he needs to be very careful. "I'm doing this my way. I'll meet him, but I'm leaving before you get there. I don't want to accidentally get caught in any of this shit." "Looks like you're finally getting smart, kid." "Just be ready. I'll call you with the location. Then I'll excuse myself to go to the men's room, and take off. Your guys can take him then." Freddy slams the phone down and slumps over his desk as a wave of nausea hits. He knows he's just sealed Owen's fate and whispers to himself. "Please God, don't let anything go wrong. Sky'll bail you out and you'll have a hell of a story to tell all your ladies." Across town Red calls Dudu and sets up the bust. As he bumps fists with Jack, he knows that in less than twenty-four hours he'll be a rich, rich man!

EASY COME EASY GO

S TANDING CLOSE TOGETHER at the front door, slightly hunched over against the chilly evening air, Catlin and Schuyler watch a beat up taxi cab pull up under the portico. Dodge and Dart sit at attention, ears pricked, at their masters side. As the cab pulls to a stop Owen steps casually out the rear passenger door, guitar case in hand, and stands waiting for the driver to retrieve his luggage from the trunk. Emphatically shaking his head no, the driver looks nervously at the dogs.

In disgust Owen asks him to pop the trunk, and gets his own bag out then hands the man a few bills, and coughs in disgust as the old cab lets out a toxic burst of smoke, as it trundles back up the hill.

"Welcome back, bro. How was your trip?"

"Not too bad. I caught that new direct flight from Atlanta. Good service, and the food wasn't too bad. Gimme a ticket for an aeroplane, bro!"

Patting the dogs, and giving Catlin a hug and kiss on the cheek, Owen reaches over to hug his brother. Again, Catlin's thinking it's amazing that they can even be brothers, let alone twins. The two are like heaven and hell. Oh, you can tell they're related by looking at them. They have the same turned up nose with a sprinkling of freckles across the bridge, and the same strong jaw and perfect teeth, but that's where the similarities stop. Sky's eyes are kind and seem to almost twinkle, while Owen's eyes are shifty, and never seem to gaze directly at you for more than a second or two. Schuyler is tall, strong and tan. Owen is just, well Owen.

Grabbing the bag, Schuyler leads the trio inside, dogs following at his heels.

"Why don't you put your stuff away, and wash up. We're having drinks in the den. Come hang out with us."

ENOUGH

CATLIN, SCHUYLER AND Owen sat around drinking beers and waiting for dinner to be served. Rosa was preparing one of Sky's favorite meals.

She'd coated a beef tenderloin in a shell made from a gummy mixture of sea salt, fresh thyme, cracked peppercorns, egg whites and flour, then had roasted it in a very hot oven just long enough for all the flavors to be locked in. Schuyler and Cat both liked their beef pink. Almost raw. She'd added tiny new roasted potatoes, tossed lightly with olive oil, fresh rosemary and garlic, and a brace of al dente asparagus. It was a simple meal, but prepared to perfection it was exquisite. For dessert they'd have clotted cream and raspberries freshly picked a few hours before, by Senhor Matsuko, their resident gardener.

After dinner Cat, Sky and Owen retired to the den once more.

"I gotta go meet Freddy, but before I go Sky tells me your parents are going out of town for a few days after Carnaval. Do you think I could borrow your Dad's golf clubs while I'm here? I don't got a dollar tonight."

"Are you crazy? He won't even let Celia clean them. Why don't you just buy your own clubs, Owen? It's not like you don't always have plenty of money!"

"Told ya, don't got a dollar. Wont'cha cut me some slack, Catlin?"

Making a visible effort to keep her temper in check Catlin got up to leave the room. At the doorway she turned. "It's just that you're always mooching something. I don't know how anyone puts up with you." Trying to side-step an argument, Schuyler changes the subject and Catlin leaves the room. "Jeez Owen, you know better than to ask for anything from the old man. He's a royal pain in the ass." Moments later Catlin bursts back into the room, and from the expression on her face, she's ready for bear! Holding out a Ziplock bag filled with pills in one hand, and several sheets of the imprinted ecstasy in the other, Catlin shouts.

"What the hell is this?"

"Oh honey don't trip, you better calm down. What are you talking about?"

Waving the bag, she spins to face Sky.

"This. This is what I'm talking about. I told you he was dealing drugs and here's proof."

"Come on Cat, chill. Those are my prescriptions. What were you doing in my room? In my room?"

"This is not your house. It's not your room."

Raising his eyebrows questioningly, Schuyler faces Owen. Putting his hands up in mock surrender, Owen smiles.

"OK Easy, baby! Whoa, calm down. You guys know I like to partay. A couple a people asked me to bring them some stuff. It's all right. It's all right. No big deal."

Catlin is livid. "No big deal? It is a very big deal. Don't you tell me to calm down. And don't call me baby!"

"Chill out! I didn't know you'd be so upset. No, no, no, no, no. I won't do it again."

The argument escalated.

"Don't tell me to chill out! Who the hell do you think you are? Always mooching, a low-life loser!" "Hey! I'm like Fuck you! Who made you God?" The anger was palpable and contagious as Schuyler put a restraining hand on Catlin's arm and turned to face Owen. "God, Owen, what the fuck? What were you thinking? Don't we do enough for you?" "Are you kidding me? It's just a few pills don't get pushy." As the volume escalates, along with the argument, the dogs growl softly and their hackles rise as Catlin keeps shouting at Owen.

"Crazy! Crazy? You're fucking crazy. You never pay for anything, but you always say you're loaded. Do you think everything is a free ride on your brother's back? You've just always been a slug."

That shut him up and Owen put his hands up once again, backing out of the den. "You know what? I don't need this. I'm outta here. I'm not putting up with this shit. It's always been the same old thing. Just cause he's two minutes older than me, he's always been the "good one". He's always the best. How can I ever measure up? I'm gonna pop that shit."

"Measure up? Owen you're an ass. There's a big difference between measuring up and being a total free-loader. Catlin's right. You need to take some responsibility and grow up."

"Fuck you both. I'm out of here. I won't stay where I'm not welcome. I'm movin' on. Going. Going. Gone."

Owen storms out and into his room, hastily gathering a few things, stuffing it and the Ecstasy into his carry-on. He angrily flings his backpack onto the ground and slams the door. Cat and Sky sit stunned listening as his footsteps echo down the hall and he shouts for Ronaldo. A door slams, then it's quiet again. The dogs stand at alert by the door, still growling softly.

"Well that's just great."

"Hah. Well good riddance is all I can say. Your brother has been real hard to deal with. Where do you think he'll go?"

"I don't care as long as I don't get stuck with some huge hotel bill in a few weeks."

"Yeah, well you better call a few places and make sure they don't let him bill his room to you!"

Outside a few minutes later Owen watches sullenly as Ronaldo loads his luggage into the back of the family station wagon.

Slipping into the back seat he digs around for his cell phone, and fumbling, calls Freddy. "I'm on my way. Your effing sister just tore me a new one. Soon and very soon, I'll be there." Looking out the window, Owen sees the blue Fiat. He recalls having seen it several times before, and doesn't like what he's thinking. As Ronaldo passes the car Owen sees the burly driver speaking into his phone.

"The kid is on his way Boss, but he saw us." "Fuck! Goddammit! Don't follow him. We can't risk spooking him. Freddy will call us as soon as he gets there, and we'll catch up then." Shrugging his shoulders, and scratching his head, Dudu looks at his partner and lights a cigarette.

Sitting at the bar Freddy looks around anxiously as he gnaws on his bloodied cuticles. He hasn't seen anyone suspicious, and though he's nervous he just wants to get the whole thing done and over. He looks at his watch again.

In the car and mumbling to himself, Owen is distracted. He covers his face with his hands, shaking his head "no". "Ronaldo, take me to the airport. Something's not right. I'm outta here."

Several minutes later, Owen sits savoring the spicy taste of some empanadas at the airport bar, and chatting with his buddy from the band. Handing over the ream of paper, and several baggies of pills he tells him. "You can hold my ice. Now let's say you owe me somethin'. I'll be back this way again." They shake hands and the guy leaves, as Owen stares at his plate thinking. He does some quick calculations in his head. He's going to lose his profit, but at least he won't be stuck with everything.

He probably should have called the fat Frog, but Owen didn't feel like explaining the big brouhaha with Cat and Sky. It was just as well. He never liked that fucker anyway. In fact he couldn't understand how the sleazy guy ever made it into their circle of friends. He never had trusted him. He should've tried to reach Freddy too but he didn't 'cause he didn't want Freddy calling the house and finding out what went down either. They'd be pissed, but they'd get it all straight later.

Owen purchased a ticket to Atlanta and settled down in the first class lounge with a cold beer waiting for his boarding call. With any luck, jet lag wouldn't knock him out. He'd be back at the family compound at Fort Argyle and canoeing on the Ogeechee with that cute little hairdresser he'd banged last week, and this incident would be a thing of the past.

Back at airport bar Owen's cell played a Rolling Stones tone on the plush banquet seat. A passing waiter retrieved the small phone, and shutting it off, placed it in the "lost and found" basket by the front register. Whoever had forgotten it would be back for it soon, he thought.

THIS IS GETTING SCARY

EXPECTING OWEN'S CALL, Freddy picked up his phone as soon as it rang. "Where the fuck are . . ." Hearing Red's angry voice, Freddy signals the bar tender for his tab and throws a wad of cash on the bar as he makes his way through the crowd. "I don't know what happened! He didn't show up. He was supposed to be here three hours ago. I just called his cell and some guy answered at a bar at the airport." "What? What the fuck are you talking about?" "I have no idea. The guy said there was an American there a couple of hours ago eating with a friend. He must have forgotten his phone." Red realized what had happened. Somehow after seeing the Fiat, Owen had gotten spooked and high-tailed it out of town. The whole effing deal was falling apart. Not even bothering to say good bye, Red disconnected the call, leaving Freddy in a greater panic as he left the bar. "What the hell is going on?" "Calm down, Jack. We still have a back-up plan. Get the car we're taking a ride."

A cold Brahma beer in his hand Henri opened his apartment door surprised to see Red and Jack standing there. "Hey guys! What are you doing here? Come on in." He opens the door wide, and both men muscle past him. A puzzled look crosses Henri's face as he reaches into the fridge to grab a couple more beers. He turns to face the men. "How'd you know where I live? I never told you." Red grabs Henri's meaty arm and propels him to the window. Pulling the curtains aside he points down at the blue Fiat. "See that car down there? Those are narco cops." "What? Holy crap. They're watching me? I gotta get outta here." Bewilderment replaces the look of fear in his eyes as he turns to Red and Jack again, who stand calmly sipping beers by the kitchen table. "What the hell? Who are you guys?" Red and Jack burst into laughter. "Man I love that movie. And here we are again." Jack ushers Henri to his couch. "You better sit down." After thirty minutes explaining the situation to Henri, Red is convinced he finally gets it. "You're the one left holding the bag. So there's only one thing left for you to do."

ALONE AT LAST

S ITTING QUIETLY ON the patio, Cat and Sky snuggle, talking about the fight with Owen. Relaxed now, too, the dogs lay sleeping peacefully at their feet.

"God. That sucked."

"All his life Owen has been destructive and confrontational. He'll get over it. It'll be alright. Don't worry about him."

"I can't waste any time worrying about him. I've got a big show next weekend. I've got three days to prepare."

"That's right. It's Oly's big coming out party. You're both going to be great."

"Thanks for the vote of confidence Bibi. From your lips to God's ears."

"Come on, it's chilly out here. Let's go inside and see if there are any of those berries left-over. I've got a sour taste in my mouth." Giggling suggestively, Catlin agrees. "Mmmm. Let's get some whipped cream, too. I can think of a few other things to get rid of the sour taste in your mouth." "That sounds even better. Let's skip the berries and go straight to the cream. You need to get to bed early."

"It doesn't sound like you're going to let me get any rest, though"

Pulling Catlin to her feet, they entwine their arms and walk lazily into the house. As they pass through the den the phone rings, and Schuyler reaches down to pick it up. Making a slicing motion across her throat, Catlin continues walking towards the kitchen. Looking back at Schuyler she mouths.

"Don't take long. I may be sleeping if you take too long."

"Hello?" A pause, then. "Hey Henri, how are ya my man?" He listens for another moment then continues. "Nah, we're just hanging out. We just had dinner a while ago. We're planning on getting to bed early. Plus we had an altercation with Owen."

Henri's internal radar goes into over-drive. He has to see Owen tonight.

"No shit. What's up with that?"

"Oh you know Owen. No big deal. It'll blow over. What's up with you?"

"Actually, Owen was supposed to bring me a special card for my camera."

"Well he split. We don't know where he went. Can I help you with anything?"

Thinking fast, Henri improvises.

"I have to go to Rio tomorrow for a last-minute photo shoot. I'm on the eleven o'clock flight tonight. Are you sure he didn't leave anything there for me?"

"Ah, shit man. I don't think so. But I'll take a look around. Can't you get whatever you need in Rio?"

"No. No. I ordered it especially from him. He's got to have left it for me. Can I come over and look around? I really need this man."

"I don't know, man. Catlin's kinda tired. She's got a big show this weekend, and . . . ."

Desperate, Henri interrupts again. "Sky. I really need your help. I wouldn't ask if it wasn't a big deal. I won't be in your hair. I'll just come over and take a look in his room. I'm sure he left it for me."

"Aw, shit, man. All right. But make it quick ok?"

"You got it. Thanks man I'll be right there. Thanks man."

"Yeah, yeah. You owe me. But don't get your hopes up, I think Owen took all his stuff. See ya." As Schuyler walks through Owen's room, he sees Owens backpack where it apparentlyslipped to the ground behind a chair in his hurry to leave.

Hanging up the phone Schuyler takes a long swallow from his scotch. Walking back towards the entryway, he wonders what Cat will say about Henri coming over. After briefly glancing inside the back pack and seeing nothing but Owen's Ipod and jumbled accessories and cables, Schuyler flips the backpack onto a chair by the door.

"Honey. That was Henri. He's got some big photo shoot in Rio this weekend. He says Owen brought him some special gadget for his camera and he needs is desperately. He's coming over to look for it."

"Awwww. We were going to go to bed early. Plus I've got all this whipped cream. He probably just wants some of Owen's drugs."

"Maybe. But he's a good guy. I looked through Owen's room. No drugs around. He left his back-pack behind though. There's a bunch of electronic stuff in there. Maybe it is in there. We can still get to bed early, and I'm countin' on this being a sweet night."

"Oh, all right. I'm going to go ahead and take a quick shower. Just don't let him stay, ok?"

KAREN KEILT

IT'S NO BIG DEAL

BARELY TWENTY MINUTES later, Henri's car came speeding down the dirt road, dust billowing in it's wake. Henri paid no attention to the car parked in the dark, under a leafytree along the side of the road. It wasn't a busy street, and occasionally lovers would park in the secluded area to get a few moments alone. At the top of Schuyler and Cat's driveway, he clattered noisily over the cattle guard set into the entrance where Dodge and Dart sat at attention. When the red taillights moved slowly down the hill, both dogs accompanied him and resuming their endless patrol of the property perimeter.

Stepping out of the car under the dark portico Henri was nuzzled by the dogs he'd come to know so well. If it had been anyone else the dogs would have kept him pinned in his seat, until someone arrived at the door to let him out. They were great guard dogs, well trained, and scary looking as hell, but they were the most loving dogs Henri had ever known. He'd always admired how they seemed to adore both Cat and Sky and he wished for the day he could own dogs like them.

Henri enters the foyer, quickly spotting the back-pack on the chair. Rifling through it he glances around nervously then places a baseball-sized foil-wrapped bundle into the bag, and slings the back-pack back onto the chair.

Heading into the big den, Henri's greets his friends, holding up a small memory card between his thick fingers. "See? I told you he would have it! Owen wouldn't let me down."

"Well, consider yourself lucky. "'Cause he's been doing a lot of that lately."

"Oh, come on Cat. You're so hard on him. He's not a bad guy."

"He's pretty lost Henri. He hasn't held down a job in years. Sky offered him a job, and he said he'd take it, but then something always came up instead." Wanting to deflect another argument about Owen, Sky offers Henri a drink. Standing in the softly lit room, Catlin senses something in Henri's demeanor that doesn't sit right with her. "Are you alright, Henri? You seem awfully tense." "No. No. I'm fine. It's just this job is really important. I want to be sure I have everything I need, you know. I've got a lot on my mind." "What's the shoot? Something for Red and Jack?" You've been working a lot with them haven't you?" Taken aback by Catlin's question Henri wipes a bead of perspiration from his brow.

"Uh, yeah, in fact. It is." Clapping his arm around his friend's holders, Schuyler laughed. "Then you've got nothing to worry about man. They're great guys. Easy going.

Come on, have that drink and you can be on your way."

Wiping his forearm across his brow, Henri declines, and thanks his friends for letting him interrupt their plans. As Catlin and Sky watch him climb into his car, and give them both a quick wave, Cat turns to Sky.

"It must be a full moon. That was totally weird. Didn't you think?"

"Oh I don't know. He was sweating bullets!"

"He's been rushing around and packing, trying to be ready to leave I guess. He's a little overweight. Big guys sweat. Don't read anything into it." Catlin and Sky watch as he turns his car around, then followed by the ever vigilant dogs drives slowly up the hill and out of sight.

As the taillights disappear they enter into the house closing the big wooden door shut with a resounding thud.

Outside, just a few feet from the cattle guard, Henri stops his car and reaches to the back for a darkly stained wet package on the floor.

Carefully lifting the messy parcel to his lap, he removes two big raw, red, hunks of beef, and lowering his window tosses them out to the dogs who watch warily. As he watches Dodge and Dart devoured the meat, then sit hopefully licking their chops for more. Brushing away unexpected tears from his eyes, Henri puts the car in gear and continues on across the gate and into the street.

Driving slowly, Henri pulls up next to the blue Fiat. Not wanting to make eye contact with the two men inside the car, he looks away.

"Well, well. If it isn't our French friend. You made it right on schedule, as promised. Did you do it?"

"Yes. It's all there. In the back-pack in the entry hall."

"Right. Good boy. Have fun in Miami. Don't burn your white ass."

Staring at Henri through the glass as his window buzzes shut, Red puts the car in gear and revving the engine drives away spewing up a cloud of red dust into Henri's open window. Tears still glistening in his eyes, Henri dives off too watching as tail-lights disappear in the darkness.

Down below in the big house, Schuyler steps towards the bed, and turns to face Catlin.

"See honey, it's only nine thirty and we're going to bed as promised."

"I still think something was wrong with Henri."

"Well, I don't think. He was just anxious about this job. That works out fine for me. I know just the thing to do with all those hours we would have lost if he'd still been here."

Pulling her into his arms, he grabs the hem of her sweater, and slowly pulls it up over her head.

Later, Catlin and Schuyler lie tangled and sweaty on the wrinkled white sheets.

"Catlin. You're so beautiful. Look at you. You're all sweaty."

"Hmmph. I don't sweat. I transpire."

"Oh, right I get it. Portingles. I think you mean perspire, don't you? I adore you baby."

"Bibi, I adore you too. Hold me, and let's go to sleep. I always want to feel like this. Safe. Here with you.

DESCENT

D AWN WAS PEELING the wispy layers of fog away from the treetops, and suffusing the sky with a soft amber glow when the blue Fiat made it's way down the long hill. It was closely followed by another dark sedan, and both cars stopped for a moment to look at the two dead dogs laying motionless by the side of the drive. They want to be certain the dogs are dead, and it's evident they are; bloody foam coats their muzzles and the sharp teeth that no longer pose a threat to anyone. The men in the cars look, but say nothing as they glide down the hill.

They park under the portico making their way unmolested to the front door. It's never locked. No one could ever have gotten past Dodge and Dart without causing a ruckus that would have awakened the entire household. Seven men stand clustered together just inside the front door conferring in soft voices.

As if waiting for this moment, Owen's back-pack instantly becomes the center of attention. One of the men scoops it up, and peers inside, all eyes on him. Smiling smugly he nods. "The frog came through." He zips the backpack shut and slings it over his shoulder.

While three men stand guard admiring the exquisite crystal chandelier in the center of the room, the other four cautiously make their way towards the kitchen and through it, to the servants wing of the house.

Shortly, two men return, pushing and prodding Ronaldo ahead of them. One man viciously shoves his gun into Ronaldo's side, no doubt leaving a nasty bruise and causing the loyal servant to wince in pain. He knows better than to utter any sound. The other two men had informed him in no uncertain terms that his family and the other servants would pay a deadly consequence for any stupidity.

The men speak for another moment, going over their plans, then march the terrified houseman down the hallway toward the master bedroom. The drapes are drawn and the room is in total darkness, but as their eyes adjust quickly to the dark, they see the forms of Catlin and Schuyler cuddling close in sleep. Prodding Ronaldo, he urges him to wake his boss.

"Senhor Grant. Mr. Schuyler. There are some men here to see you." Turning over groggily to face Ronaldo, Schuyler squints open an eye and is shocked to see several men standing in his room and sits up instantly awake. Pulling the tangled sheets and blanket to his chest, he stutters as he speaks, whether out of fear or confusion is not certain. "Ronaldo, what is it? Is everything all right? What's going on? Who are these men?"

Disturbed from a deep sleep, Catlin also sits up, and as the sheets fall from her bare breasts the men murmur. Looking to Schuyler for some sort of explanation, she scrambles to cover herself with the sheets, leaning back in fear.

"Sky what's happened? Has there been an accident? Is it Owen? Is he all right?"

Pushing Ronaldo away the large man grabs his crotch suggestively.

"The only fire is right here sweet thing. Now get up, both of you. Out of bed." He points his weapon casually, but it's menace is clear.

Schuyler scrambles out of bed, self-consciously covering his nakedness, slipping quickly into the jeans he'd casually tossed aside before going to sleep. Catlin huddles on the bed, the sheet pulled tight to her chin. Schuyler reaches for her, but the large man grabs his arm and pulls him away from the bed.

Letting go of Schuyler he reaches inside his jacket pocket and pulls out his detective ID shield.

"I am Detective Jorge Ramos. These are my men. We are here to search your house for illegal narcotics."

He nods his head at Catlin telling her again to get out of bed.

In a brave attempt not to let the men intimidate her, Catlin demands a robe, which she tells him is hanging on the back of the bathroom door. The detective shrugs at one of his men, who sullenly retrieves the robe and tosses it on the bed. Schuyler moves to stand in front of Catlin as she tries to dress with some dignity. Pointing again the officer, the Detective tells him to take Ronaldo back to the kitchen and to wait there.

"We're from the Center of Narcotics Enforcement. We have evidence you've been operating a narcotics ring and we're here to locate the drugs and arrest you. This can go easy or it can go hard. It's up to you."

Completely awake, finally able to catch his breath, and thinking somewhat more clearly, Schuyler demands to call his attorney. "I'm afraid the only person making any more demands here is me. You'll do as I say." The burly detective waves his weapon closer to Schuyler, making it clear to everyone in the room that he will not hesitate to use it. "OK, first things first. Where are the drugs?" Schuyler and Catlin are so surprised by the suddenness of this line of questioning, they are speechless. Recovering somewhat, Schuyler finally replies. "I have no idea what you're talking about. We have no drugs here." "You must be looking for Owen. He's Sky's twin brother." Catlin's eyes drill into Schuyler in an "I told you so look." The detective guffaws loudly. "Oh that's rich. My twin brother did it. I have to say, I haven't heard that one before." Seeing the back-pack slung over the detective's shoulder, Schuyler points to it. "That's my brother's back-pack. Where did you get that?" "Oh this? It was on the chair in the foyer. It looked like it might be important." Tossing it to Schuyler he adds. "Why don't you do the honors?"

Detective Ramos clears the top sheet and blanket off the bed. "Go ahead. Open it. Here. So we have witnesses", and smirking he adds, "and don't get the wet spot." Gritting his teeth in anger and embarrassment at the outrage, Schuyler unzips and dumps the back-pack, his eyes widening in horror, as the foil-wrapped bundle rolls onto the sheet in the middle of a jumble of cables, and ear buds.

"I just looked in there last night before we went to bed. That wasn't in there!"

"What is that Sky? Where did that come from?"

One of the officer's picks up the small bundle and hands it to his boss, then literally disappears into the woodwork, leaning against the doorjamb. He's the type of guy you'd forget the moment you passed him on the street. Slightly balding, with no remarkable features; his small, dark, beady eyes, and his well worn drab brown shirt and pants, make him almost invisible.

Detective Ramos carefully opens the silver ball, gasps in mock surprise, then slowly dips his finger into the yellowish-white powder. Holding his finger under his nose, he inhales deeply and then wipes the powder on his gums and turns to Schuyler once more.

"Where's the rest?"

"Rest? What? I have no idea where this came from! I swear I looked in that bag last night. It was empty except for the Ipod stuff. I told you that's not mine!" Schuyler's brow creases in worry. Something's definitely not right here, and it's getting worse fast.

"Yeah. Twin brother. Right." The detective's deep booming voice echoes in the room, scaring Catlin more than ever, making it hard for her and Schuyler to get a word in. "Don't give me any shit! I told you we have all the information. We have your little surfer boy friend in custody. We know you bought fifty grams last night. Where is it?" "That's insane. I don't know what you're talking about! Surfer? I . . ." "So you do admit you know him? You must be in some drug induced state of amnesia is that it?" "No. No. We quit. We only tried it a couple of times. Cat's going to be in the Olympics. We never even really meant to try it."

Lunging at Schuyler, Detective Ramos backhands him across the face, sending him flying into the wall next to the bed, and knocking the lamp from the bedside table. Shards of porcelain and glass shatter at his feet, and Catlin screams in shock.

"Sky! Schuyler. Oh my God. Are you alright?"

She rushes to his side but is stopped mid-stride by the burly detective. He grabs her arm and twisting it painfully behind her back. As Schuyler tried to stand up the other officer pulls his gun, and presses it to his forehead, holding him tightly in place on the ground.

Tears streaming from his eyes, Schuyler cries out in obvious frustration and pain.

"Let her go. Let her go. I'll do whatever you say. Just let her go! I have money."

"Well, now that's more like it. Nothing like a little respect. Let me explain this again. Last night we arrested your friend Henri. He was in custody for a couple of hours."

Wide-eyed Catlin and Schuyler glance quickly at one another. The look wasn't lost on the detective.

"That's right. We got him just after he left here. He told us, you'd just made a huge buy and he came over here to get some for a trip. Now we know you either have it here, or you've already sold it to someone else. Tell us where it is, or you'll be in bigger trouble than you've got now."

"He's lying. He must be trying to protect someone."

"Trust me, he's not lying. We had a very good conversation." Smirking evilly, the detective added. "We had a very persuasive conversation with him, and I'm certain that he couldn't be lying. And after that he was useless to us. We let him go."

Both Schuyler and Catlin got the message. The Brazilian police are notoriously corrupt and brutal. They were known to use inhumane tactics to get what they wanted, whether it was truth or not. They were not beyond torturing suspects to get what they wanted.

"Look we want to cooperate, too. But I honestly have no idea what you're talking about. But I'm sure we can come to some understanding, and maybe we can pay you for your trouble."

Schuyler had switched tactics trying to placate the men by seeming eager to help, and could pay to make all this go away.

"Don't play the "dumb gringo" card with me. Do I look like an idiot to you? I want the truth."

"That's the truth. We've been around some friends who use cocaine occasionally, but it's just for fun. No one gets hurt." Spreading his arms out in supplication he cautiously got to his feet.

"Take a look around. You can see that we're respectable, productive people. My wife just made the National Olympic team. She'll be representing Brazil."

"I don't care if she's the next female astronauta. You're both drug addicts and I can't believe anything you say. Get me the rest of the drugs or we tear this place apart and still have take you downtown anyway. Make it easy on us all."

Detective Ramos waves at his men, and they begin searching. Catlin's eyes widen in fear, as she remembers the small glass vial. She'd never thrown it away! As if in slow motion one of the men pulls open the drawer in Schuyler's dresser, and after rummaging briefly pulls out the partially filled glass vial.

In an uncanny replay of what had happened in Freddy's apartment a little less than one year earlier, Catlin was thinking that this might be a routine matter of greasing the right skids, Catlin tried something else. Turning to face the man who was still applying painful pressure to her arm, she spoke softly so that only he could hear.

"Look, why don't we all calm down here. There's no need to get carried away. We can resolve this another way. We have US cash in our safe. We can make a deal here. Maybe this was all just a huge mistake. You may have the wrong house all together, right?"

Desperately trying to turn the situation in their favor, Catlin smiled at the officer.

Scratching his rough chin thoughtfully, the detective released her arm, breathing rancid fumes directly into her face. It took all her determination, and some serious acting skills for Catlin not to turn away.

"Well, well. It looks like someone has some sense in this family after all. How much cash are you talking about?"

Breathing a sigh of relief Catlin turns to Schuyler smiling. Fishing a shirt from a chair by the fireplace, Schuyler slips it over his head and motions for Detective Ramos to sit.

"I think I have about ten thousand dollars US cash in the safe."

Ramos laughed. "Beer money. I thought you were a smart man, that you were willing to discuss this serious matter with respect. I can see that I'm wasting my time." He started to get out of his seat.

"Wait. Wait. Maybe I'm mistaken. Maybe it's more. It might be as much as fifty thousand. And if there isn't that much, I can certainly get it."

"You're making more sense now . . . that's starting to sound like beer, dinner and a movie too." He laughed. One of the men accompanied Schuyler to the den, where Schuyler opened the safe and pulled out a stack of dollar bills. He quickly counted it, realizing it was only thirty seven thousand dollars.

They had been dipping into the money in the safe over the past year for new furniture, their honeymoon trip, and the amount had dwindled quickly. Trying not to be discouraged Schuyler carries the money back to the bedroom where Catlin waited nervously under the steady gaze of Detective Ramos.

While Catlin had been sitting stoically, waiting for Sky to come back, she had tried to figure out just how this had happened. She had a feeling that somehow Owen was involved, but she simply couldn't make the pieces fit. She wanted to ask Schuyler, or even this "detective" but she was afraid that she might say something that could be used against them, so she wisely kept quiet. They'd have plenty of time to get to the bottom of this later.

They would figure everything out in a few hours, and put this all behind them. She's known trying cocaine had been a mistake, and briefly she cursed Freddy for ever bringing it into her life.

As Schuyler enters the room, she jumped up from her seat and ran to hug him. She truly felt comforted and safe in his arms.

"I only have thirty seven thousand here in the house." He handed it over and added.

"But I can get the rest. Let me call my attorney and he'll bring the rest over in a couple of hours. You and your men can come back after lunch and we'll take care of this."

Ramos threw his head back and slapping his thighs, bellows a huge belly laugh, joined by his men.

"You must think me really stupid and incompetent. I'm not that stupid that I would leave you here with your smart American attorney. Call him now. If he can bring the money here to me in an hour, we have a deal. If he cannot, you're coming with us."

Ramos got up and angrily slid the patio doors open storming outside to catch his breath by the pool. The sky had lightened, but it was a dismal, damp cold day.

Tilting his head, he orders his men to keep a sharp eye on the girl, while Schuyler made his phone call.

Dialing a number on his cell phone, Schuyler listened anxiously as the phone rang repeatedly on the other end. Fearful that no one would answer or that Dean Whitaker would be out of town, Schuyler was relieved when a groggy voice finally picked up the phone. He practically shouted at him.

"Dean, it's me. I need your help. I'm in a jam, and I need your help now."

Taking a deep breath he listens, then more calmly explains the situation in hushed tones. Again he listened briefly, then hung up. He looked at Catlin, and shook his head from side to side, and mouthed "I'm sorry."

"Sorry. What do you mean? Won't he do it? What's going on?"

Schuyler explained to Catlin that his attorney had advised him that giving the money to these thugs was tantamount to giving it away. It could simply disappear, and they would still end up in jail, or worse it could be construed as a bribe, and they could be charged with that, too.

Whitaker had strongly advised against giving them anything. He advised Catlin and Schuyler to go along with whatever the men said. He suggested that they go downtown, and said he would meet them there as quickly as he could.

"No. No. That's impossible." Catlin was becoming extremely distraught. Her cries brought Detective Ramos back inside.

"Sky! There's no way we can go downtown with them. This is not the US. You don't know what they do here. My father's told me all about what can happen. No. No! We can't go. Schuyler, don't let them take us. Do something!"

"Silence!" Detective Ramos had had enough. He pulled his gun again and was brandishing it menacingly.

"What the fuck is going on here?" he shouted.

"Look. My attorney has advised me to go downtown with you. He's going to meet us there. If you put everything in writing, and we are assured that no charges will be filed, he will bring you the money. There is no reason for Catlin to come with us. She can stay here."

Calmly now, Ramos responded.

"Your brain must be addled by all the cocaine you've shoved up your nose. That offer is only valid here. If we go downtown the dollar amount is going to increase significantly. That's it."

Taking his cuffs off his belt he throws them across the room to one of the officers who catches them deftly, and just as easily slips them around Schuyler's wrists. Without a word, the other man comes up behind Catlin roughly pulling her arms behind her, cuffing her as well.

"Wait. Please. Let her get dressed. Please she can't go out like that."

Finally showing a trace of humanity, Ramos nods his head, indicating that Catlin should get dressed. Quietly, tears streaming down her cheeks, Catlin retrieves her jeans and sweater from the floor, slipping into them quickly. Sitting down onto the floor, she slips on her socks and her new Frye boots thinking of the wonderful trip she and Sky had taken to New York in October, where she'd bought them on Fifth Avenue. She had an ominous feeling that life as she'd known it was about to change, and as the group walked down the hallway to the kitchen, the foreboding would not go away.

The group halted at the front door, and one of the officers left to gather the rest of their men. Alerted by footsteps echoing on the brilliantly polished marble floors, in the otherwise silent house, the officers were greeted by their two colleagues, escorting the group of servants.

Startled at the sight of his boss in handcuffs, Ronaldo blurted out. "Senhor Grant! What's going on?"

Showing more confidence than he was feeling, Schuyler replied in a calm voice.

"It's nothing, Ronaldo. There's been a misunderstanding. We're going down to the police station with these officers. Please call Ms. Catlin's parents and tell them what's happened. Call Senhor Freddy, and tell him where we are."

He didn't mention anything about Owen. Like Catlin, Schuyler had been trying to put things together, and had come up with a plausible explanation why this was happening to them. In his heart, Schuyler knew that his and Cat's brief foray into the world of cocaine, had not attracted this much attention. Someone else brought the drugs to their home. Something else was going on here.

All he could think of was that somehow they had been set up. Bribery, graft, and payoffs were routine, every day events in this part of the world, and Schuyler had heard many of the horror stories. It was not inconceivable that someone had discovered the extent of Schuyler's wealth and traded that information to the police. Henri had mentioned that the disgusting woman Freddy had recently met had seemingly disappeared. Was it possible that she had somehow tailed him when he left her apartment? Or even worse, had something Owen started gotten him and Cat in this predicament?

Schuyler couldn't quite put his finger on it, but he knew there was some other forces working here, and he was reluctant to mention Owen's name, as a tiny worm of doubt was telling him that Owen was somehow involved.

As the servants watched in silence and shock, the officers pushed Catlin and Schuyler through the front door, roughly loading them into the parked cars.

Catlin had started crying, and was inconsolable as the cars turned around under the portico and started heading up the hill.

As they neared the top of the driveway Schuyler spotted the lifeless forms of Dodge and Dart alongside the driveway. At one point during the initial confrontation, he had briefly wondered how these men had managed to get in to the house without alerting the dogs. All the chaos and confusion had put that thought out of his head and he hadn't thought of it again until just now when he understood they had been poisoned, so that they would not be able to set off any alarm.

Inconsolable and unable to stop weeping since they'd gotten in the cars, Catlin had not looked up, so Schuyler turned in his seat as best he could, shielding her from the sight of her two beloved pets and protectors, lying dead along the side of the driveway.

Schuyler whispered in her ear, and trying to reassure her that everything would be alright.

"Dean is going to meet us at the police station, and he'll have us bailed out in no time. You'll see."

Schuyler had been thinking about certain remarks made by Detective Ramos in their bedroom. It seemed to him, that he was trying to pin dealing on Catlin and Schuyler.

He knew that dealing would carry a stiffer penalty than simply using, and he tried to convey that message to Catlin. The truth did not matter here but he knew that anything they said could be twisted to look differently, so they had to maintain their innocence from the start. Leaning close to Catlin he tried to make her understand.

"Catlin, you cannot mention Henri or anyone else ever doing drugs here. They cannot ever know we even tried it, or anything about Owen. They found the shit in our house, so they have us on that, but never, never admit it. And don't mention any other names. OK?"

Catlin agrees, nodding her head.

The reminder of the car ride is silent except for Catlin's continued soft sobs.

LIFE AS YOU KNOW
IT IS OVER

THE ENTOURAGE OF cars pull to a stop in front of a decrepit-looking five-story brick building. From the outside it looks like most of the other old buildings on the busy main street in one of Sao Paulo's oldest sections. The building hasn't been cleaned in years, and the grime and pollution from the steady flow of city buses, and non-stop traffic has deposited a layer of sediment over every visible surface.

The building is fortified, with even it's windows covered by ornate wrought iron bars, even the bars are covered in filth, rust and grime.

Catlin cannot bear to look up as they mount the steps into the building, and pass through the metal detector. Alarms sound, but the Detective pushes them through, waving his gun and pointing at the handcuffs on the two prisoners. Groups of officers and detectives watch as the small group walks past, and is herded into an interrogation room.

They usual suspects brought into the building are not normally attractive, seemingly clean-cut kids, such as this young couple in their midst, and many of the officers are interested by the arrival sparking a buzz of conversation and whispered remarks in the damp, chilly hallway.

Detective Ramos slams the interrogation room door shut behind them, rattling it's hinges and hardware, and motioning for Catlin and Schuyler to take a seat at the massive, scarred table.

For a few moments no one speaks. The door opens and a short, husky man enters the room. He's carrying a sheaf of papers, which he hands to Detective Ramos.

Catlin looks questioningly at Schuyler who just shakes his head and mutters to her under his breath.

"We're not signing anything. We're waiting for our lawyer. He'll be here in a few minutes. Then we'll talk."

Without saying a word, both men stare at Catlin and Schuyler, and if it's intimidation they're after, their technique is effective.

Catlin and Schuyler are both visibly shaken, Schuyler is the first to protest. "This is not legal. We have rights you know. We can't be held like this. Our lawyer is supposed to be here. Where is he?"

Detective Ramos slams his fist on the table.

"Rights? You have no rights in here! You think because you are rich, you deserve special treatment? No one gets special treatment in here. Everyone is the same. Don't forget you are in my house now, Guilty until proven innocent!" Angrily, he slides a pile of papers to Catlin, and the another, in front of Schuyler.

"Not anymore! That's not the way it is anymore. I'm entitled to my attorney." Ignoring Schuyler Ramos continues. "These are your confessions. Fill them out, and afterwards you can see your lawyer." He punctuates his remarks by slamming two pens down on the table.

Though it seems impossible to be shocked by anything else, Catlin and Schuyler are stunned by this newest demand. "I told you. We're not confessing to anything."

Schuyler quickly turns to Catlin. "Remember what I told you in the car. Don't say anything."

Fear evident in her eyes, Catlin nods in agreement, saying nothing.

Reassuring her and himself, Schuyler continues.

"Cat, if you write anything, just write about what happened this morning. How these men came to our house. We're not dealers. Don't ever admit to anything like that. We're going to get out of here. They can't keep us. Don't worry."

Realizing quickly that Cat will do anything without Sky to guide her, Detective Ramos decides to separate the couple. Signaling to one of his officers they confer in hushed tones for a few moments, then Ramos moves menacingly across the room to stand behind Catlin.

"Get him out of here." Two thuggish cops pull Schuyler's chair back, dragging him to his feet, and roughly push him out the door, while the Detective lays a restraining hand on Catlin's shoulder, holding her firmly in her chair, and causing a frisson of pure fear to travel down her spine. Smiling wickedly does his best Schwarzenegger imitation, and his accent give it even more menace than possible. "I'll be back."

Alone Catlin spends the next several hours agonizing over their fate. A few minutes after being left alone, she had realized that pounding on the door, and screaming was getting her nowhere. She had to be brave. She had to be. She knew that Dean would be there soon to bail them out, and then this would all be straightened out. Surely by now Ronaldo had also reached her parents, and though Catlin was fearful of their reaction to the situation she was sure that she would hear her father's booming voice shortly, and he would make everything all right. Because of his childhood friendship with Jose Barros, Catlin was certain her father could make this entire mess "go away". Her only fear was that he might be tough, and decide to let her "learn a lesson". That was always his parenting style. "No" she thought, "He would never put me through that." Her parents would never allow her stay in jail. Had they been in the States, maybe, But here? Never. Walther had often scared both his children with horrific tales of the atrocities committed in Brazilian jails and prisons, advising them to always be prepared with a bribe, carefully stowed in a glove compartment, or with a drivers license. But Catlin didn't need to recall her father's horror stories. Every day the newspapers carried stories of police brutality and abuse. Every day it seemed, you read about the disappearance of a group of homeless children, whose only crime had been begging and committing petty crime on the streets of Sao Paulo in order to survive.

Business owners feared those petty crimes and robberies would cause them to lose customers, so they often banded together and hired vigilantes, or paid off corrupt officers, to "take care of the problem". She also remembered that a group of college students had disappeared from the site of a peaceful demonstration just a few short months ago. The newspapers, and TV news covered the disappearance for a few days, and just as quickly it became a rumor, and then was no longer news at all. For a second, Catlin even wondered if she'd imagined the entire event. No. She knew she hadn't.

Corruption was a well known problem in Sao Paulo, and all over Brazil. This was Brazil's "skeleton in the closet". The population was soaring; inflation temporarily halted, yet salaries stayed the same. Blue collar workers were paid low salaries, and it was common practice to do just about anything to increase a family's income. With five, six or seven hungry mouths to feed, an extra real was welcome, and no one asked where it came from. Brutality, corruption, violence and crime were steadily rising. Catlin knew that she and Schuyler were going to pay a hefty price for their mistake. Her greatest fear was being left at the mercy of corrupt police officers who had a grudge against people like her. People with money.

THE FIRST DAY

THEY WERE KEPT in holding for hours. Catlin alternated between screaming in despair, banging her fists on the locked wooden door, and sitting slumped on the floor with her back against the wall. "Literally", she thought. "My back is against the wall. Where is everyone?" Her back and legs ached painfully. Her wrists were chaffed and raw, and cold from the cement floor was seeping into her bones. She could hear activity in the hallway and offices beyond the big wooden door, but it seemed as if she had been forgotten, her cries and pleas were ignored.

Schuyler was having a tough time too. He kept imagining the very worst. Where was Catlin, what were they doing to her?

He knew he had put on a brave front for her, but he was scared shitless. He'd heard rumors of the torture and rapes and beatings. Even an American newbie, a tourist knew what to do in a traffic stop or at the first hint of any trouble with the police. Always carry a couple of crisp hundred dollar bills. Be ready to slip them into the hands of the police officer, and be humble, be apologetic. A couple hundred dollars was usually enough to get you out of any scrape. He knew this was not the usual scrape.

Schuyler started second guessing his attorney's advice. Should they have simply waited at the house, and handed over another twenty or thirty grand? Would this all be over now? Or would they be here facing bribery charges on top of everything else? What about Catlin? Was she OK? How long had they been here? What was going on?

He got up again to pound on the door once more. All he got for his efforts was a bruised fist.

After what seemed like several more hours, the door was opened and several men entered the room. Schuyler was so startled, that at first he didn't notice that one of them was impeccably dressed Dean Whittaker.

In the drab, dingy room, Dean's designer suit and brilliantly starched white shirt seemed more detrimental than advantageous. It seemed to shout "Money! Lots of American dollars here!" Even though he was a larger-than-life guy, the environment diminished him, and Schuyler knew that never in his wildest NYU Law dreams, had Dean envisioned himself bailing his top client out of a cocaine bust in downtown Sao Paulo, Brazil.

Dean was a lawyer's lawyer. Top of his class, a contract litigator and exceedingly capable of negotiating the toughest international business deals. Now Schuyler wondered if he was completely out of his league in this environment, and if they should hire a local criminal defense attorney. Eventually, Schuyler knew they would be making a pay off, and wondered who was better equipped to find the right person or persons to pay. Schuyler had hired Dean based on his reputation and moxie in the boardroom, he had a feeling that this sleazy job had him way out of his comfort zone. Schuyler thought he looked a little green, his voice didn't resonate with it's usual booming timbre.

"Don't worry about a thing, Schuyler, and don't say anything. Now that I'm here, we're going to do this by the book. We have some paperwork to present to the judge, and then we'll have you and Catlin back home. It'll be an hour, tops."

Relieved by Dean's words, Schuyler stood up and expelled a lungful of air. His worried expression softened for a moment, but only for a moment, as one of the other men in the room spoke.

"An hour. Tops. That's a good one." Looking at his colleagues, the officers laughed. "I don't know how you're going to pull that off Mr. Lawyer, sir." He lowered his voice conspiratorially as he moved to stand inches away from Dean. "You do have papers to present to the judge, but you see, it's three o'clock. His honor has gone to Guaruja for the weekend. He won't be back until Monday morning. Maybe even Tuesday."

Sputtering, Dean demanded to speak with the officer in charge. He motioned to Schuyler that he would be right back, and turning on his heel like a Gestapo commander, Dean Whittaker left the room, followed by the lazy, laughing detectives.

As the door slammed shut again with a resounding thud, Schuyler slumped down into the chair, and suddenly threw up, spattering his shoes and his pant legs with the reek of last night's scotch.

Hours later, hands again tightly cuffed behind their backs, Catlin and Schuyler were herded down the corridor of the old police station. Hunched over painfully, stiff from hours of sitting alone as they awaited their fate, Cat and Sky were both numb.

Occupants of each office stopped whatever they were doing to look at the rich American drug dealer, and his Olympian junkie wife. They were shoved into a room at the end of the hall, to stand silently as an officer removed first Schuyler's cuffs, then Catlin's.

Pushing them each roughly against the blank white cement wall, the officer placed a small placard into Schuyler's hands, then turning him to face the room nodded at the photographer standing at the back of the room. A flash went off and Catlin started, realized their pictures were being taken. She was being booked and finger-printed like a common criminal. How had it come to this? As the officer pushed Catlin into place with the dated card, he shoved Schuyler to a table where his fingerprints indelibly pressed onto a dated file card. Then it was Catlin's turn.

Now, Catlin was in a complete state of shock and didn't resist at all. Her blue-green eyes stared blankly at the opposite wall, and didn't even blink when the flash exploded brightly in the room.

But a light came into her eyes in a moment, as she heard a familiar voice just outside the room. Pushing her way through the door, with surprising strength and quickness, Catlin hurtled down the hallway, stopping still a foot away from her stern father.

"Daddy!" She flung herself at him, and huddled to his chest, but Walther stood stiffly, looking down the hallway at Schuyler. He quickly turned to the officer who had followed Catlin, and held out a restraining arm.

Where Dean's five thousand dollar suit, had done nothing to elicit respect from the men, Walther's steely voice cut through them like a knife. "Step away from my daughter. Now." Looking nervously over his shoulder to his commanding officer for some indication of what he should do, the young officer shrugged. Catlin raised her arms around her father's head and clung to him crying in relief, and embarrassment into his neck. "Daddy. I'm so sorry. Please forgive me. I don't know what we were doing. I'm, sorry Daddy. I'm sorry. Please forgive me."

For a moment Walther looked like he would respond to her pleas, and gather her in his arms, but the steely look strengthened in his gaze, and he spoke instead to the detective.

"Get Mr. Barros." "I'm sorry, sir. Mr. Barros is unavailable at the moment." "Do you know who I am? My name is Walther Lauria. I am a close personal friend of Mr. Barros, and I demand to speak to him, this minute." Speaking clearly, and softly, the detective addressed Walther without backing down, the tension between the two men palpable. "Of course I know who you are, sir. And I mean no disrespect. But Mr. Barros is not here. He's left town this morning, and I'm afraid he cannot be reached." "I don't care where he's gone. Barros and I grew up together. I want you to get in touch with him, and tell him what's going on."

Taking a calming breath, he continued.

"I am leaving here with my daughter and my son-in-law. We will take this matter up when Jose is back in town. Enough of this charade!"

Detective Ramos slowly stretched his neck side-to-side, annoyed, holding his temper in check, and walked closer to Walther speaking softly, yet loudly enough for everyone to hear.

"I've told you, I cannot reach Mr. Barros at this time. I believe he may be sailing.

"I know this is a difficult situation. Your daughter and your son-in-law were apprehended earlier with a very large quantity of cocaine. They are under arrest, and until this matter is resolved legally they will remain here. I have to tell you that if you continue to interfere, I will have no choice but to arrest you as well."

"Daddy That's a lie! We did not have any drugs!" Walther raised his arm to silence her, and the detective having fulfilled his obligation to be respectful shouted at his men. "Cuff her and get them out of here."

Catlin clung desperately to her father, screaming for him to help her. To not let them take her away! She cried hysterically, pleading and begging, while Walther stood ramrod straight, anger boiling in his steely blue eyes. Catlin wasn't sure if he was madder at her and the embarrassment she was causing the family, or at his inability to remedy the situation immediately. Walther was unaccustomed to not getting his way.

The officers dragged Catlin down the hall, pulling Schuyler along, too. He tried his best to reassure her that everything would be sorted out soon. That Dean would have them out of there in matter of hours.

Turning the corner at the end of the chipped and stained linoleum floor, the officers stopped at a padlocked wooden door.

Detective Ramos made a big show of unclipping a huge ring of keys from a chain on his gun belt, and slowly unlocking the padlock, then pulling open the metal hasp. His eyes dripping disdain bore right into Walther for a moment, then he stepped through the doorway, pulling Catlin and Schuyler kicking and screaming behind him.

A clamor arose from somewhere deep below them in the passageway. The door slammed shut behind them and they were dragged down a dimly lit hallway to a set of stone steps.

It was cold and dank, but there was an evil odor rising from the depths.

It was the rancid stench of unbearable pain, fear, and death, and Catlin's skin prickled in horror and she recoiled in panic as she fought to keep from being led into that hell.

Her screams echoed hollowly, falling on deaf ears as the small group made it's way to the bottom of the steps. They came to a metal gate set crudely into the concrete walls, and Detective Ramos banged loudly on the bars with the butt of his gun.

"Open up. We have some new guests for you."

The man who ambled to the gate looked like a B-horror movie director's idea of hell's gate-keeper. He was round and squat like a toad, with yellow skin and horrific bulging red eyes. Beneath his ragged, once gray wife beater tee-shirt, his skin was pasty, covered in a sheen of sweat. He was flabby, but strong, and had once been muscular.

His red rimmed eyes peered at the small group on the other side of the metal bars, and his mouth opened in sickly imitation of a smile.

"Welcome! More guests? How nice of you to choose to stay with us! Come in, come in."

With a flourish of his jangling keys, and the screech of rusty hinges, he swung the heavy metal gate inward, and bowed low in a parody of an elegant hotelier welcoming his favorite guests' for visit, as the guards shoved Catlin and Schuyler down the remaining steps and into the jail.

Catlin was paralyzed with fear, and shivering uncontrollably. Schuyler tried to comfort her. "We'll be out of her soon. Don't worry about it. This is all a mistake. Your Dad and Dean are working it all out. Be strong, Cat. Be strong." She trembled, her eyes growing huge as the jailer swung the gate shut with a clang, and gripped her arm pulling her away from Sky. "Since we're going to be seeing so much of one another, let me introduce myself. My name is Antonio Tobias, and the boys here all call me Toninho or TTTiny. But don't let that fool you. I may be short, but I'm not tiny." His laughter boomed and echoed on the concrete block walls, as he suggestively grabbed his crotch.

At first Catlin and Sky both thought he was stuttering, but in a moment they realized that he had tried to say his nickname in heavily accented English. TTTiny. And it stuck. His pals behind the counter laughed and repeated it. "TTTiny."

"Here let me show you to your "rooms"."

Catlin and Schuyler desperately tried to breathe through their mouths to avoid the fetid odor that assaulted them as Tiny made a sweeping gesture indicating they should proceed ahead of him.

From what they could see, the jail appeared to be divided into three sections. The wide open area they were in now, was a processing area, consisting of a long counter that ran the full length of the room, coming to an end at a small, barred square window. Behind the counter two guards sat watching, as Tiny approached the work area.

Banging his fist on the counter he shouted for the new paperwork. A stained coffee pot wobbled on a filth encrusted hot plate, and Catlin flinched in horror, as a large rat dashed for cover. On the far side of the counter Catlin could see three sagging desk chairs, piles of papers, a battered and archaic computer screen, a dented file cabinet, several mugs, and overflowing ashtrays. On the wall behind the counter, a peg board was covered with old newspaper clippings, keys, and various scrawled notes and a tattered and grease-stained, nudie calendar.

As she watched in horrified fascination one of the men, banged on the keyboard, then smiled a reptilian ragged-tooth smile, and handed a printed form across the counter to his boss.

"So. Gringos. You two look like you should be on the cover of Veja or something. Hmmm. Drugs. Of course. You rich kids never learn. It looks like Daddy couldn't bail you out of this one, hey? OK, let's get going. I want to get you settled in your "rooms" before dinner is served."

The guards laughed and Tiny pulled Catlin towards the corridor at the end of the room. "Wait!" Schuyler's voice was tinged with panic, but he spoke quickly and surely to the man in charge. "Look. This is a mistake. I know you've heard that before, but we'll be out of here in 24 hours. Our attorney is working on it now. My wife is very delicate, she cannot survive in one of your "rooms". Please. Let us stay together. I'll make it worth your while." Tiny dropped Catlin's wrist moving to stand in Schuyler's space with his bulging stomach pressed against him. It was all he could do to keep from gagging in the wretched man's face, but Schuyler knew Catlin's life depended on him at that moment. The toad-like man peered up at Schuyler and mumbled under his breath. "How can you possibly make it worth my while? What can you give me? What have you got?" Schuyler quickly pulled out the crumpled wad of bills Dean had handed him just as they were hustled down the stairs. "It's all I have right now, but my attorney will bring me more. It's a show of faith. Let us stay together, I beg you."

The wad of cash disappeared, and Tiny sneered at Schuyler, but then jerked his head, indicating that Schuyler and Catlin should stand against the wall while he conferred with his men. Moving with deceptive speed, Tiny walked behind the counter and the three men spoke together for a few moments. Catlin and Schuyler huddled together against the wall. They watched as the three men divided the bills, then tore up a sheaf of paperwork.

Catlin and Schuyler looked at each other in awe, realizing that the three men were going about their business, ignoring the two worried and scared prisoners in front of them. Tired of standing, they slumped to the hard concrete floor, whispering.

Distracted by sounds Catlin had previously only heard in her darkest nightmares, she turned her head away from Schuyler and looked to her right. About fifty yards away, a corridor opened in the wall. Catlin wondered if it was a bathroom. She was desperate to go, but knew she would hold it for as long as she could. And then she would hold it some more. She'd always thought her father was a tyrant for not letting them stop to pee on car trips to the beach or the family farm, but now she silently thanked him, as she knew she would be able to keep the urge in check a little longer.

As if he was reading her mind, Tiny looked over at her from behind the counter. Their eyes locked for a moment, and Catlin quickly looked down, but not before she had recognized the sexually implicit look in his eyes that any woman, any where in the world would understand. Schuyler's head slumped to his chest for a second and then his head jerked back up, as he too, caught the lewd expression on Tiny's face.

Sensing tension in Catlin's body he turned his cheek into Catlin's messy hair, murmuring soothingly. "This will all be over soon. I promise. I know your Dad and Dean will have something worked out very soon, and we'll be home in time for dinner. Try to relax." "I can't relax. That monster over there keeps looking at me. I'm so scared." "Honey, I'm right here next to you. There are two other guards with him. There's nothing he can do, we'll be out of here soon."

Occasionally, the three men would pass by Cat and Sky on their way to do some gruesome errand in one of the two corridors. By now Catlin had decided that the corridor fifty yards to her right housed women's cells, and the corridor fifty yards to their left housed the men's cells.

She had been too afraid to do anything but cling to Schuyler at first, but now as she had relaxed just a little, she started listening to the sounds coming from those corridors. From the women's side she heard a soft continual sound. At first she thought it was some kind of radio or taped music, but after listening intently she realized it was a woman constantly keening the same three words over and over in a sing-song voice that never varied in pitch or timbre. "Marcia, my baby. Marcia my baby."

Intuitively, Catlin wondered if this woman had been taken away from her child, and how a child cold survive in this world with out her Mommy. Then in horror she thought perhaps this woman was here because she had murdered her child. Was she an addict who had killed her child in a drug induced rage? Was she one of the hundreds of exploited single mother's who roamed the streets of Brazil prostituting herself or her child to pay for a loaf of bread? Had she killed her child because she could no longer stand the idea of watching while some pig abused her daughter then left them both discarded? Catlin knew unspeakable horrors happened every day on the mean streets of Sao Paulo, and had often read about the horrors of "dead babies in bathtubs and bathrooms." She knew she was letting her imagination run wild, but there was no way she could stop it.

Catlin tried to burrow further into Schuyler's shoulder, as if his warmth could shield her from the sounds echoing a few feet away. Even though she got some relief from him, she knew she would hear that keening in her head for the rest of her life.

No sooner than Catlin was able to will herself to ignore the cries, than a loud ruckus erupted from both corridors. Men and women shouted and yelled. Metal clanged against metal, the thud of bodies pressing against other bodies and the impact of flesh on flesh rose louder and louder with every passing second. The men behind the counter carried on as if they didn't hear a thing. One continued to flip through the lifeless glossy pages of an old magazine, while the other stared listlessly at a small color television incessantly blaring the screams and shouts of contestants on a banal game show. Tiny seemed to be sound asleep, his chair back balanced precariously on three legs. Yet his beady eyes popped open, startling her as she stared at him from across the room.

And once again, he smiled an evil smile at her that chilled her to her very core. What little sun there had been that day had slowly disappeared behind the grimy window, and now sitting on bare concrete, in the subterranean room, a chilling ache permeated her bones.

She finally tore her eyes away from his snake-like gaze as she heard a commotion at the barred entry gate, and a stench unlike anything she had ever experienced assaulted her. She saw a disheveled, fat man was banging on the jail gate with the metal soup ladle.

"Come on, come on. Open up. I don't have all night to feed these miserable fucks. I want to get home to my wife. Open the fucking door or everyone goes without supper!"

"Hold your pants. I'm coming."

The chair slammed down scraping concrete, and Tiny ambled over to the gate, flipping his long metal chain of keys as he walked. Unlocking the bolt and swinging open the gate he peered into a gigantic cauldron, that somehow the man managed to carry with little difficulty. The cauldron was charred and blackened on the bottom, and looked as if it had never been cleaned since being put to use.

Bits of a grayish sticky substance coated the sides, and one or two dried out husks of red bean stuck to the handle like vomit on the side of a toilet bowl. "What's for dinner tonight? Inhaling deeply and sighing, Tiny rubbed his fingers beneath his large bulbous nose.

"Ah. Your specialty. It looks like a gourmet dinner of red rice and beans. The aroma is superb. Tell me dear chef, what is your secret to the earthly delight?" His loud booming laughter overpowered the cells for a brief moment, then the clamor rose to a frenzy again. Both men laughed, and looking over at Cat and Sky, kept up a light banter as the cook ladled huge gobs of the disgusting mixture into various, saucers, bowls and mugs that had been brought out of the corridors by the two other guards. Stepping away from the pot for a moment, the cook stepped over to Catlin and Schuyler, inspecting them like he would a side of rotted beef. He prodded Schuyler with the toe of his slime encrusted shoe.

"What have we here? Has this old dump finally exploded from over-crowding? Are you two ready for dinner? Or are you two being cooked for someone else's dinner?"

He reached down and thrust a filthy bowl full of the rancorous mixture into Schuyler's lap. Both Catlin and Schuyler gagged at the odor; it was all they could do to keep from throwing up. The dented metal saucer was full of what looked to be white rice which had yellowed from age or whatever rancid oil had been used in it's preparation. Mixed in with the rice were a few red beans that had boiled until they became rock hard unpalatable pellets. In the middle of the gruel were one or two small pieces of something else. As Catlin looked in disgust she thought it may have been small torn chunks of meat, covered in fur, and looking for all the world as if it had simply been ripped from a small animal.

Unable to pretend that they would eat any of it, Schuyler held the dish up to the cook.

"Thank you. But we'll pass. My wife is feeling a bit nauseous, and I think if I were to eat, she might, you know, have a bad reaction." Laughing the cook took the plate away.

"Well, don't you worry. I'm sure someone else will be happy to get your portion. And you won't be turning your nose up at this tomorrow. You'll be plenty hungry by then."

As he walked away the clamor from the men's cells erupted again, even louder if possible, and the man grunted as he passed the plate to one of the guards. Catlin and Schuyler looked at one another in disbelief, and he muttered under his breath. "That was disgusting. Don't worry sweetheart, we'll be out of here in no time, and Rosa will see that we have a wonderful dinner as soon as we get home." "I can't believe that's what they give to these people for food. I'd rather eat the beef hearts and rice stew Rosa makes for the dogs."

LIVING THE VIDA LOUCA

T HE AROMATIC SCENT of sizzling garlic, onions and beef wafted in through the open window accompanied by the stirring beat of a Latin salsa band.

Henri lifted his head deeply inhaling the sounds and smells of Miami's infamous South Beach. Looking at the digital clock perched next to the big bed, he sighed and stretched thinking he might go down for a bite to eat and to check out the action. He stepped in the steaming shower and let the cascade of water wash away all the worries of the past few days.

After a harrowing few moments while waiting to clear passport control at Guarulhos airport, Henri had boarded a Varig flight to Rio with connections to Miami, and had drunk himself into a stupor on the plane.

Just around four o'clock in the morning he had convinced himself that Schuyler's battery of attorney's and his deep pockets would get him out of anything Detective Rodrigues, Jack Kelly, or Red Tucker could throw at him.

He convinced himself that Schuyler had enough money on hand to sate the greed of the local cops, and that he and Catlin were at this very moment sitting down to a delightful dinner prepared lovingly for them by their household staff. And finally, he was certain that if the circumstances had been reversed, Schuyler would have betrayed Henri just as easily to save his own skin. For a brief moment he missed Bette's comforting big boobs, and the knowledge that she was waiting for his call, but just as quickly he dismissed any thought of her, he stepped to the window and looked out at the twinkling lights and hustle and flow of traffic and beautiful people on Atlantic Boulevard. Henri thought of the tough times in his childhood, and yeah, maybe he'd had to resort to some questionable measures to survive at times, but hey, that's what survival of the fittest is all about, n'est pas? He was a survivor after all. This was his milieu, and he was beginning to feel that this town would be good to him. Turning to look in the full length mirror, he smiled at himself, winking seductively at his reflection.

Holding out his hand to an imaginary woman, he mimed an introduction.

"Gerard Dupree, Fashion Photographer. I just got back from a shoot with Giselle in Rio. I need a mojito to unwind, and get my head back on. Isn't travel a bore?"

He practiced rolling his r's even more than usual, everyone loved his accent, and without another thought for Catlin and Schuyler, walked out the door to the bustling street below, and his exciting new life. After all, he thought, a positive attitude can get you through anything.

MEA CULPA

FRANTICALLY PACING THE length of his apartment, from the door to the window and back, Freddy nervously picked at his cuticles until his fingernails were bloodied and raw.

Since he'd received the phone call from Ronaldo at the crack of dawn this morning, he'd been wide awake, unable to eat or drink. He couldn't think. His mind was churning in a thousand different directions, and for the life of him Freddy couldn't come up with any answers.

He couldn't wrap his head around the news that Ronaldo had given him. Where were Owen and Henri? The houseman hadn't mentioned them at all, and Freddy had been too afraid to ask any questions.

The phone had rung relentlessly throughout the day, but Freddy hadn't had the courage to answer any more calls. Every time the answering machine picked up, Freddy dreaded hearing the voice he knew he would hear.

Predictably that voice was his father ordering him to call him right away. Freddy heard a muttered curse, before the line went dead.

The next call was his mother. Her tone was anguished. She was completely distraught.

She begged Freddy to pick-up, and then after a moment she implored him to call as soon as he got her message. Even in her pain, Colleen had perfect manners, leaving the date, and time of her call.

Thirty minutes later his father called again, this time sounding desperate, and when the phone rang again a few minutes later it was his desperate mother once more.

"Freddy? Where are you? Something terrible's happened. Catlin and Schuyler. Oh my God, I can't even think about it. I'm so worried about you. Are you OK? Freddy? Freddy, call me please."

He still hadn't called anyone. He alternated between flinging himself anxiously around the apartment, to sitting in a corner rocking back and forth like a demented mental patient.

How could this have happened? What the fuck was going on? Were those god damned cops coming for him next? He was scared and had to figure out a way out of this mess. His life was over. He could kiss his great job and all his new friends goodbye as soon as the news got out . . . . Jesus! The news! He quickly turned on the TV and flipped through the unfamiliar channels looking for the news.

Finding only commercials, he ran over to his desk and flipped on his computer, quickly surfing the local news. Then he found it. Holy Shit. It was Cat! And Sky. Right there. Front page news. She looked like a shell-shocked bomb victim. Her huge eyes didn't register the flash from the camera, Sky looked stoic, numb. God how had this happened?

Ever since Ronaldo had woken him with that frantic phone call at dawn, Freddy had tried to reach Red and Jack but neither one was taking his calls. Freddy knew it was only a matter of time before he'd have to face his own demon. Walther.

He had no idea where he could go, but he needed quiet where he could think! Jesus, what was he going to do?

MOTHER'S LOVE

"WALTHER. THERE MUST be something you can do. Give them the money they want. However much it is, you have to give it to them! You have to get her out of there!"

"I'm doing everything I can. I've left messages for Jose. As soon as he gets them he'll make arrangements to get the kids home. He's gone to his beach house; you know he doesn't turn his phone on when he's there. He's probably sailing, and there's no way to get in touch with him. We just have to wait until he comes back."

"I can't bear the thought of my baby in one of those hell holes. I don't care what they're saying she did. You know what they do in those places. She'll be raped or worse. They'll destroy her. You've got to do something!"

Pulling his wife to her feet, Walther wrapped his arms around her and held her tight.

Colleen had always been strong, and that was where Catlin got her strength too, he realized, but now it seemed as if Colleen's spirit was dead. He needed her in one piece. Gently stroking her back he murmured into her perfectly coiffed hair.

"Shhh. It'll be all right. I promise you. We'll get them home safe and sound, very soon. Schuyler won't let anything happen to her. He's smart and Dean told me he gave him some cash. He'll take care of her, don't worry. I need you to be strong, because we're going to be bombarded by reporters. If it looks like you've fallen apart, they'll tear her apart too."

As if on cue the phone rang. A moment later, Celia tiptoed softly into the room. "Sr. Lauria. There is a Mr. Marcos from the riding federation on the telephone. What shall I tell him?" "I'll take it Celia. Give me a minute." He steered Colleen to an arm chair next to the couch and lowered her softly into the seat. Taking her chin in his hand he raised her tear streaked face to meet his gaze. Tears glistened on her lashes as she looked up at her husband of 32 years, mascara and tears streaming down her face.

"I promise you, I will get her out of there, and everything will be fine. I'm going to talk to the Federation. I need you to get Freddy. We need to figure out how on earth this could have happened."

Walther turned to the telephone, and Colleen wiped her face. She steeled herself to the battle that lay ahead.

SAILING, SAILING OVER THE OCEAN BLUE

A STIFF WIND SLAMMED into the sloop rigging of the 28 foot, O'Day Sloop, the "Hunraken". Smiling gleefully, Jose Barros saluted the pirate flag snapping in the wind, and laughed out loud.

The dark blue fiberglass hull was in excellent condition, and it solidly slapped the dark blue waves as Jose headed further away from shore, into the dark blue Atlantic. He'd been sailing since he was a boy, yet unlike most of his sailor friends, who prayed for clear skies, and gentle breezes, Jose lived to sail in dangerous conditions, and rough seas. He liked sailing alone, and he never told anyone where he was headed. Only after hours of drinking his favorite Liquor de Poie did he ever share some of the stories of his dangerous exploits with close friends.

Years ago, on a whim he had started to follow news of hurricanes forming off the coast of Africa. When it seemed poised to strike, then he would quickly motor north, planning his arrival in the Caribbean to coincide with the storm's arrival. Some might say he had a death wish, but he did it to prove to himself that he was man. He did it to prove that he could do battle with nature, indeed with some of the deadliest forces of nature, and still emerge alive. Victorious! He had done battle with some of the biggest named storms, and had documents to prove it, hanging on his office wall.

Each time one of his boats had capsized, he had clung to a small raft or preserver for hours. He had somehow always miraculously been plucked from the grasp of the sea by some coast guard boat or another, just as he knew he would be. As usual he surprised his rescuers by immediately asking for documentation that he had been in the storm, rather than thanking them for saving his life, like most survivors would. Each time he got a new boat, he would name it in honor of the Mayan God of hurricanes . . . . Hunraken.

Thinking back to his close calls with Eloise, Hugo, Alberto and George, Jose silently cursed the calm 2007 hurricane season. He prayed for another monster storm like Katrina. He'd had his eye on a brand new 32 foot Ferretti Yacht, and now that he would be getting his big cash pay-day, he would be able to trash this boat and get something better.

Taking another swig of the potent pear liquor, straight from the bottle, he laughed like a madman, thankful that he could be himself out here on the open ocean where no one could see him.

Briefly he wondered how his "friend" Walther was doing now that his precious daughter was in jail. He would give anything to see how the princess super-star was doing right about now. They thought they were so much better than everyone else. Hah.

They were worse than everyone else, their money gave them the freedom to get away with murder and to do what they pleased. But not this time. This time Walther would pay.

Jose didn't have anything against Catlin. In fact the kid seemed to be the genuine article. She had worked hard to get on the national team, and to make a name for herself in one of the most difficult and dangerous competitive sports in the world. It was Walther he wanted to bring down a peg or two, and this was the only way he was able to do it. By taking his family. After all, Walther had taken the only thing that had ever mattered to him.

Seething, he recalled the long-ago night when he and Walther had met Colleen at a dance at West Point. As usual Walther had wrangled an invitation to the exclusive party and had brought along Jose, his trusty side-kick.

As they'd swaggered into the large ball room, Jose's eyes had immediately been drawn to the petite brunette, standing quietly in the midst of a group of co-ed's. Her shoulder length hair was curled demurely, a small white daisy affixed with abandon. She wore a shoulder baring black satin gown, that hugged her figure, and then blossomed at her waist falling in waves to her knees. She looked at Jose, too, but lowered her eyes after just a moment, and he knew there had been a spark, as they made their way across the room to the small group.

Walther confidently made introductions all around, paying little attention to the shy young woman. It was only later, after Jose had confessed his attraction to her that Walther seemed to develop an interest. A few months later Walther made another trip to New York, and when he returned she was his wife, and Jose never even had a chance to tell her how he felt. He'd been furious, and never forgave his friend, but he'd never mentioned it either. All these years, he had been biding his time, waiting for the perfect moment to destroy him. And now, finally that time had come. Now, he'd have the last laugh. And maybe if his plan worked he was able to completely destroy the family, Colleen would come running to him for comfort.

Another wave sent spray flying, shaking Jose from his reverie, and he pointed the boat gleefully into the rough, gloomy waves.

THE FIRST NIGHT

IT WAS IMPOSSIBLE to tell time. Catlin knew there was a clock behind the desk, but from her low vantage point, she couldn't see it without moving around and calling attention to herself. Catlin didn't want to call any attention to herself or Schuyler. It had been several hours since the prisoners had been given their evening meal, and in the time since the noise level seemed to lower. Catlin had somehow relaxed a little bit convinced by Sky tomorrow Dean would bring the necessary paperwork to get them released.

She and Schuyler had talked about everything they were sure was being done, and though she had been very frightened to think she would be spending a night in jail, the events and stress of the day and night before were making her drowsy and she caught herself nodding her head.

A bolt of fear shot through her, she knew that she had to remain awake and vigilant. She nudged Schuyler so that he would do the same.

"I'm awake." He grumbled under his breath. "I just closed my eyes for a few minutes. They're burning, I can't stand this glare anymore. Don't they ever shut off the damn lights in this place?"

"I'm scared Sky. Don't go to sleep."

"Don't worry. I won't. I can't sleep here."

"I'm freezing."

"Yeah. Me too. Snuggle closer."

Sky and Catlin hadn't spoken to their guards since dinner. But now Sky looked up across the counter, and caught the eye of the third guard. He nodded when Sky opened his mouth to speak, then raised his finger to his lips, and got up and stretched. Coming around the counter, the guard knelt on one knee in front of them.

"What do you want?"

"Look. My wife is freezing. Is there any way you can get us a blanket? And can we take off these hand-cuffs? We're not going anywhere."

"A blanket. This is not the Copa!" He laughed and looked over his shoulder at his boss. Tiny nodded his head towards the women's corridor, and threw across his ring of keys across the counter.

The skinny wizened guard unlocked their handcuffs then leaned back on his haunches, as Cat and Sky rubbed their chaffed, raw wrists. Without saying another word he got up and shuffled down the far corridor. Cat and Sky huddled closer together and Sky wrapped his arm around her shoulder. They were briefly startled when a filthy burlap sack landed in a heap at their feet. Looking up, Schuyler nodded his thanks, but the guard had already returned to his post behind the counter and didn't look at them again.

The burlap bag stank of rot and fear and Catlin was afraid to put it close, but they were both shivering now so they huddled in it's meager cover.

Schuyler held her and rocked gently back and forth as tears started streaming down her cheeks again.

Several hours passed agonizingly slowly, while Schuyler and Catlin mumbled and murmured to one another. Finally unable to keep his eyes open for another moment, Schuyler drifted to sleep. The last thing he heard was Catlin begging him to please stay awake.

"I'm just going to rest my eyes for a few minutes, Cat. I'm not going to sleep. Nudge me if you need anything."

Leaning back against the wall, Schuyler's mouth gaped open and he snored. When he was slept like that, a bomb could go off in the room, and it wouldn't wake him. Scared, yet determined to be brave, and to let him get some rest, she closed her eyes too.

Suddenly Catlin was lifted to her feet, a damp rag was pressed tightly into her mouth. She felt wet breathing in her ear, and shuddered as she felt the sharp tip of a knife pressed into her neck at her rapidly pulsing artery.

"Not a sound if you know what's good for you. One sound and I'll stick you with this, then slice his throat too."

Toes dragging the concrete, Cat was carried to the women's corridor. She knew she was dead if she flinched.

"That's right. No noise. If you make a sound I'll kill you both, and no one will ever ask any questions. You know that's the truth. We didn't search you when you came in, but I have to be sure you don't have any hidden weapons or drugs. I don't think rich boy wants to see this."

Catlin had to be strong. She could control a thousand pound horse, she was in great shape. She'd been kick-boxing for years, and knew she could beat this monster if she could just get a little leverage. Adrenaline pumping through her veins, Catlin fought to stay alert for any opportunity to escape. But then what? What would happen to Schuyler? What if the other two guards woke up? Would they come to her aid, or join their boss? Barely moving her head she looked desperately toward the desk, but both other men were also sound asleep, snoring. There was nothing she could do.

Catlin was more afraid than she'd ever been in her entire life; she'd never felt so completely vulnerable or terrified. She squeezed her eyes shut and tried to block everything out of her mind. Tiny dragged her to the end of the long women's corridor.

If any of the women saw her, they made every effort to conceal it. In here it was everyone for themselves.

At the end of the corridor Tiny stuffed another rag into her mouth. He pressed himself against her. Kissing and slobbering on her neck and face, he unbuttoned her jeans and pulled them down around her knees. She gagged, becoming a shell as a sob escaped her throat. That was all the encouragement he needed and he cracked her head against the rough stone wall leaving dizzy, disoriented and helpless. She heard his zipper and felt him against her thigh.

Biting her lips, Cat tasted blood and he slammed into her, and roughly pawing at her breasts and buttocks. He finished quickly, slumped against her, then reached down between her legs rubbing her viciously. He pulled his hand up to his nose and breathed in her scent.

"Mmmm. Rich pussy. Smells just like regular pussy."

CELEBRATE

IN HIS SLEAZY motel room, Jack Kelly thrust his hips and shuddered, collapsing on top of the half naked hooker lying beneath him. Dripping sweat, he extricated himself and tossed a sodden condom onto the floor. He rolled onto his side looking at the woman. She hadn't looked too bad at the strip club last night, and now he realized she looked even better than he thought. But she was young.

He was afraid to ask just how young, but her budding breasts, and tiny flat stomach told him she was still in her teens. The only thing that made her look less than a child was the garishly smeared make-up, and the totally blank look in her eyes. He was just about to ask her some questions when his phone rang.

"Yeah?"

"Get over here. We got to talk. And get rid of that under age cooze you have in your room."

"Jesus, Red. Don't you ever relax? It's just a little celebration. Besides if I hadn't taken her home, who knows where she would have gotten her next meal?"

"Whatever. Get in here. Now."

Jack flipped the phone shut patting the young girl on the hip. She immediately started getting down on her knees, ready to take him in her mouth.

"Mmmm. Sorry, baby. Gotta go." He sighed and pushed her off the bed. Throwing what little clothing was on the floor at her, he reached into his wallet and pulled out a handful of bills.

The girls' quick hand snatched the proffered bills as soon as she saw them, and stuffed them into the waistband of her skin tight short-shorts.

Slipping into his jeans and pulling a gray sweatshirt over his big head, Jack escorted her to the door, kissed her goodbye, then knocked softly on the door adjacent to his own, looking wistfully over his shoulder as the young girl sauntered away.

"What's up?" Peering left and right down the empty hallway, Red pulled him inside then closed the door, and motioned for Jack to sit down. "That fuckin' kid is making me nervous. Yesterday he wouldn't return my calls, and now he's been calling every hour, saying we have to talk." "Tell him to fuck off. If he keeps calling tell him I'll pay a visit to his fancy office and shut him up." "He's not at his office. He's threatening to spill the beans. It sounds like he's losing it."

"Then we do what we have to do. I know how to make him shut up. Permanently."

"We can't kill him. We have to make him see reason."

"Fuck. I just want to celebrate this score. What do you suggest?"

"First of all, it's too early to celebrate. I haven't seen any pay-off yet."

Pumping his fists in the air, Jack did a poor imitation of Tom Cruise. "Show me the money! Baby, show me the money."

"Shut up you idiot, and go take a shower, you stink. Then let's figure this out. We gotta convince college boy to keep his cool."

ATTORNEY CLIENT PRIVILEGE

D EAN WHITTAKER LOOKED anxiously around the small room while he waited. The scraping sound of the door opening announced Schuyler's arrival and he was shocked at his client's appearance. One night in the jail had etched worry lines and deep circles under the handsome young man's eyes.

"Dean. You gotta get us outta here." Schuyler hugged his friend, and for a moment it seemed as if he wouldn't let go. Schuyler regained his composure, sitting down at the metal table.

"I hope you have good news for me. Cat is in bad shape. She hasn't said a thing all morning, just has a vacant look in her eyes. Yesterday she was crying non-stop, and seemed to still have some fight in her, but today . . ."

"Schuyler. I'm afraid I don't have good news. I went before the magistrate today, but he refused to let you out on bail. I didn't offer to surrender your passports because I think that would be a mistake. Cat's Dad has been trying to track down the Commander, his friend, Jose Barros, but apparently the guy is out sailing, and there's no way anyone can reach him. He won't be back until Monday."

"Monday? There's no way we can wait until Monday! That's three more days. Cat will never survive, and quite frankly, I'm not sure I will either. We haven't had anything to eat, we haven't even been to the bathroom. You've got to get us out of here. What about the money?"

"Schuyler, that takes time. You know that. We don't have the kind of cash they want on hand. They want two million."

"Two million! Jesus. Can they make us pay it?"

"No of course they can't make us pay it, and we might be able to negotiate that down a bit, but if we don't pay what they want, you will be stuck in here for who knows how long. It could take too long." He didn't finish his thought, but Schuyler understood the attorney's meaning. Schuyler slumped forward, banging his head on the rusted metal table. "How on earth did this ever happen? Did you find Owen and Henri and tell them what's happened?" "They're both in the States. They both landed this morning. Owen in Atlanta, and Henri in Miami. You didn't know about that?" "What? That's impossible! Owen just got here from and Henri has a photo shoot in Rio this weekend."

"Sorry Schuyler. It's beginning to sound like you've been somehow set-up. When I couldn't reach either of them my office did a check with immigration control; they're both gone."

Shaking his head in complete disbelief, Schuyler muttered to himself. "I was set up by my own brother? There must be something else going on. This is not possible."

Turning to face Dean he shouted at his friend.

"I can't believe this! You've got to find out what's happened and you've got to get us out of here!"

"There may be one other thing I can try. I haven't notified the consulate yet, although with your faces on the front page of every newspaper in Sao Paulo, I won't have to. I can ask for extradition. We can try to get you sent to the States, and you can face whatever real charges there may be, if there are any, there. It could be easier to deal with than this."

"Do that. Do that! Get the paper-work filed right away. I've got to get Catlin out of here!"

Speaking quickly, Dean continued. "There's one small hiccup in that plan. Since Cat was born in Brazil, even though she's an American citizen, the government here doesn't recognize her American citizenship. She'd have to stay behind at first. Only at first. Once you're there, we appeal to have her released as your wife."

"No way! There's no way. Don't ever mention that again. If she can't come with me, forget it. I'm not going anywhere without her. She'd be dead as soon as I left." "There are no other options, Schuyler. We do that or we give them the money. But hang in there. I've got my entire team working on this." "It's going to take a few days to get the money together, then get it into the right hands without leaving any trails." "Get it. Get the money, now. Do whatever you have to. Get us out of here, Dean, I'm counting on you. We're counting on you. Our lives depend on you." A guard escorted Schuyler back to the staircase, and once again he climbed back down to hell on earth.

KAREN KEILT

THAT'S MY SISTER!

F REDDY LAUNCHED HIMSELF through the hotel room door the moment it opened and he saw Jack and Red.

Though he was initially surprised by the attack, Jack caught Freddy in a choke hold, and twisted his left arm up behind his back, then quickly shoved him back inside, throwing him roughly on the hard wood floor, and pressing his gun to Freddy's temple all in one swift motion.

"Don't ever forget who you're dealing with Mother Fucker!"

"Shit. That's my sister! She's in that jail! How did that happen? That wasn't supposed to happen! Do you have any idea how they treat people in there? I don't think she'll last. She won't survive."

Jack lifted the gun away from Freddy's head, looking down at the sniveling man.

"You got yourself into this. And you got your sister into it, too. You should of thought about what you were doing a long time ago."

Hanging his head in despair, Freddy replied. "I just wanted to prove to my father that I didn't need his money. I was tired of him always telling me what to do. Of him telling me that I'd never be a man like him. I didn't want anyone to get hurt."

He looked up at the two detectives with tears streaming down his face and begged for their help.

"Please. There must be something you can do. I don't want to lose my sister."

"Too late for crying Freddy.

"It's not our problem. The best thing you can do is go over and talk to your old man and convince him to get the money together. The sooner you pay the piper, the sooner your sister will be home. A few days in the slammer isn't going to kill anyone, and I have it on good authority that they're getting special treatment."

TALK TO ME

S ITTING NEXT TO Catlin on the floor Schuyler was very worried. Catlin was in a daze, and he was trying to figure out what else they could possibly do. The telephone on the counter rang jangling his already frayed nerves and Schuyler looked up.

He watched as Tiny answered then nodded several times before mumbling something to the guard who had given them the burlap sack the night before. Schuyler watched as the young man came over to them and nudge Catlin with the toe of his boot.

"Get up. You two have a little interview to attend."

Sky pulled himself up, then reached down pulling Catlin to her feet beside him. Her eyes weren't focusing properly, and she seemed more detached from her surroundings. He was becoming increasingly worried.

"Cat. Snap out of it."

After a few scary moments of silence, her eyes seemed to refocus and Catlin turned to look up at Schuyler with a somber expression.

"Where are we going?"

"I don't know. Let's just go. Maybe Dean managed to get us out of here after all."

Nodding her head, humming softly to herself, Catlin followed along as the guard led them through the gate and down a corridor behind the staircase.

The stone floor was worn smooth, and though there was very little light back there, Schuyler could see scuff marks, scratches and stains on the dirty, mucus-colored walls. They came to stop in front of a huge wooden door. The guard slipped the ring of keys from his belt, and opened the door. He shoved them into an empty room. The room was windowless. On the opposite wall from the entrance, was another wooden door.

There were no furnishings. In one corner were two empty liter soda bottles. The bottles were discolored and the labels had long since been ripped off, giving no indication of what had ever been in them. Looking at the bottles made Schuyler think about how thirsty he was, and of how desperately he needed to go to the bathroom.

The guard told them to wait and went out, slamming and bolting the door behind him. Catlin stood just inside the door, while Schuyler walked across the room to pause at the second door. Cautiously he put his head against it, listening for any sound. Though he could see it was padlocked, Schuyler reflexively pulled the handle to open it.

Unable to open the door, and hearing nothing, he gave up and walked around the room once more, coming to stand again next to Catlin.

"Cat. Are you OK? You haven't said much."

"I'm OK." She mumbled. "Just tired."

"You haven't said much since I told you about my meeting with Dean. He gave me some cash, and I think Tiny will let us use it to buy some food. Do you think you could eat? As soon as we get back from whatever we're doing here, I'm going to see how much it will cost us to get a sandwich, something."

He moved to hold her, and she stiffened in his arms. Just then door unlocked, and Detective Ramos and his henchmen stepped into the room.

In a jovial booming voice he announced "Well, well. Our little love birds. How are you enjoying our little "hotel"?"

The three men laughed, sharing a private joke, then Ramos walked over and stood close to Catlin. He lowered his voice and spoke directly to her.

"Is there anything you need? Is there anything we can get you?"

Sensing an ominous change in the room, Schuyler moved to put his arm around his wife trying to maintain a conversational tone of voice.

"We want to cooperate. We're both very uncomfortable. We would appreciate a bathroom."

Detective Ramos barked at Schuyler.

"There you go again! Asking me for special treatment! You're no better than anyone else. Piss on the floor if you have to, or use one of those bottles over there. That's what they're for. We'll turn around."

Schuyler ushers Catlin over to the corner of the room, shielding her body from view with his, thinking he had to be dreaming. Thinking he had to wake up. Schuyler thought Catlin seemed disturbingly detached, as she lowered her pants and peed slowly into the bottle.

Sky was afraid her psyche was shutting down in an attempt to cope with the dismal situation. When she was done she simply stood there for a moment before pulling up her pants, then stood quietly while Schuyler relieved himself in the same manner. He didn't want to think about what either of them would do if they had to do more than just pee. They turned to face their captors who had been watching all along.

"All comfy? We have some questions for you. The sooner you give us the right answers the better off you'll be."

"We're not supposed to answer any questions without our lawyer."

Ramos nodded his head at Schuyler and before he knew what was happening, he was pinned against the wall, a night stick pressed firmly under his jaw, cutting off his airways. For the first time that day, Catlin reacted, but slowly, and Ramos grabbed her by her hair yanking her back into his arms before she'd taken a second step toward Schuyler. Fear erupted in her eyes, and as her head was tilted up she screamed.

Ramos sucker-punched Schuyler in the kidneys. His knees buckled and he would have dropped to the floor if he hadn't been held up by the night stick.

Gagging, his eyes bulging, Schuyler thrashed as he tried to get away, but the two men held him in place punching him again and again as Catlin continued screaming in horror.

"Who were you selling to? Where is the rest of the cocaine?"

Rather than give Schuyler a chance to answer, he punched him in the mouth, and Schuyler spit a few teeth through his bloodied lips.

"This is your last chance. Tell us what we want to know."

Schuyler was frantic. They weren't giving him a chance to answer the questions. They didn't have note books or recording devices. This was purely entertainment. Their entertainment. He managed to look over at Catlin, seeing that one of the cops now had one huge paw on her breast, that she was rigid with fear. Using every bit of strength remaining in his body, Schuyler flung himself toward Ramos, and managed to break away for an instant. Just as he thought he was going to be able to get away, something smashed the side of the head, and he went down like a load of bricks. Just as he lost consciousness he looked over at Catlin and saw that she was thrashing wildly in the cops' grasp. Then gratefully everything went dark. Fully alert Catlin desperately tried to remember what she's learned in kick-boxing class, but was incapable of thinking clearly. She tried to jam a finger in his eye, but he caught her wrist and bent it backwards. A searing pain and loud pop, told her he'd broken a bone. She screamed and kicked wildly and was hit viciously by the night stick falling stunned, to the ground.

When Catlin came to she was slumped in a corner of one of the women's cells. Someone was tugging at her feet. She realized one of the women was pulling off her Frye boots. Looking around she saw there were ten other women in the small dirt floor cell with her.

"Help me."

They all turned away. It was impossible for her to tell their ages. None of them made eye contact with her. She didn't have any strength in her to struggle, and she knew there was no way she could over-power the woman anyway. It was useless to pretend she could.

She might as well save her strength for any other more important battles that might arise. Catlin needed to find out what had happened, and find out why she was here now, and not with Sky.

Looking at the women who was stealing her shoes she asked.

"Do you know what time it is?"

She got no answer, so she kicked out the woman. That got her attention, and earned her a little respect.

"Ah. I see you've got some balls."

"Look. Take my boots. I don't care. I just need to know what time it is. What day is this? Where is my husband?"

"Time doesn't matter here. All I know is they bring us food twice a day, and you've already missed one of those times. I think it's Sunday, and your husband is in the cells on the other side of this wall."

"If you shut up and listen you can hear him. He's been calling your name non-stop for hours. I'm surprised no one has gutted him over there yet."

Catlin listened intently, and sure enough she heard Schuyler shouting her name over and over.

"How can I answer him? How can I let him know I'm OK?"

Trying to stuff her fat legs into Catlin's slender boots the woman shouted at the top of her lungs, and the women's corridor immediately hushed.

"Shut up bitches."

As soon as the clamor was silenced, the woman began to screech like a monkey. All the noise and chatter from the men's corridor was silenced too.

The woman stood up, and clomped over to the cell bars. She had picked up a metal mug and used it to rap on the bars, the clanging tone echoed down the corridor and through the jail.

"The gringa is alive and here. Now shut the fuck up."

Despite her injuries and her frame of mind, Catlin smiled, and nodded at the women.

She knew Sky had gotten the message. She couldn't stand not knowing how he was, she had seen him beaten but she knew he was strong, and that he would bounce back quickly. With a new resolve, Catlin swore that they would not defeat her.

She would survive, and she would pay a debt for her mistake. But she didn't deserve this.

No one did. If the rest of the world knew that this kind of treatment went on every day in cities and towns all over Brazil there would be a huge outcry. How had the government managed to keep such a dirty secret all these years? As soon as the question formed in her mind she knew the answer. Money. Catlin put her head down on the dirt floor in despair, and in a matter of moments she was sound asleep.

On the other side of the wall, Schuyler managed to keep the one eye that wasn't completely swollen shut open just enough to watch the predators in his cage. The rest of the cash Dean had given him was gone and so were his shirt, sweater and shoes. He lay in a bloodied undershirt, and his torn, filthy jeans and socks.

He had fully wakened as one of the men in the cell was attempting to remove his socks, but Sky had given him a powerful kick that sent the scrawny, muttering man scurrying back across the cell. Now they watched him like rats, their beady eyes seeming to glow softly in the foul air.

Schuyler felt better now that he knew Catlin was OK. He had to believe that she was OK.

He had to believe that they hadn't done anything to her, and that they would get out of here in the morning. He was pretty certain it was Sunday night, but he could just as easily have lost another day. He knew he had drifted in and out of consciousness, and he was worried that he had sustained a serious injury, possibly a punctured lung. He knew he had a couple of broken ribs, he was having difficulty breathing, and he had coughed up a handful of dark red blood, and that had him worried. He also knew he had to get something to eat, but he was afraid he had missed dinner again. If he was unable to get any food, he would get weaker and weaker.

The only facilities in the cell were a dark reeking hole in one corner, and to the right of the hole a pipe in the wall dripped vile brackish water.

He had managed to get a handful down, but it had made him gag, and the reflex sent shock-waves of pain spinning through his torso. He told himself to tough it out. He knew he could do it. He had to do it for Cat.

TIME? DOES IT MATTER?

C ATLIN HAD BEEN awake for hours with horrible stomach cramps and shooting pains in her abdomen. She prayed it would pass.

The first day they had been in the jail, they'd heard the most pitiful wailing coming for hours from the men's corridor. Trying to distract herself from the relentless pain Catlin tried to figure out the size of her cell. The space could be crossed in a few strides. The ground was hard concrete, covered by a two inch layer of dirt. Looking at the 12 women crammed along the walls and laying on the ground, Catlin deduced that over the years, bits of the crumbling walls, decaying food, and soiled clothing had all coalesced to form a surface a bit softer than the concrete, but so disgusting, she realized this line of thought was getting her nowhere.

The walls were marked with obscene drawings, and names etched with whatever crude implements were available, even what looked like it could have been bloodied fingers. No one stayed near the hole in the ground. Catlin understood that the stench that had been so overpowering when they first arrived had finally seeped into her very being, and she could almost feel the filth lining her nostrils and her mouth, but somehow she had become immune to the wretched odor.

Catlin tried to imagine why these women were here with her, and how long they had been there.

As if by some unspoken code they rarely spoke, doing so only to bark a gruff warning or to keep a stray hand form encroaching on their space. Cat thought that mostly they looked like prostitutes, their scant clothing barely covering their bodies, leaving their breasts and genitals almost completely exposed. They didn't seem to notice or care. Their bodies were covered with scars, festering wounds and needle tracks. Their faces were empty of emotion or expression their eyes blank and vacant, staring at nothing, withdrawn, uncaring, dead except for a pulse.

These women had probably lived in poverty their entire lives. They'd been beaten and sexually abused for as long as they could remember and in most cases had turned to prostitution as the only thing that could keep them fed and alive.

In most cases they looked to be many years older than Catlin but she knew that most of these women were probably still young girls. If they had turned to drugs it was because their lives were so completely inhumane and unbearable, it was the only way they could stay numb. With a shock Catlin realized for some of these women, being here was better than being out on the streets.

Catlin put her head down in shame. Shame that she'd risked throwing away a life these women couldn't even imagine. Shame that she could be so stupid and so spoiled. Shame that she'd used drugs for recreation and fun. To be cool. She cried. In that moment she saw a vision of Dona Claudia. She didn't cry for herself, she cried for these women, and for the men in the cells on the other side of the wall. Catlin prayed in shame.

BACK TO WORK

JOSE BARROS WOKE up to the sound of a thousand birds outside his window. It sounded like a flock of parrot's had taken up residence in the tall royal palms that shaded the roof. They were beautiful birds, but they could be a real pain in the ass with all that squawking.

Laying in bed, he lifted his head and looked out the sliding glass doors, as the first rays of light split the horizon, and the sun seemed to boil up out of the sea.

Ignoring the birds, he stepped into the cascading shower, framed by clear glass walls, and let the water beat the remaining sleep out of him, as he watched the sun complete it's climb into the sky. He toweled off and dressed in his crisply pressed military uniform, then made his way downstairs and out to his car.

The servants were not up yet, but he had to be in the city before the day officially began at nine o'clock and he wanted to beat any traffic.

He knew there would be no traffic at this early hour, he gunned the engine of the SUV, and took off in a cloud of dust. He hoped to still be ahead of the commuter curve, by the time he reached the cities outskirts in a couple of hours.

TIME FOR ANSWERS

S CHUYLER WAS STARTLED from sleep by Tiny who dragged him to his feet, and threw him out of the cell. Landing on his side sent a bolt of pain so sharp through his injured ribs and torn lung that Schuyler thought he would pass out again.

Ignoring the puddle of blood on the ground, Tiny propelled him through the open barred gate. Pinpricks of light exploded behind his eyes, as Schuyler stumbled along from one wall to the other until they reached the wooden door. Tiny pushed him through the door. There, he would have collapsed in a heap if the three detectives hadn't reached out breaking his fall. Through the gray haze, and shooting pains, Schuyler could smell the alcohol they had recently consumed rolling off their bodies. He wondered if they had been to a party and was confused about why they were there.

"Come on. This time maybe you can stay awake long enough to talk."

Detective Ramos had moved across the room and held the other door open. They half-pushed and half-pulled Schuyler into the small room.

It was dark, and Schuyler could barely make out what was in the room. It was a smaller windowless room with a dirt floor, and what looked like two construction saw horses. An iron pole was balanced between the four foot span between the two saw horses, resting in crude notches.

Unsupported, Schuyler collapsed on the ground, trying to catch his breath, listening to it bubble in his chest.

In a raw voice Detective Ramos told him to strip. Schuyler looked up at him dumbly, no more able to undress himself than he would be to fly. Rough hands gripped him by the arms and yanked him to his feet. Schuyler heard fabric tear, as his clothes were torn from his battered body. Then he was on the floor again, his arms were pulled behind his back and tied to his ankles. He felt the sting of the rusted bar tearing skin as it was shoved between his elbows and his knees, then suddenly he was in the air. Schuyler didn't feel anything anymore. The room was spinning, the lights were flickering on and off. Something hot burned through his veins, and for a moment he thought he smelled meat roasting on an open fire. The last thought he had before he passed out was that he hoped Catlin got something to eat.

"Get him out of here. We're not going to get anything from him. He's good for nothing. Useless. Bring me the girl."

Even in his haze Sky realized that none of this mattered. It had been a set-up from the beginning.

CRUISING ALONG
SINGING MY SONG

I N HIS SUV, Jose switched on his cell phone, put it in speaker mode so he could listen to his messages. There were several from his assistant, warning him that Walther Lauria was trying to reach him. The only message he returned was from his American friend Red Tucker. The phone rang a couple of times, then Red's sleep-heavy voice boomed in his ear.

"Good morning my friend. You called. How can I help you?" "Hello Jose. How's it going? What time is it? Where are you?" "I'm in my car on my way back from the coast. It's five o'clock now. I should be in my office by seven o'clock, if I don't run into any traffic. How are things progressing?"

"We've spoken to Freddy and convinced him he has to go to his old man for money. They're probably discussing it all now."

"The kid freaked out, but we got him back on track, and everything's fine now. I expect the lawyer will be contacting you today to talk about making the transfer. I wanted to see if there's anything you need from me, and to keep you up to speed."

"Good. Thank you for the update. I'm sorry you had any trouble. Would you like me to send some of my men over to the kid's apartment?"

"No. Thanks. We stick to the plan. The less people who know we're involved together the better. We don't want that stupid kid getting so scared he spills his guts to his father. Have you heard anything form him?"

"My assistant left me several messages saying that Walther has been desperately trying to reach me. I think the family will have reached the breaking point, and will be prepared to make the payment as requested this afternoon or tomorrow."

"Perfect. Then we can wrap this up and get on with our lives."

"Good. I'll let you know how things progress throughout the day. I'm sure it will be a busy one. Give my regards to Jack."

He switched off the phone then settled back to enjoy the rest of the ride. Why ruin the ride with any disturbing calls at this point. Looking at his watch he saw he had plenty of time and decided to stop at his favorite bakery for some sweet rolls and coffee.

CAN SOMEONE GET
A DOCTOR?

S INCE THEY'D RETURNED from being interrogated Tiny would bring Catlin out of the cellblock to leave her sitting on the ground in front of the work guards' station. He told her he "liked looking at her." She didn't know what was worse, being in the filthy cell with women who continually eyed her like a hawk preparing to scoop up some helpless creature or sitting there scared and alone in front of Tiny. And now Catlin thought she would scream for sure if she had to listen to the agonizing pleas for a doctor coming from the men's corridor for one more second. Tiny finally got up from his squeaky chair behind the counter and stood in front of her, a twisted smile on his lips as he examined her, then laughed and ambled sloth-like down the men's corridor. She could hear a scuffle then what sounded like a body being thrown against the wall, followed by more moaning. Tiny then emerged from the corridor with blood spatter on his filthy shirt and told one of the guards to call for a doctor.

The injured inmate's moaning became background noise in the otherwise eerily quiet jail.

Several hours later a man arrived at the gate. He was dressed in a rumpled suit, his shirt the color of weak tea, his jacket sleeves rumpled up his arms. The only thing that could possibly indicate he was a doctor was the fact that he carried a battered valise. But it was old and flimsy, the leather peeling, and a pitted and corroded stethoscope drooped over the side.

After some shouting and examining of papers the guards brought the complaining prisoner out into the front area of the jail.

Cat watched in amazement, as the "doctor" briefly examined the pitiful man's face and head by prodding and probing his mouth, ears and nostril with his fingers.

After a moment the doctor opened his valise and rummaging around extracted what looked to Catlin to be a stack of used popsicle sticks bound with a blue rubber band. Taking two from the stack he jammed them into the man's nostril while the guards held the screaming man still. Catlin couldn't drag her eyes away from the spectacle and felt as if she were watching a horror movie in slow motion. The "doctor" twisted and twirled two popsicle sticks like chopsticks. Thin strands of bloody mucous collected on the stick, streamed down the man's face, into his mouth, and down his chin. Every so often the doctor would pull out the sticks and examine them in awe. Then he'd jam them back in and twirl some more. The process went on, and on, Catlin wondered where all this mucous could possibly be coming from. As if reading her thoughts the doctor muttered in amazement to no one in particular.

"I think I must be getting his brain. The inside of his head is so rotted it's all just slipping out."

Now back in the cell Catlin shook her head dispelling the memory and decided she would grit her teeth and put up with the pain. There was no way she would use the foul hole that was the toilet in the cell, and no way she would ask for a doctor. Looking up for the first time, she took inventory of the disgusting room. It looked to be about 15 feet by fifteen feet.

FREDDY COMES CLEAN

H ER EYES SWOLLEN and red, Colleen did her best to maintain her composure as she and Walther listened to Freddy explain the situation again. She still hadn't come to grips with the fact that Cat and Sky were in jail. She knew it had something to do with drugs, and something to do with Owen or another of their friends. She watched Walther, afraid that he would go over the edge and seriously harm Freddy. Blue veins throbbed and pulsed on his forehead as he grit his teeth and flexed his clenched fists while standing rigidly in the center of the room.

"Let me get this straight. You were busted in the States, and these two thugs followed you home to Brazil? Where are they now?"

"Some flea bag downtown. But it doesn't matter. They made it real clear that if we don't get the money together, Cat and Sky will rot in that jail."

"But who are they? Who are these guys?"

"I asked that question myself the first time I met them. Somehow they knew Jose Barros from some criminal apprehension convention they all attended in Boston. When they busted me in Boston I turned states evidence, then I was deported. I was told I could never go back to the States."

Colleen's hand flew to her mouth, and she bit back another avalanche of tears.

"There was no way I could ever tell you how badly I'd fucked up. I thought I was home safe but then they showed up here."

"Why didn't you just come to us when that happened? Why couldn't you come to me, your mother? Or your brother Martin? Anyone. Someone."

"I couldn't Mom. I just couldn't do it. I thought if I cooperated with them, they'd go back to the States, no harm no foul. They really wanted Owen. He was the one who was on the Brazilian radar all along. But I don't know. Somehow, he figured it out or got a vibe or something and he left."

"A vibe? Your sister is in some hell-hole, and you stand here talking to me about a vibe?" Walther exploded and advanced on Freddy fist poised to strike as Freddy cowered in fear.

Colleen jumped to her feet, restraining Walther and he spun to face her, his face set in a monstrous mask of anger. Holding her ground Colleen shouted. "Stop this!!! I can barely deal with what's happening to Catlin. Stop this, this minute. If you want to go at him, do it later! Get my daughter home first!"

Closing his eyes, Walther slumped to the couch, and head in hands shook in despair. His anguished cry echoed in the room as Colleen, reached tentatively for her husband. She handed him a glass of scotch, and he drowned it in one gulp, then shook and cried pitifully.

MAKE THE TRANSFER

D EAN WHITTAKER ANSWERED the phone before it could wake his wife. Tiptoeing out of the bedroom he was 100% awake when he heard Walther Lauria's voice, who got right to his reason for calling.

"Dean. Sorry to call so early. Colleen and I have been up half the night. We're very worried about Catlin and Schuyler." "Mr. Lauria. I'm worried about them too. I'm planning on being in Mr. Barros' office the minute it opens at nine this morning."

"Freddy has come to me with a very disturbing story, and we need to talk before you go downtown. We may have to have a money transfer in place before you get down there."

"Yes sir. I haven't been able to liquidate enough cash yet to make the transfer. I'm afraid that's going to take a few more days."

"That'll be too late. I've already been on the phone with my Swiss bank. They are prepared to make a wire transfer in the amount we need as soon as I give them the routing information. Freddy can give that to you when you get here."

"Yes. Yes of course. I'll head over to your house right away and we can take care of everything."

"Thank you Dean. We'll expect you here shortly."

When they hung up, Dean jumped in the shower. He was dressed and out the door ten minutes later.

FINAL DETAILS

SITTING ATTENTIVELY IN the Lauria living room, Dean watched the family as Freddy continued his explanation.

"Somehow the cops got to Henri, he must've traded his life for Cat and Sky. It's the only thing I can figure out." Freddy slumped into the sofa, as Colleen swallowed half a glass of amber liquid that Dean was certain wasn't tea.

Fully composed Walther interjected, "Why would they want that french faggot? What could he give them? Nothing. That was their tactic. They knew that, and knew he was scared shitless."

"You're right Dad. Their whole plan was finished. Once Owen left, they were done. But they must've scared Henri so badly, that he did whatever they asked him to. He did the last desperate thing he could've done. Somehow he convinced them to go after Cat." Colleen, Walther, Dean and Freddy sat stunned, each lost in their own thoughts.

"What I don't understand is why on earth you think Jose is involved in all this?"

"I'm not sure, Mom, but when they came to my apartment to give me the bank information, one of them, Jack, said Dad'd be totally surprised to know that his friend was after him. I asked him to explain, but the head honcho, Red Tucker gave him a look that shut him up."

Walther paced the room, barely keeping his temper in check. "That son of a bitch. He's been pissed at me for the last 30 years because your mother married me, and not him."

Freddy turned to his parents in disbelief. "I had no idea he even knew Mom. What do you mean?"

"Old history. It doesn't matter. All I want is to get my daughter out of there. Dean, make the transfer." Then Walther turned to face them all again, his commanding look riveting them in place.

"But once she's home, heads are going to roll. They have no idea who they're dealing with." Walther glared meaningfully at Freddy, who hung his head, then he looked pointedly at Dean. "And you. You never heard that."

IT'S ALL PART OF THE PLAN

S EVERAL MILES AWAY, Red Tucker's phone vibrated in his shirt
pocket. He checked caller id, then flipped it open and listened
intently. Without saying a word he walked across the room to his laptop.
Watching him Jack got off the bed to follow his partner cross the room.
Red sat at the desk and logged onto his off-shore account. As they both
watched the screen, the balance in the account went up from $1,000.00 to
$2,000,100.00! They stared in disbelief, then turned and banged fists in
the air. The phone was forgotten as Red's chair was overturned, and they
hugged, pounding one another on the back. "We did it! We're rich!" Jack
scampered around the room clutched a pillow to his chest and mouth and
muffled his shouts of joy.

Tilting his head back, eyes closed he stood still, then walked back to
the open computer. He stared down at the laptop, then stared at Red who
was standing by the closet door with his hand behind his back.

"Wait a minute. That's not right. All the money's in one account. Half's
supposed to in your account and the other half in mine. What the fuck?
What are you doing?"

He watched as his partner pulled on a pair of latex gloves. Jack's quizzical
expression turned to disbelief as Red embraced him, pillow and all, in an
awkward dance.

At the soft "pop" he looked down at his chest where a bright red stain
spread on the pillow as it fell to his feet, and Jack's knees buckled. He was
dead before he hit the floor, his head cushioned by the pillow. He appeared
to have fallen asleep right there on the floor. Except for the spreading pool
of blood.

"Nope. That's exactly right. That's exactly the way I planned it."

Callously stepping over the body, Red closed the lap top and visually
swept the room for any trace evidence. Satisfied, he snapped off his gloves,
pocketed them inside out, then opened the door and slipped out into the
bright morning.

SING LITTLE BIRDIE, SING

S HE HEARD THE scrape and shuffle of heavy feet, and the jangling of his keys before she saw him. The other women did too. She felt a twinge of fear that made her shrink into the wall, and she noticed that the other women in the cell were also suddenly still.

Looking in at Catlin, Tiny announced.

"Time for visitors."

For one second Catlin allowed herself to hope that Dean had come for them. Or her parents. She looked up at him with an expectant half-smile. But she saw only evil on his face and knew that he was there for some other purpose, and she steeled herself to be strong. As the shadow of his huge bulk stood over her, Catlin kicked out viciously, her kick strong and aimed for his crotch. But she hadn't eaten and her reflexes were slow, and he brushed her leg aside like brushing away a pesky fly.

He grunted, and stuck his tongue out his mouth moving it quickly side-to-side in an obscene manner, and growled at her. He reached down and yanked her up to him so that her face was barely an inch away from his. All the horrific smells of the cell and the jail didn't compare to the rank, decomposing odor that spewed onto her face, and lodged in her throat. She gagged, and his expression turned even more hateful. He pressed himself up against her, and she could feel exactly what he intended.

"I'm saving myself for you." He whispered. "When you get back, I've got something really good to give you. And I'm going to give it to you, until you beg me for more."

While he was talking, Catlin sucked every bit of moisture from her mouth into a small gob, and with all the venom and hate and despair she could muster, she spit into his face. His big fat tongue snaked out of his mouth and he licked the spittle and smiled.

As he was dragging her past the men's corridor, Catlin shouted Sky's name, and over the raucous cries of the men, thought she heard him respond.

Tiny unlocked the bolt, opened the door, and unceremoniously shoved Catlin inside, then bolted the door shut behind her.

Alone, she quickly pulled down her jeans and peed in the plastic soda bottle. Zipping up, she heard the bolt slide free again, and turned to see Detective Ramos and his cronies enter the room.

Without preamble he told her.

"You need to do the right thing. You need to give us the names of everyone you've been selling drugs to. You need to be honest, and not try to protect anyone. I know you will still get a harsh sentence, but you will be doing the right thing, and it will make you feel better."

"I have nothing to tell you. We told you we never sold any drugs."

Detective Ramos walked and stood an inch away from her in an obvious attempt to intimidate her.

"Tell us what we want to hear, and we'll go easy on you."

Close to fainting from the terror of being in this room with these three men, Catlin turned her head away from him and gritting her teeth in preparation of the blow she expected.

Instead Detective Ramos walked away. He walked to the other door and unlocking it, swung it open, stepping inside. The other two men each grabbed an elbow, carrying her in behind him.

Dreadful fear coursed through her in waves unlike anything she'd ever known before when she saw the interior of the room. This is where they brought Sky, she thought, but she couldn't make sense of what she saw.

"Strip."

Catlin didn't move.

"Strip!"

He screamed at her. Still she didn't move. She couldn't move. Her feet were bricks, mortared to the dirt beneath them. He walked over and yanked her arms over her back, as the other two men tore off her clothing. Released, she crouched naked and trembling, trying to cover herself.

Tears streamed down her face, and she looked hopelessly around the room for some way to protect herself from what she thought was going to happen.

Kicking her fiercely, Detective Barros sent her sprawling face down in the dirt. She hunched into a fetal position, scooping up two handfuls of the loose soil.

The two men grabbed her arms, pulling them behind her back, then tied her wrists to her ankles. She had no chance to throw the pitiful dirt and it fell useless to the ground. Before she could understand what was happening they stuffed a sodden rag into her mouth. The delicate skin behind her elbows and knees tore as they shoved a rusty bar between her elbows and knees. Trussed like a bird they lifted her up. Catlin tried desperately to free herself, managing only to tighten the cords that bound her. She couldn't breathe. She feared she would asphyxiate yet steeled her will. *"I'm strong. I get through this. I can do this. Focus."* Her muscles were stretched beyond endurance. The cords and wires binding her ankles and wrists dug into her flesh. The men lowered the bar onto the saw horses backing away towards Ramos. She was exposed and vulnerable, and though she knew she would tell them anything they wanted to know, she couldn't speak. Desperately Catlin tried to spit out the gag. She moaned into the rag pleading with her eyes. *"Oh my God. I'll tell you anything. Anything. Please stop. Please stop!"*

Detective Ramos had pulled a wooden backed chair to face her, and sat, leaning towards her.

"Now, you will sing like a bird. Everyone does."

He nodded at the two men who reached for a car battery on the ground beneath her. Two wires extended from the terminals. Touching the ends together the wires sparked and sizzled.

Eyes wide in terror, Catlin watched as the two wires closed in on the nipple of her right breast. For a fraction of a second she felt a sting, like a bite from an angry bee, then the electricity coursed through her, and she arched her neck convulsing in agony. Her muscles spasmed pulling her body apart, arching her back further than it was meant to go. They held the wires in place until she thought she could bear it no longer, only then pulling them away. Catlin tried to breath through the gaps at the sides of the rag, and through her nostrils, but she just couldn't get enough air.

"Again."

For what seemed like eternity to Catlin they shocked her over and over until Catlin could smell her own flesh burning. She prayed she would die. She was certain that her screams could be heard through the walls and upstairs to the police station. Why didn't anyone come to help her?

She realized they had stopped and she tried to focus her gaze on the torturers. Her thoughts were jumbled and confused, she could almost grasp a thought and hold it, then it would fade away in searing pain. Through the haze she thought she saw the detective's hand in his crotch, and a look of pure evil on his face.

His deep voice was hoarse as he mumbled.

"More" he said. "She still won't talk. Give it to her."

The man with the wires approached Catlin and she saw he was not going to place the wires on her breast. He smiled as he looked in her eyes lowered the wires, turning on the current.

Pain screamed through her body, and Catlin convulsed in agony. They shocked her wrecked body over and over. When she woke up she was lying on her side in the cell. She was only awake for a moment, then gratefully, she passed out again. Several more times she seemed almost able to move, but when she did, gratefully the pain would take her back down into the darkness.

THE PARROT'S PERCH

Finally, she woke to a soft hand caressing her brow. It was her mother! She murmured soothing words, and ran a silky square over her face, her lips, her eyes.

"Aw baby. You're awake. Shhh. It's alright. Don't close your eyes. You've been sleeping so long. Stay awake. Stay awake."

Catlin blinked and her mother was gone. She smelled the poisonous fumes from the hole in the ground. She moaned and looked up. The other women were watching her form across the room. She struggled to sit up, and saw blood on her torn T-shirt. She wore only the shirt and soiled panties. Her legs and arms ached, and she couldn't focus her eyes. She shook her head, but a shooting pain screamed in her skull and she moaned again.

"The Parrot's Perch." The voice from across the cell was disembodied, and seemed to come at her from every direction, yet she knew it was one of the women. Slowly she came into focus.

"They put you on The Parrot's Perch. That's what they call it. There's no reason for it, except to get their rocks off. You'll be dizzy and confused for awhile. You need to drink water. Try to drink this."

The woman put a small plastic cup in her hand, and closed her fingers around it, but Catlin couldn't make her hand move to her mouth, and the cup dropped from her hand and she passed out again.

There was no time here. She thought the guards had stuffed bits of stale bread through the bars earlier. The pain in her stomach had continued to grow, and through a dizzy fog she wondered what was happening with Sky. They had a silly thing they did when they knew they were going to be apart. They would set up a coordinated time, and at the appointed hour would stop whatever they were doing and send one another mental kisses. They hadn't had time to set anything up, but Cat thought she "felt" Sky thinking of her, and so she closed her eyes, and sent him a loving embrace and warm fluttery kisses.

MISSION ACCOMPLISHED

J OSE BARROS STARED at his computer screen, and took a deep breath. The money was supposed to be in his account by now. Furtively he looked over his shoulder to be certain no one could see him as he quickly tapped in his seven key password. Nervously drumming his fingernails on his desk, he waited for the page to load. His account number appeared on the screen, and he clicked on it. More moments passed, and then the page loaded. And there it was. One million dollars. He closed his eyes and clenched his fists. Yes! He got it. It was over.

A knock on his door startled him, and he quickly moved his mouse, minimizing the screen on his desk top. "Yes. What is it Jorge?" Holding the door open, Jorge announced, Mr. And Mrs. Lauria were waiting outside the door.

Standing, after quickly glancing at the screen once more to see the balance again, and to hide the page Jose smoothed his crisply creased pants, and as Walther stepped into his office, took his hand in both of his.

Unaware that Walther and Colleen knew of his complicity Jose clasped his friends' hands who stiffly embraced him. After a moment they separated, and Jose moved to embrace Colleen.

"Walther. Colleen. I am so dreadfully sorry. I just heard this morning."

He indicated a pile of forms and the newspaper on his desk. "We are processing them out right now. I cannot believe this happened. I would never imagine that Catlin would get . . . but never mind . . . . Oh if only I hadn't gone sailing."

As if on cue his cell phone rang. Looking at the caller ID he apologized.

"Excuse me. Just one moment. I've been expecting this call."

"Yes? This is Commander Barros."

He listened thoughtfully for a moment, keeping a grim expression on his face.

Walther and Colleen sat quietly across his desk, listening unobtrusively to the one-sided conversation. Both Colleen and Walther could have won awards for their performances.

"Yes. I verified it just this moment. Everything seems to be in order. Of course. Yes, I am very pleased. You've done an excellent job. He listened another moment then continued.

"And thank you too, for your hard work and planning. Your diligence and creativity were put to the test, but you passed with flying colors. Congratulations Sir. Have a pleasant trip."

He put the phone down.

"I'm sorry. That was about my boat. It had a problem, but it's been resolved now."

He looked up as Jorge came running into the room a horrified expression on his face. Without excusing himself, Jorge leaned over and whispered into Commander Barros' ear.

"What? There must be some mistake! How could this happen? Are you certain?"

Glancing at the Lauria's the young man answered quietly.

"Yes sir. Quite certain sir. I'm very sorry, sir." He backed up and left the room, closing the door behind him.

A moment later out in the hall he heard Colleen Lauria's, sorrowful wail and the scraping of chairs. Jorge had just told his Commander that Schuyler had succumbed to his injures and was dead and Catlin was being rushed to a hospital. Jorge briefly wondered if there'd be any fall-out on this case, and shrugged his shoulders as he walked down the hall.

"My baby. What have you done to my daughter?"

LEAVING ON A JET PLANE

RED SHUT OFF his phone and sat back as the jet's big engines revved for take-off. He smiled, hugging his bag to his chest, and closed his eyes dreaming of the island beaches that was his destination.

He had worked hard to get this. He would live the life he'd always dreamed of, and maybe even offer to consult with the island's police force. Just to keep his hand in the game.

Looking out the window, he gave a little wave as the unending Rio skyline disappeared beneath the clouds. He smiled at the passing stewardess and ordered a cocktail. He could get used to this first class shit. He wouldn't miss any of the old life. That was for sure.

THE PARROT'S PERCH

T WO MONTHS LATER Freddy sat in the library with his father. The two men nursed shots of scotch and looked out the sliding glass doors to the garden, where Catlin sat straight and still on a stone bench her curled fingers pale and rigid, the color of marble on the edge of the seat.

"What are you going to do about Barros?"

"Jose always told me he wanted to die at sea. He'll get his wish. I have a wish too. I want to find all the people responsible for what happened to Catlin and Schuyler."

"Does Mom know about this?"

"No. Your mother doesn't need to know. She can't take any more. She's too worried about Cat."

"How is she? How is Cat doing, Dad?"

"The visible bruises and wounds are fading, but she's not good. They had her for forty-five days. She has horrible nightmares, wakes up screaming every night. She's always taking showers. Says she can't get clean. The doctor's say it's a classic reaction. She comes here every day, but she won't talk to anyone. She just stares at that damned bird. Maybe you should talk to her."

He waved his hand absently at Freddy, and resumed nursing his drink.

That was it, he'd been dismissed. Things it seemed, were back to normal as far as his father was concerned. Freddy hadn't had the courage to tell Cat what had really happened. He wondered if she knew. *She'd said she and Sky had tried to figure it all out when they were in jail. And of course the damn lawyer knew everything. He wondered if he'd told Cat. Maybe she knew about his involvement. Shit.* Freddy slowly got up and put down his glass as he stepped toward the patio door.

He walked outside and stood quietly several feet away from his sister. Her arms were bare and he could see what looked like burns on the back of the pale, translucent skin. She was so thin. She probably wasn't eating either. She didn't hear him. Didn't turn around. She was staring intently at the vibrant macaw pacing back and forth on it's perch.

He thought he could hear her mumbling and didn't feel like he should interrupt her, but he did. "Catlin. I'm so sorry. I can have those guys killed you know." Catlin turned and faced him briefly, red eyes fierce. "No." She turned away again, and Freddy knew he'd been dismissed yet again. Catlin walked stiffly to the parrot's perch. Bending slightly and slowly as if she was in pain, she reached for the bird's manacled claw. The wild bird flapped it's wings furiously, and bit her hand with it's wicked beak. Catlin didn't seem to notice as she opened the manacle and unclasped it from the birds' spindly yellow leg. With no concern for her safety she lifted the large bird in her arms then heaved it with all her strength up into the gray sky.

The beautiful bird flapped it's wings hard, and flew out over the yard and pool, then up and over the tallest palms. Catlin watched until the bird was out of sight. When she finally turned around tears streamed down her face and she was alone. A hint of a smile lifted the corners of her lips.

Karen Keilt was born in Sao Paulo, Brazil and now works where she lives with her husband in Carefree, AZ and Gloucester, MA where they enjoy hiking with their dog Curly, amateur photography, working-out and Anusara Yoga.

760 - 702-6167

Edwards Brothers, Inc.
Thorofare, NJ USA
October 3, 2011